BIRDS OF NEW YORK

OVER 100 PLATES

LOUIS AGASSIZ FUERTES

FOREWORD BY
ROBERT McCRACKEN PECK

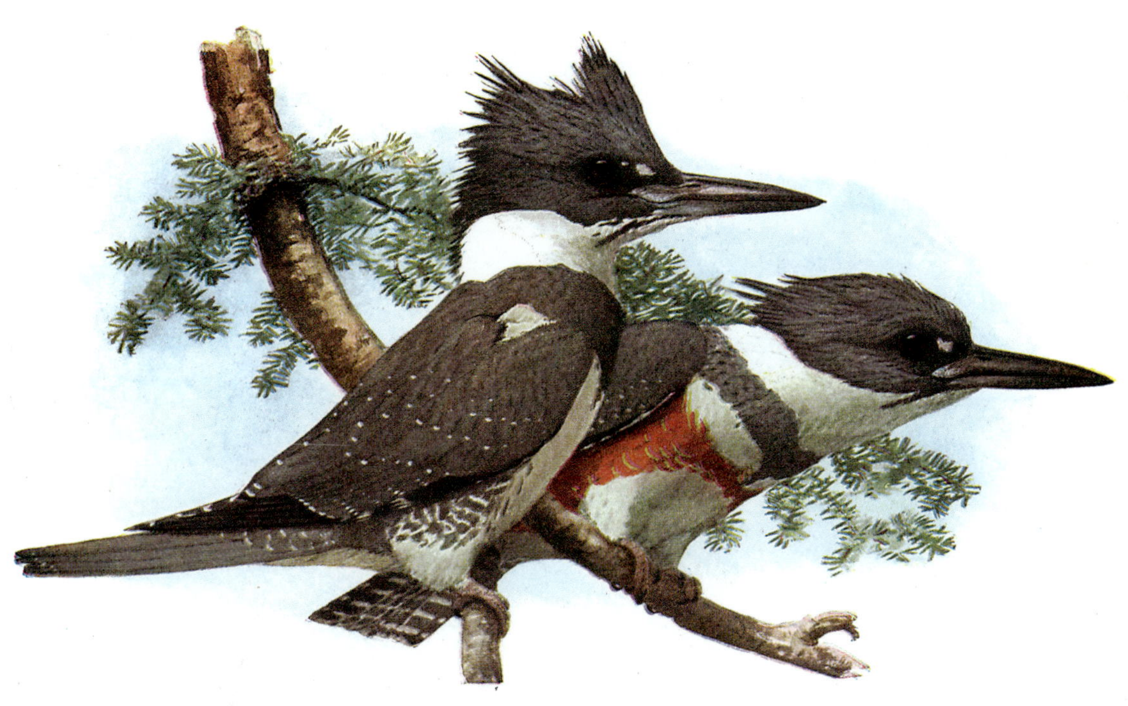

DOVER PUBLICATIONS, INC.
MINEOLA, NEW YORK

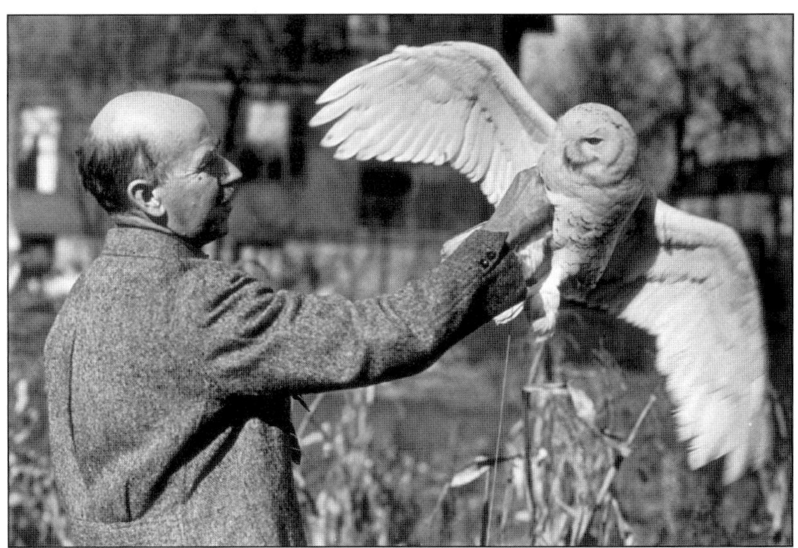

Louis Agassiz Fuertes with a live snowy owl, ca.1920
Louis Agassiz Fuertes Papers, #2662. Division of Rare and Manuscript Collections, Cornell University Library.

Copyright

Foreword copyright © 2019 by Robert McCracken Peck
All rights reserved.

Bibliographical Note

This Dover edition, first published in 2019, is a republication of all 106 plates from the work originally published by The University of the State of New York State Museum, Albany, in 1925. The plates were originally published in two volumes of *Birds of New York* by The University of the State of New York, Albany. Vol. 1, containing plates 1–42, was published in 1910, and Vol. 2, containing plates 43–106, was published in 1914. Some of the plates have been reduced in scale to better fit the book's trim size. A new Foreword, written by Robert McCracken Peck, has been specially prepared for the present edition.

Library of Congress Cataloging-in-Publication Data

Names: Fuertes, Louis Agassiz, 1874–1927, author. | Eaton, Elon Howard, 1866–1934, author. | Eaton, Elon Howard, 1866-1934. Birds of New York.
Title: Birds of New York / Louis Agassiz Fuertes ; foreword by Robert McCracken Peck.
Description: Dover edition. | Mineola, New York : Dover Publications, Inc., 2019. | Originally published: Albany : The University of the State of New York State Museum, 1925. The plates were originally published in the 2 volume Birds of New York, by Elon Howard Eaton (Albany : The University of the State of New York (plates 1–42), 1910; (plates 43–106), 1914). | "Over 100 Plates."
Identifiers: LCCN 2019013461 | ISBN 9780486837406 | ISBN 0486837408
Subjects: LCSH: Birds—New York (State)—Pictorial works.
Classification: LCC QL684.N7 E3 2019 | DDC 598.09747/1—dc23
LC record available at https://lccn.loc.gov/2019013461

Manufactured in the United States by LSC Communications
83740801
www.doverpublications.com

2 4 6 8 10 9 7 5 3 1

2019

Foreword

by Robert McCracken Peck

In the long history of wildlife art, few painters have matched—and none have exceeded—the brilliant originality and strength of the bird paintings made by Louis Agassiz Fuertes (1874–1927). In his short but influential career, Fuertes painted thousands of pictures of birds from North America and around the world. A group of 106 watercolors—made to illustrate Elon Howard Eaton's classic, two-volume *Birds of New York*—are among the best known of those that established his reputation as America's most admired wildlife painter.[1]

An Early Interest in Nature

Fuertes was born and lived most of his life in Ithaca, New York. His father was a professor and dean of engineering at Cornell University. Fuertes was a student at that school and would later become a popular member of its faculty. From an early age, he reveled in the wildness of the New York countryside, studying nature and keeping a small private "zoo" of wild animals under the family's front porch. As a teenager, his interest in observing birds expanded to painting, and what began as a method of study quickly became a passion. Like John James Audubon, the artist-naturalist who most influenced his early work, Fuertes was essentially a self-taught artist. He studied the hand-colored engravings in Audubon's great book, *The Birds of America*, in his local library and adapted that artist's artful compositions and meticulous attention to detail to his own paintings.

Two Mentors in Science and Art

During a glee club trip to Washington, D.C., in 1894, Fuertes was introduced to Dr. Elliott Coues (1842–1899), one of America's leading ornithologists. Coues was enormously impressed with Fuertes and his paintings and encouraged him to pursue his interests professionally. It was a turning point in Fuertes's life, for although he had long enjoyed bird painting as a hobby, he had never considered it as a possible career. "Ever since that first interview with Coues," Fuertes later recalled, "[I] never thought of any other profession." At least in part, it was thanks to Coues's early support that Fuertes would never need to.

---

[1]*Birds of New York* was published by The University of the State of New York in 1910 (Vol. 1, containing plates 1–42) and 1914 (Vol. 2, containing plates 43–106). So popular were these illustrations that they were republished in *Birds of America*, edited by T. Gilbert Pearson (New York: The University Society, Inc., 1917).

Fuertes's other early mentor was Abbott Handerson Thayer (1849–1921), an important American artist whose theories on the optical properties of color and light were of special interest to Fuertes. Following his graduation from Cornell University in 1897, Fuertes received his first formal instruction in painting from Thayer. With Coues's advice on scientific matters and Thayer's instruction in art, Fuertes's innate talent was nourished and refined, advancing his work to new levels of excellence. Within a few years of his graduation from college, he had become America's acknowledged master of bird painting.

A Flourishing Career at Home and Abroad

Over the next thirty years, Fuertes received painting commissions from the U.S. Biological Survey, the National Audubon Society, the American Museum of Natural History, *National Geographic* magazine, and the Departments of Education in both New York and Massachusetts, to name just a few of his many patrons. His studio work was informed by frequent outings in the country and longer research trips to Alaska (1899), Texas (1901), the Bahamas (1902), California (1903), Jamaica (1904), the Canadian Rockies (1908), Mexico (1910), Colombia (1911 and 1913), and Abyssinia/Ethiopia (1926–27).

Fuertes's Evolving Style

Fuertes's earliest paintings emulated Audubon's in composition and technique, but his style became more relaxed and original as his confidence and experience grew. His greatest strength was capturing the characteristic postures, gestures, and even personalities of his subjects. With a few easy brushstrokes in watercolor or gouache, Fuertes could suggest the essence of a particular bird. He based his avian portraits on scientific study skins, his careful observations of birds in the wild, and a near-photographic memory of their diagnostic postures and behavior.

Fuertes was delighted when he was commissioned to illustrate the ambitious Eaton book on the birds of New York, for he knew it would give his artistic production great visibility and enable him to support his growing family, but he was frustrated that the financial restrictions of the commission sometimes forced him to create images that were not as he would have wished. "Owing to the large number of species and plumages necessary to present," he explained, "it was found impossible to devote an entire plate to each species as was the first hope of all connected with the work. This accounts for the regrettable combining of several species on a plate, at times introducing anomalous conditions, and bringing birds together that seldom see each other."

"Among the water birds presented in volume 1," he went on, "the groups are for the most part not unnatural, though frequently crowded, but among the land birds in the second volume it was necessary to frankly face the situation, do the best we could, and make this explanation."[2]

[2]Fuertes's "Illustrator's Note," *Birds of New York*, Vol. 1.

A Brilliant Career and Life Cut Short

After completing *Birds of New York*, Fuertes went on to produce the illustrations for two other state bird books: *Birds of Massachusetts and Other New England States* (1925–1929), with text by Edward Howe Forbush—for which Fuertes was working on the plates at the time of his death—and *The Birdlife of Texas*, with text by Harry C. Oberholser, edited by Edgar B. Kincaid, Jr., which was not published until 1974. He was also the principal illustrator for a number of important ornithological monographs, including William Beebe's *Monograph of the Pheasants* (1922), John C. Phillips's *A Natural History of Ducks* (1922), and T. Gilbert Pearson's *Herons of the United States* (1924). His primary audience was adult and semiscientific, but he created a number of books for children as well, including *The [Thornton] Burgess Bird Book for Children* (1919) and *The Burgess Animal Book for Children* (1930). His work for *National Geographic* magazine and the illustrations he created for ornithological collecting cards distributed by Arm & Hammer Baking Soda reached the households of millions of Americans, significantly advancing the popularity of birds and the cause of wildlife conservation in the United States.

Tragically, at the peak of his artistic career, Fuertes was killed when his car was hit by a train at a road crossing near his home in New York. His wife, who was traveling with him, survived the accident. A group of paintings that he had made on a recent trip to Abyssinia, miraculously, were thrown clear of the wreck. They were later acquired and published by the Field Museum in Chicago, which had sponsored the expedition on which they were made.

The illustrations for Fuertes's watershed *Birds of New York*, reproduced here without the accompanying text, serve as a timeless record of the birds of Eastern North America and a lasting memorial to the painter who helped so many Americans come to know and love them.

Robert McCracken Peck is Curator of Art and Artifacts and Senior Fellow at the Academy of Natural Sciences of Drexel University. He has written about a number of other wildlife artists, including Basil Ede, Fenwick Lansdowne, and Terence Shortt, and the English poet and natural history painter Edward Lear, about whom he wrote a book in 2016. His biography of Fuertes, *A Celebration of Birds: The Life and Art of Louis Agassiz Fuertes*, published in 1982, is considered the definitive biography of the artist.

Index to Plates

All ⅔ nat. size

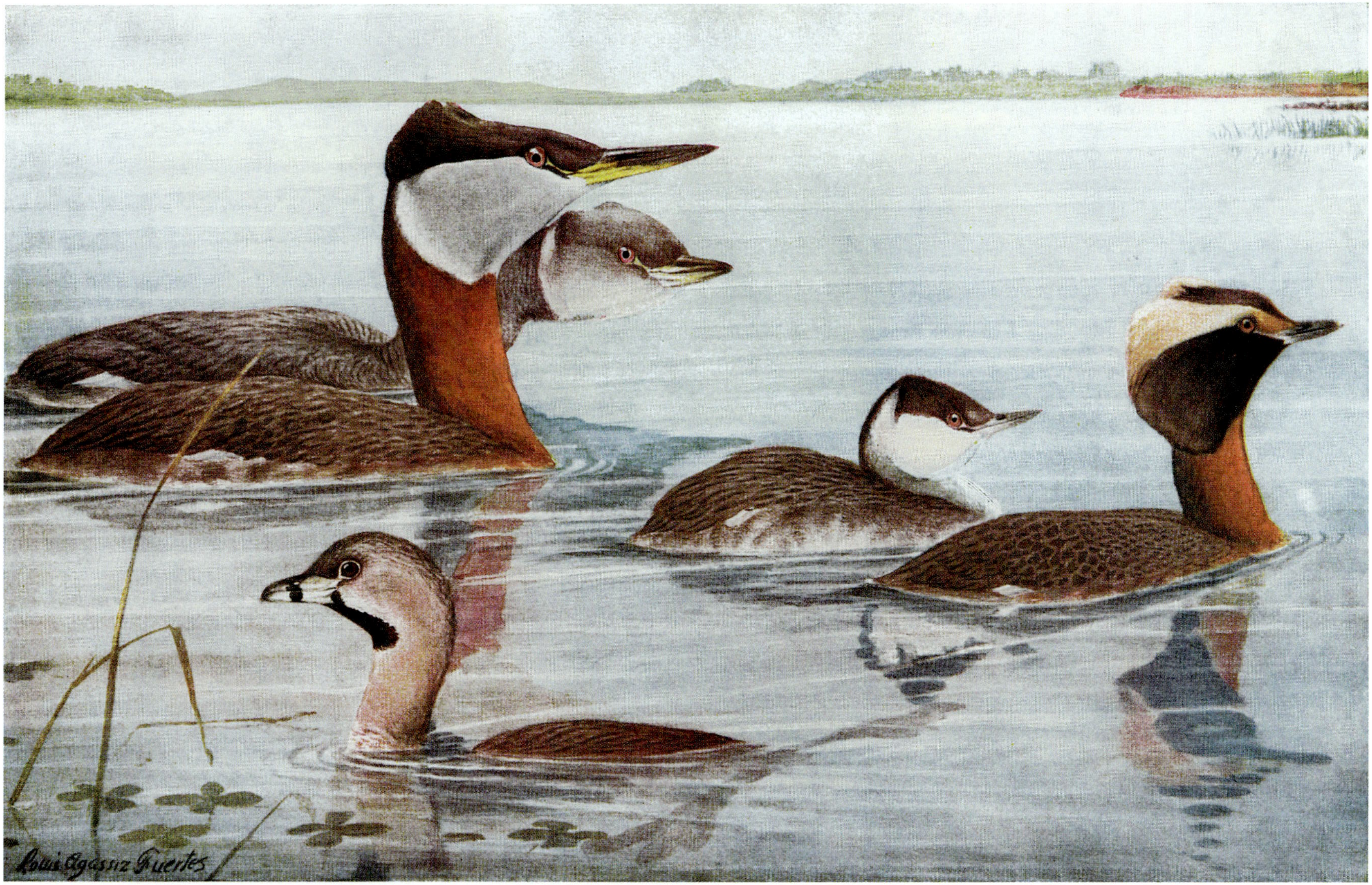

Louis Agassiz Fuertes

HOLBOELL'S GREBE
Colymbus holboelli (Reinhardt)
WINTER
SUMMER

PIED-BILLED GREBE
Podilymbus podiceps (Linnaeus)
SUMMER

HORNED GREBE
Colymbus auritus (Linnaeus)
WINTER
SUMMER

All ⅕ nat. size

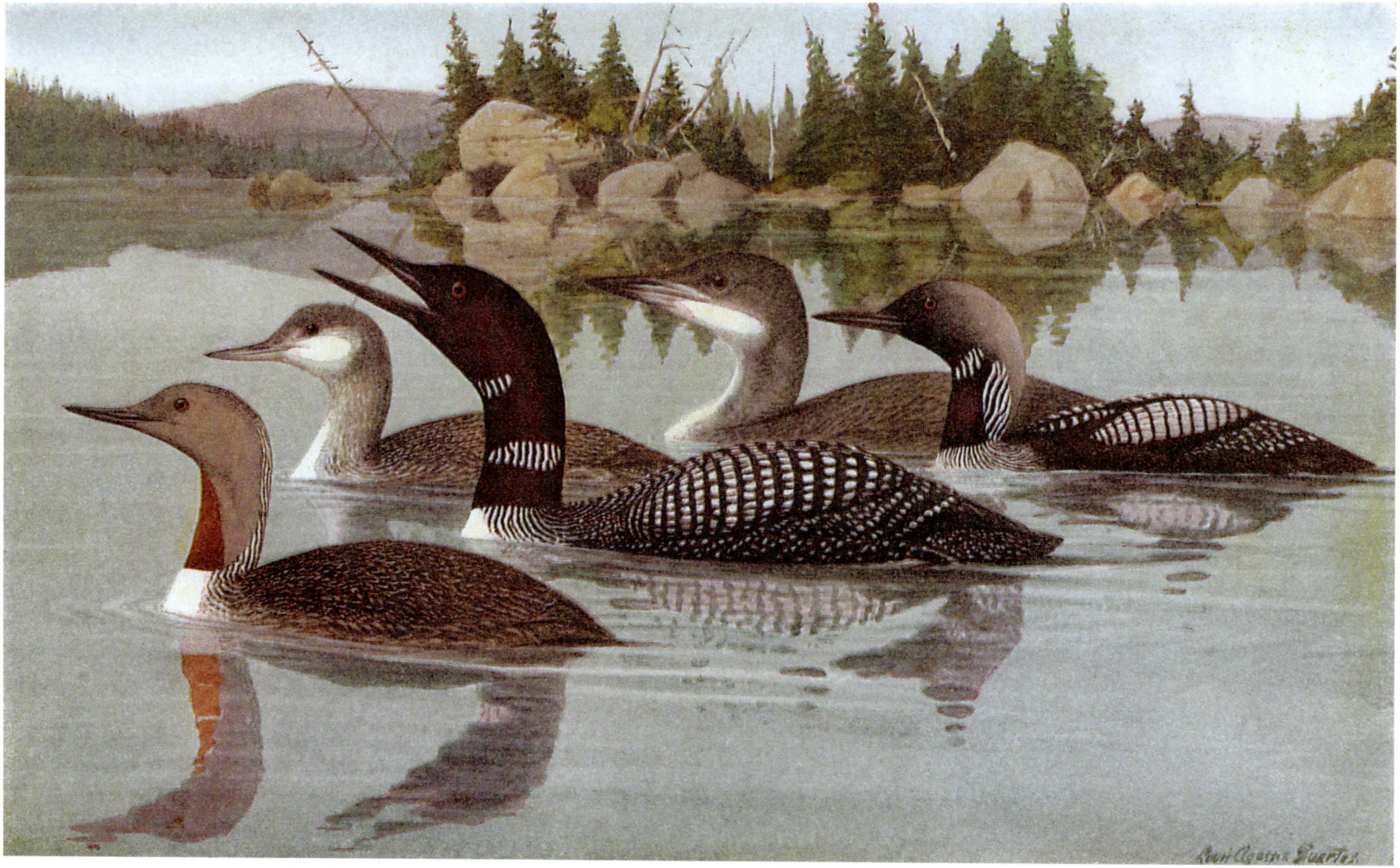

RED-THROATED LOON
Gavia stella'a (Pontoppidan)
SUMMER WINTER

COMMON LOON
Gavia immer (Brünnich)
SUMMER WINTER

BLACK-THROATED LOON
Gavia arctica (Linnaeus)
SUMMER

All ¼ nat. size

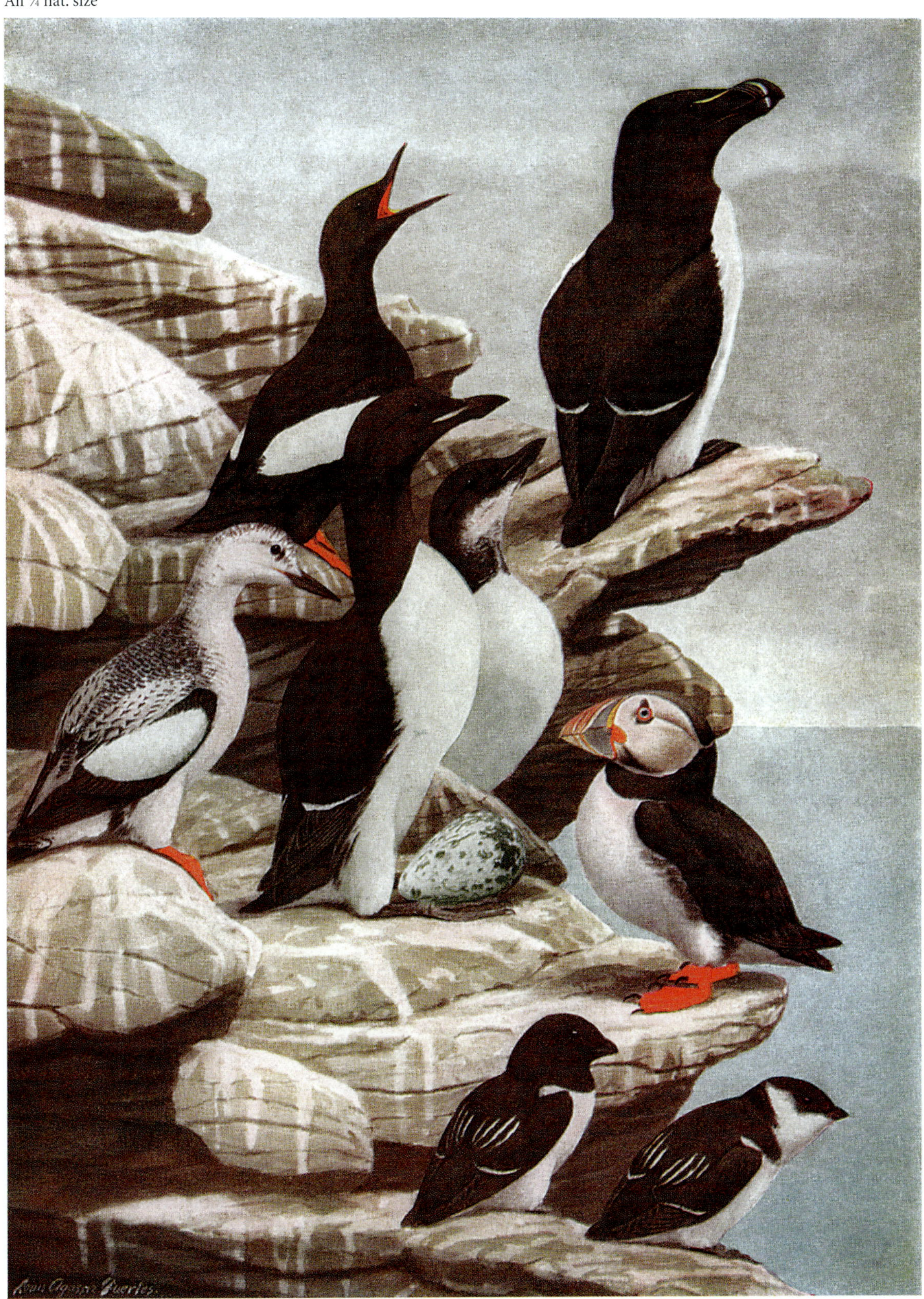

BLACK GUILLEMOT
Cepphus grylle (Linnaeus)
WINTER SUMMER

BRÜNNICH MURRE
Uria lomvia (Linnaeus)
WINTER SUMMER
EGG

RAZOR-BILLED AUK
Alca torda (Linnaeus)
SUMMER

PUFFIN
Fratercula arctica (Linnaeus)
SUMMER

DOVEKIE
Alle alle (Linnaeus)
SUMMER WINTER

All ⅕ nat. size

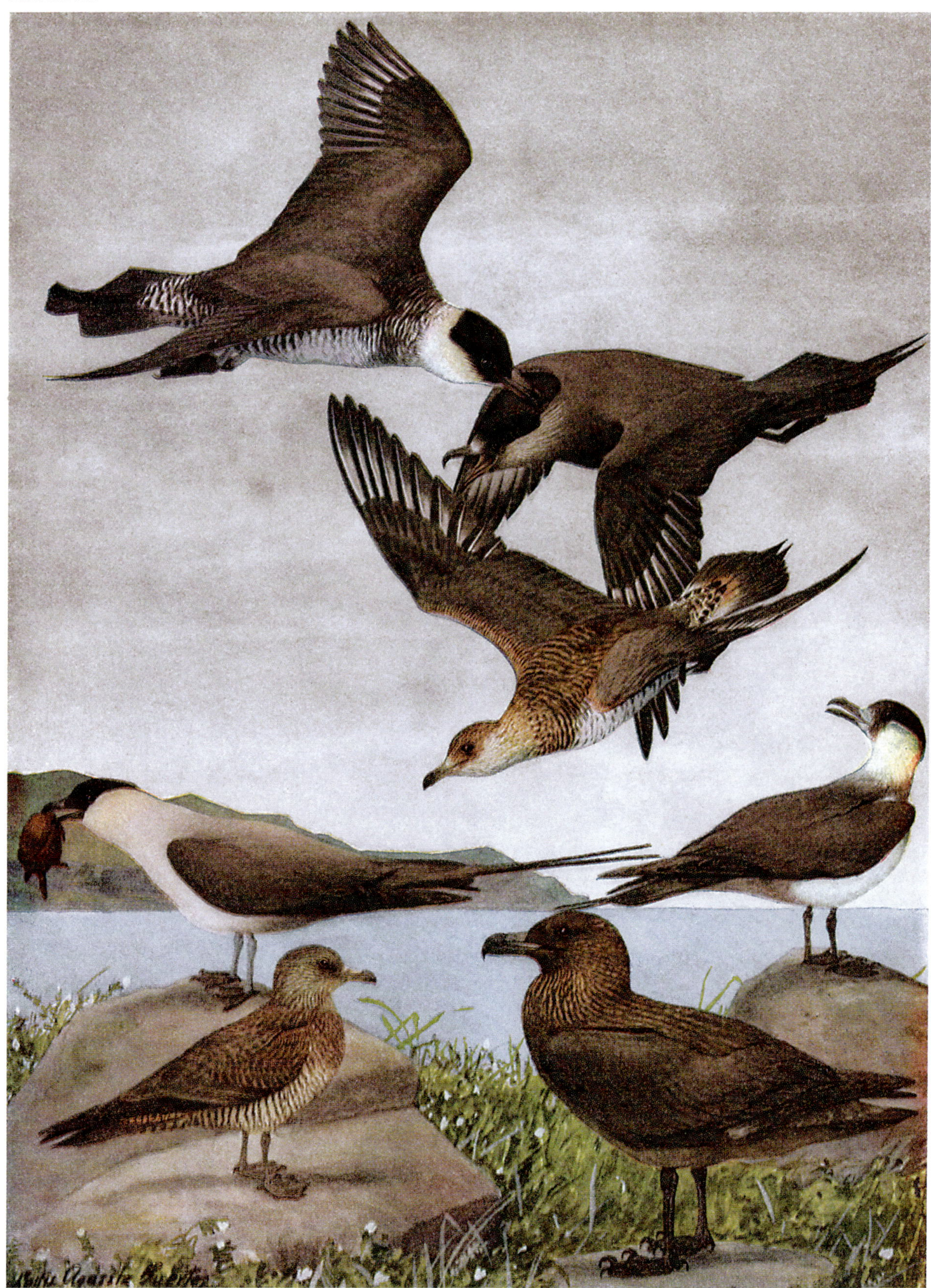

POMARINE JAEGER *Stercorarius pomarinus* (Temminck)
LONG-TAILED JAEGER *Stercorarius longicaudus* (Vieillot)
ADULT
IMMATURE *S. parasiticus*

PARASITIC JAEGER *Stercorarius parasiticus* (Linnaeus)
DARK PHASE
INTERMEDIATE
LIGHT PHASE
SKUA *Megalestris skua* (Brünnich)

All ½ nat. size

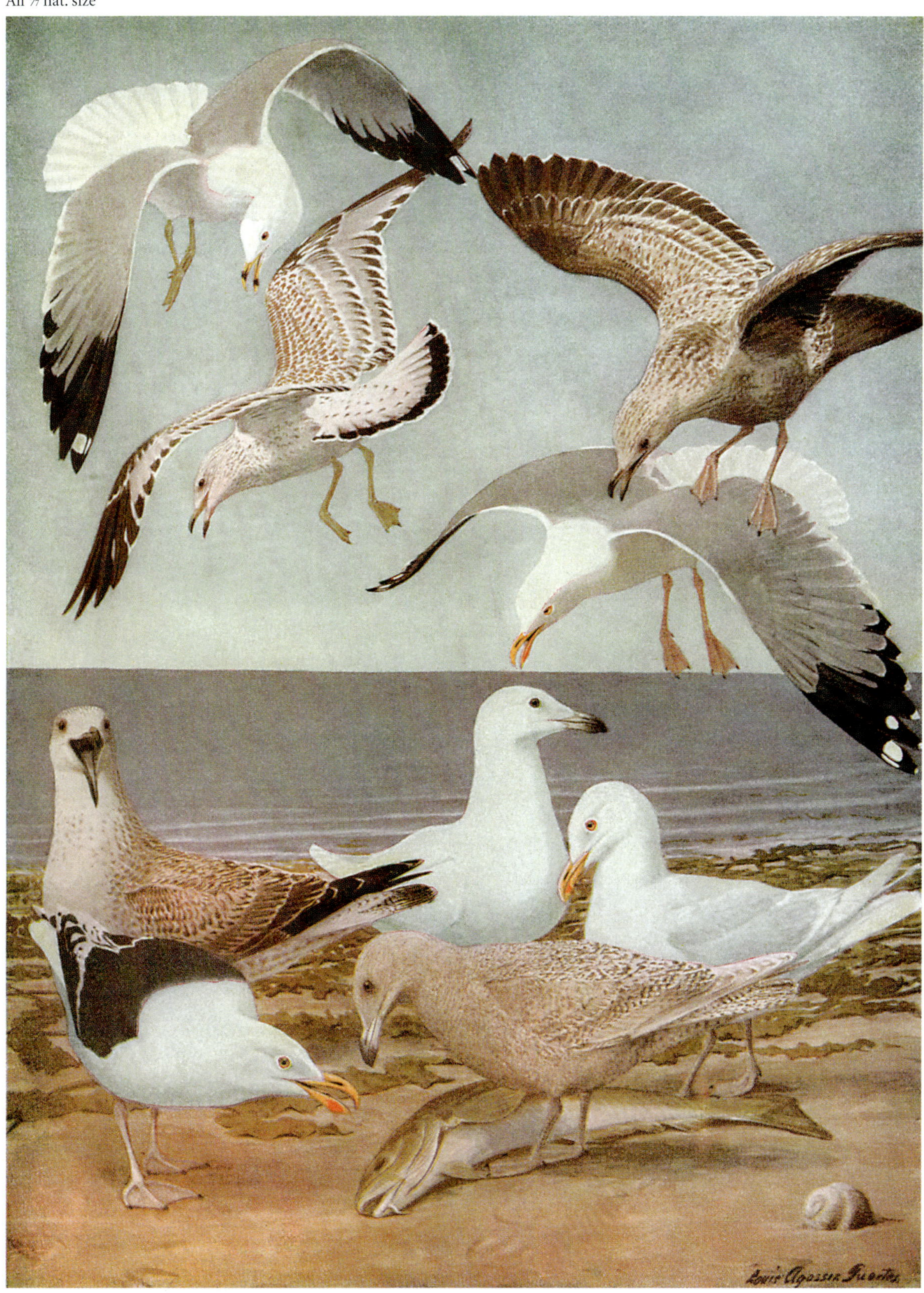

RING-BILLED GULL
Larus delawarensis (Ord)
ADULT IN SUMMER IMMATURE

HERRING GULL
Larus argentatus (Pontoppidan)
IMMATURE ADULT IN SUMMER

GREAT BLACK-BACKED GULL
Larus marinus (Linnaeus)
IMMATURE ADULT IN SUMMER

GLAUCOUS GULL
Larus hyperboreus (Gunnerus)
END OF SECOND YEAR ADULT IN SUMMER
IMMATURE

All ⅙ nat. size

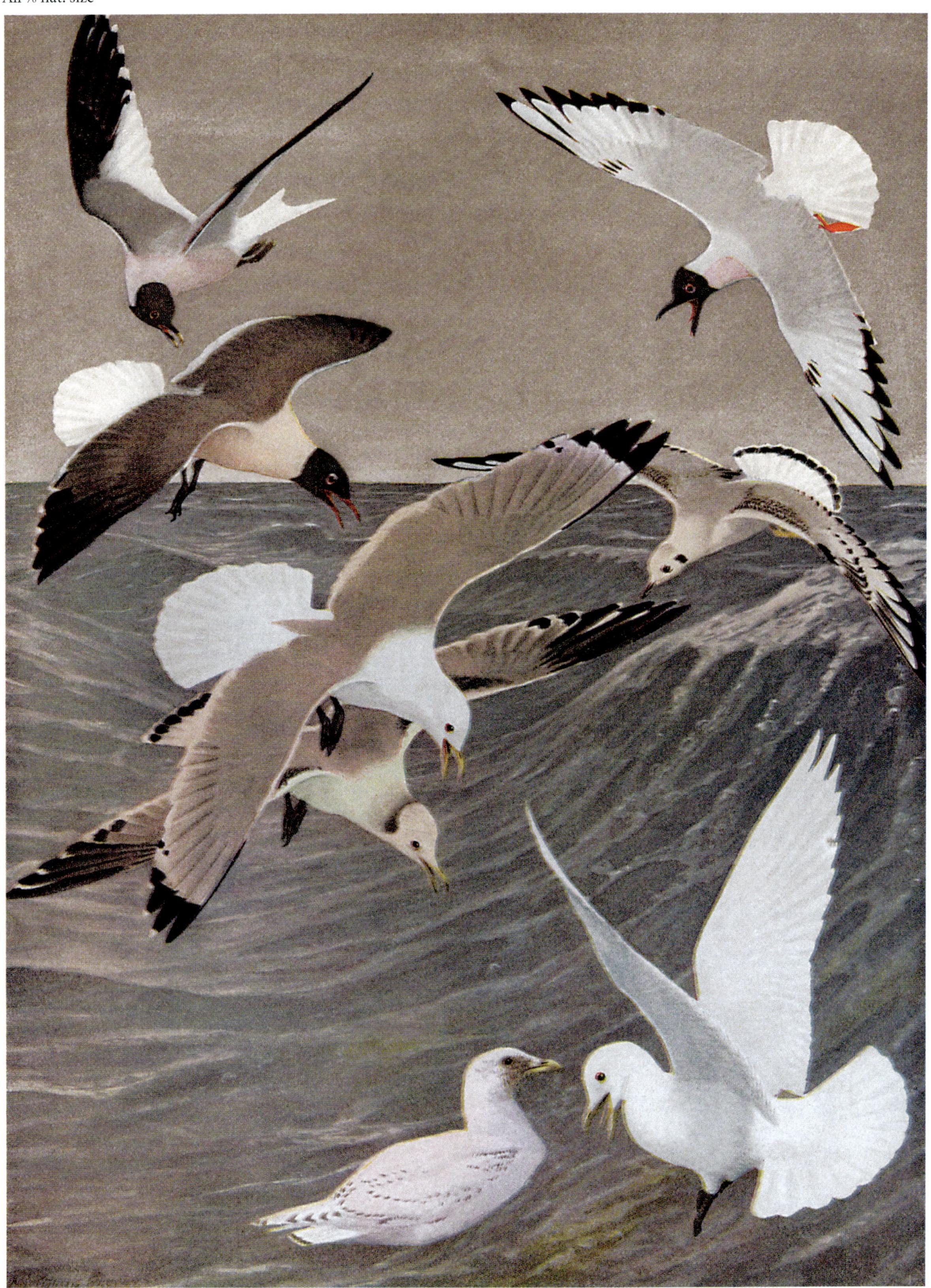

SABINE GULL ADULT IN SUMMER
Xema sabini (Sabine)
LAUGHING GULL ADULT IN SUMMER
Larus atricilla (Linnaeus)
KITTIWAKE
Rissa tridactyla (Linnaeus)
ADULT IN SUMMER IMMATURE
IMMATURE

BONAPARTE GULL
Larus philadelphia (Ord)
ADULT IN SUMMER
IMMATURE
IVORY GULL
Pagophila alba (Gunnerus)
ADULT IN SUMMER

All ⅕ nat. size

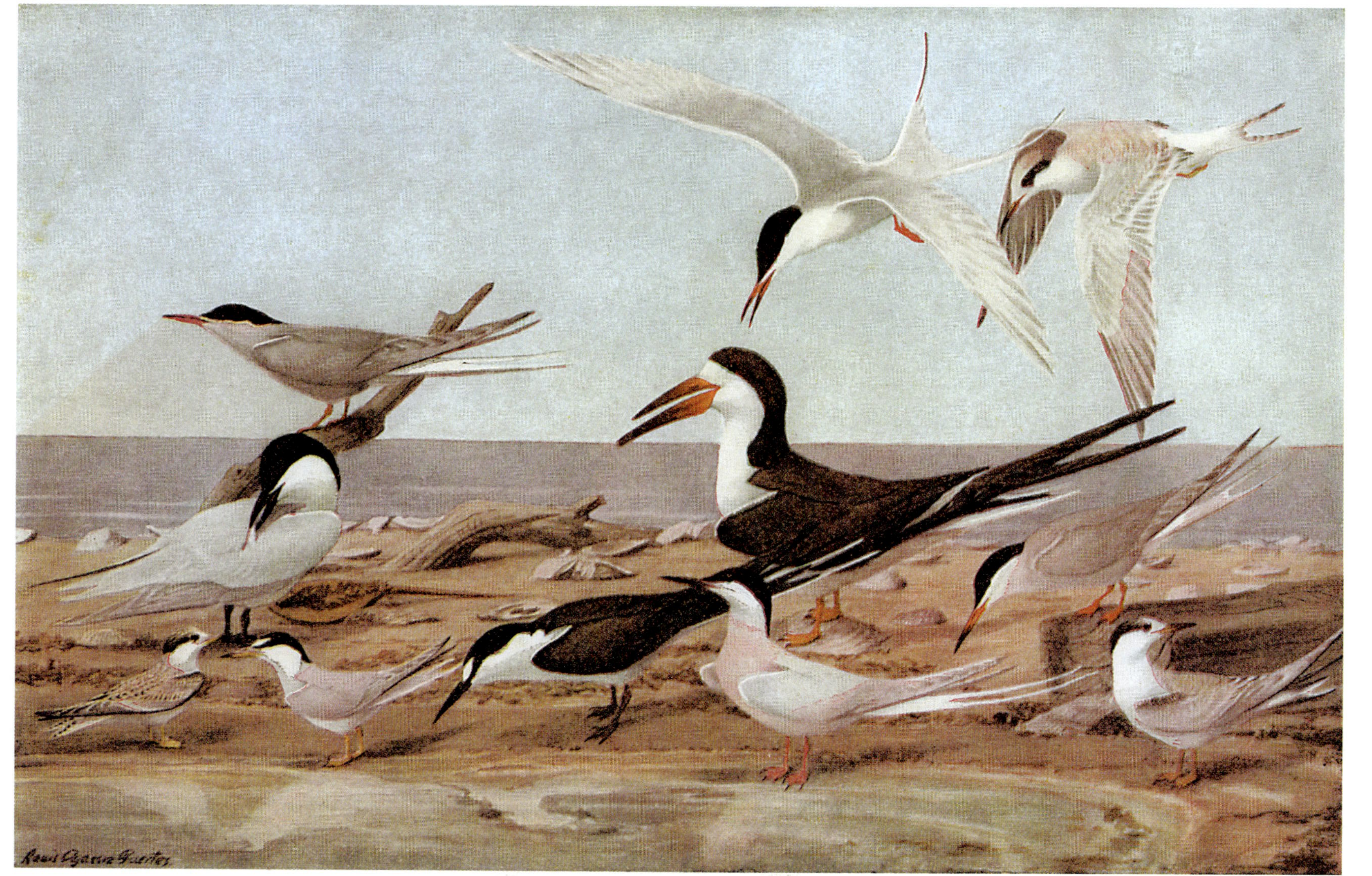

ARCTIC TERN ADULT IN SUMMER
Sterna paradisaea (Brünnich)

GULL-BILLED TERN ADULT IN SUMMER
Gelochelidon nilotica (Hasselquist)

LEAST TERN *Sterna antillarum* (Lesson)
IMMATURE ADULT IN SUMMER

SOOTY TERN ADULT IN SUMMER
Sterna fuscata (Linnaeus)

FORSTER TERN
Sterna forsteri (Nuttall)
ADULT IN SUMMER IMMATURE

BLACK SKIMMER
Rhynocops nigra (Linnaeus)

ROSEATE TERN ADULT IN SUMMER
Sterna dougalli (Montagu)

COMMON TERN
Sterna hirundo (Linnaeus)
ADULT IN SUMMER IMMATURE

All ⅙ nat. size

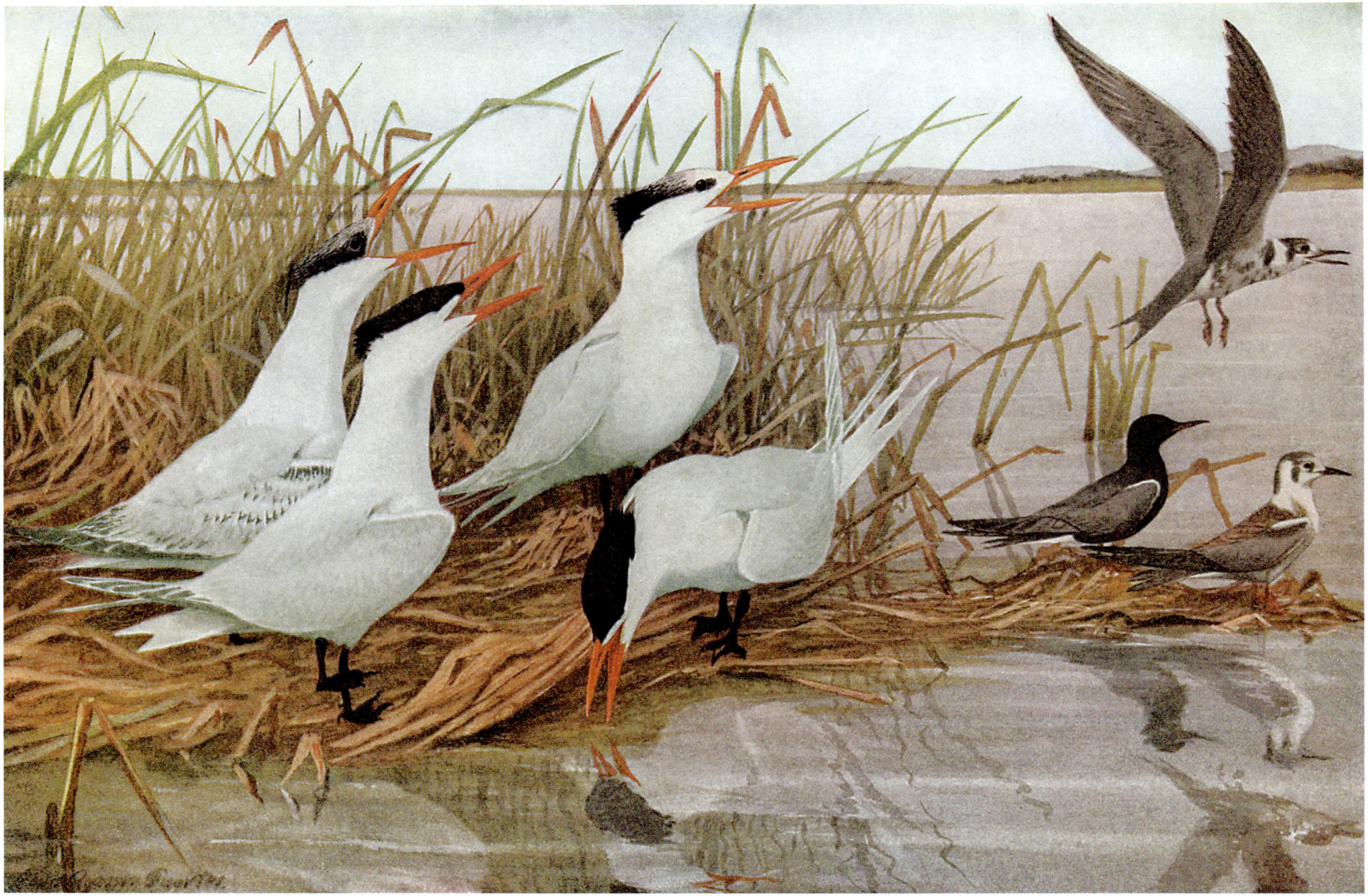

CASPIAN TERN
Sterna caspia (Pallas)
IMMATURE ADULT IN SPRING

ROYAL TERN
Sterna maxima (Boddaert)
ADULT IN WINTER ADULT IN SPRING

BLACK TERN
Hydrochelidon nigra surinamensis (Gmelin)
ADULT CHANGING TO WINTER PLUMAGE
ADULT IN SPRING IMMATURE

All ⅙ nat. size

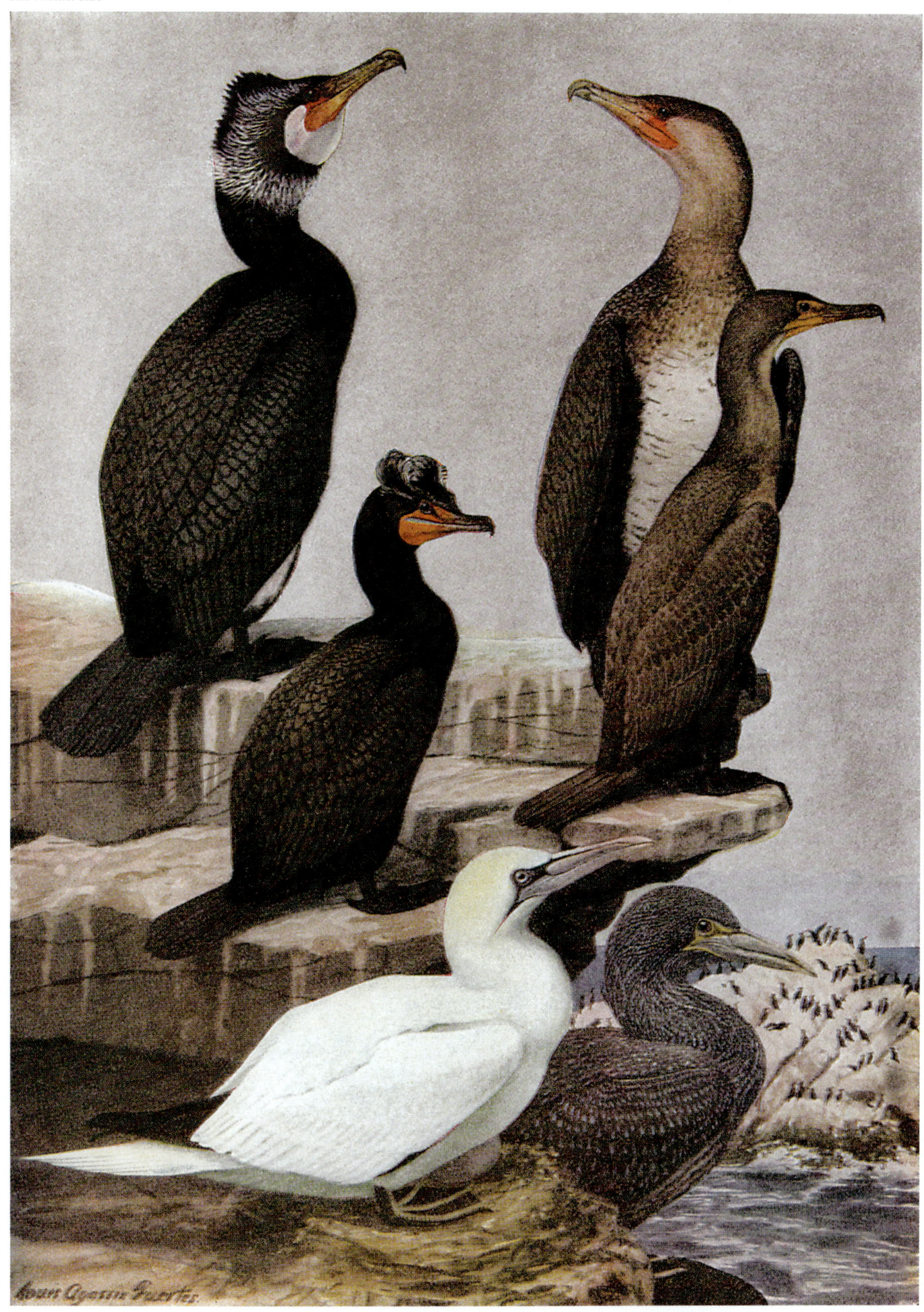

COMMON CORMORANT *Phalacrocorax carbo* (Linnaeus)
ADULT IN BREEDING PLUMAGE IMMATURE

DOUBLE-CRESTED CORMORANT *Phalacrocorax auritus* (Lesson)
ADULT IN BREEDING PLUMAGE IMMATURE

GANNET *Sula bassana* (Linnaeus)
ADULT IMMATURE

All ⅕ nat. size

RED-BREASTED MERGANSER *Mergus serrator* (Linnaeus)
FEMALE MALE

AMERICAN MERGANSER *Mergus americanus* (Cassin)
FEMALE MALE

RUDDY DUCK *Erismatura jamaicensis* (Gmelin)
FEMALE MALE

BUFFLE-HEADED DUCK *Charitonetta albeola* (Linnaeus)
MALE FEMALE

Both ¼ nat. size

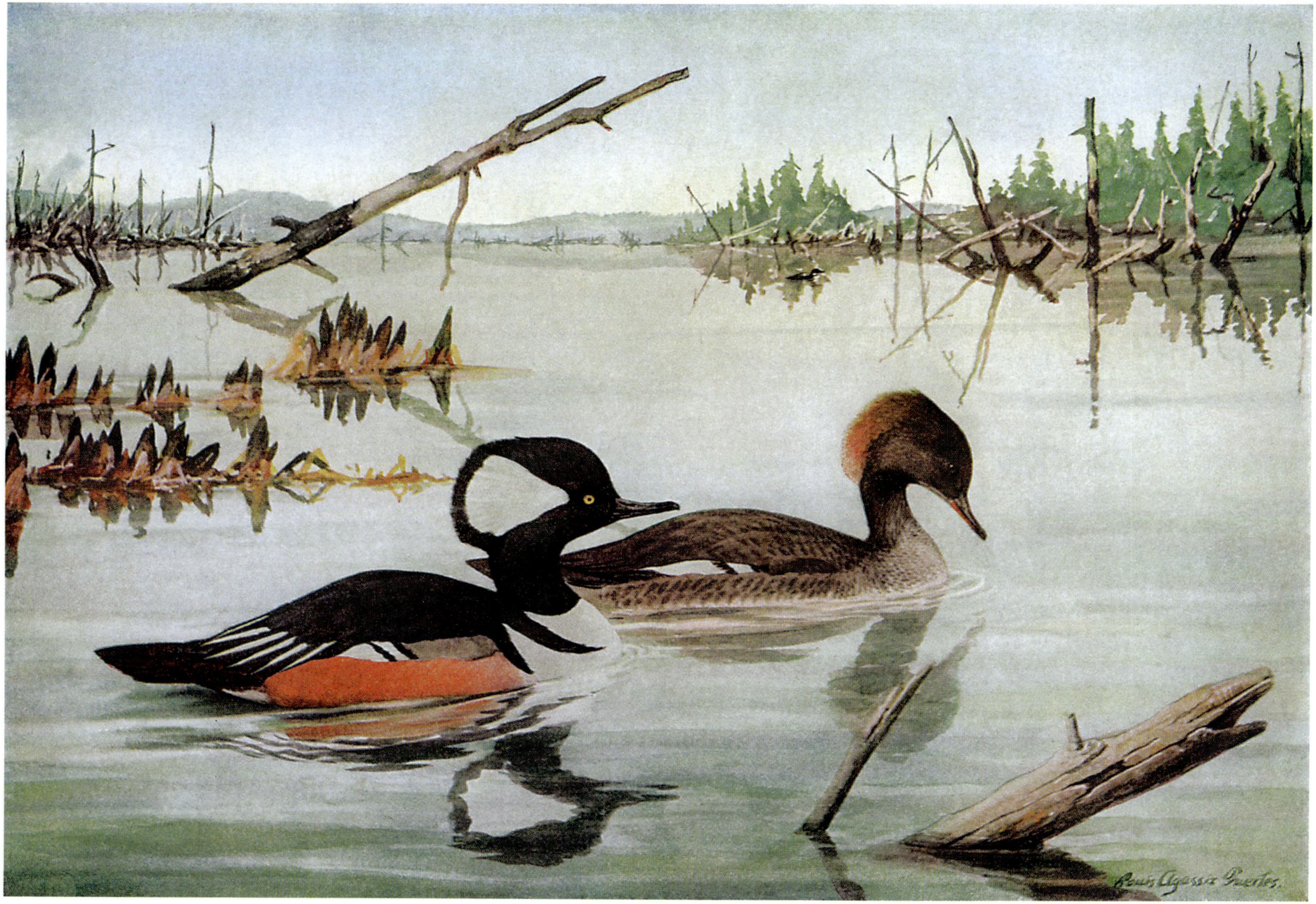

HOODED MERGANSER *Lophodytes cucullatus* (Linnaeus)

MALE FEMALE

All ⅓ nat. size

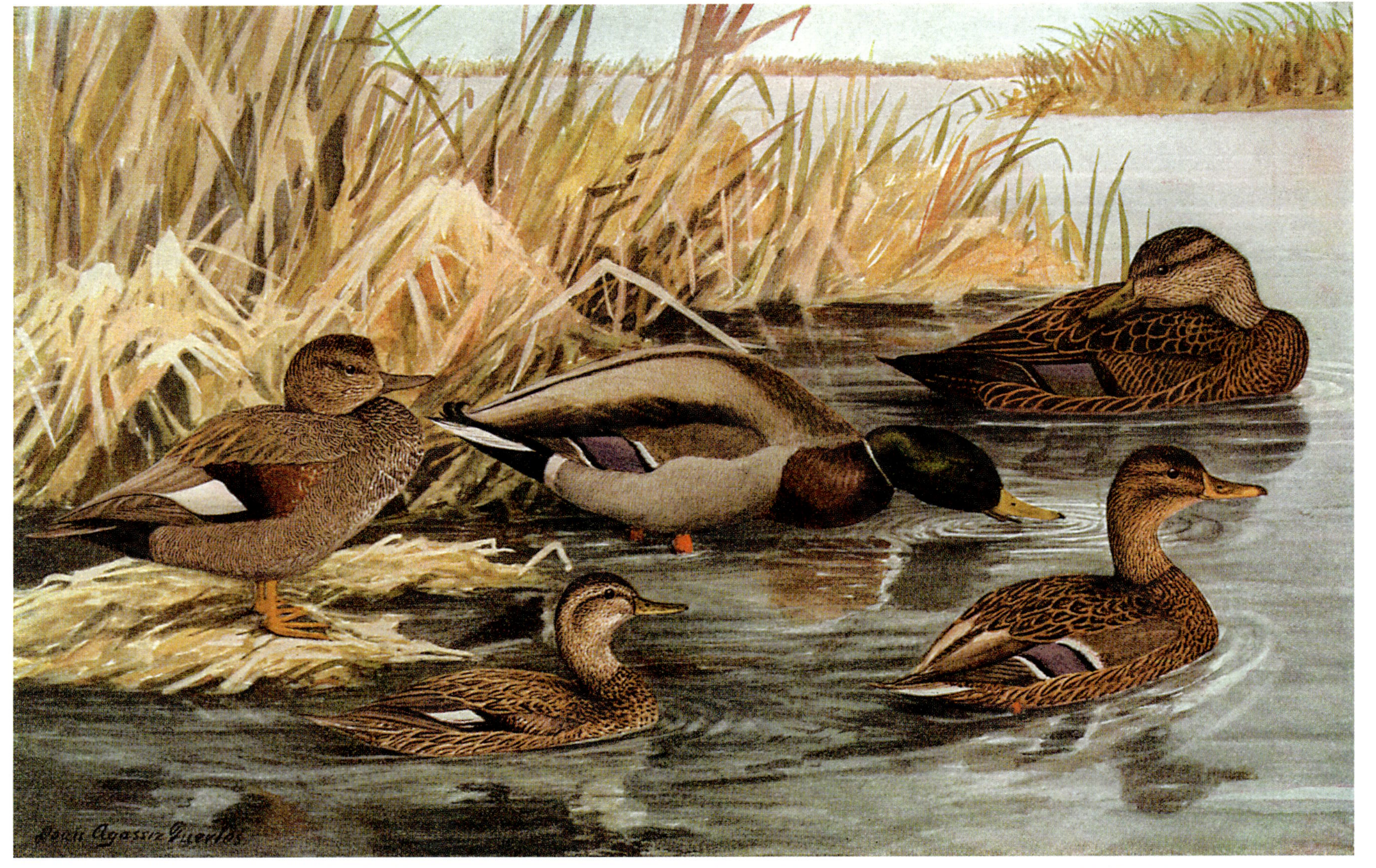

GADWALL
Chaulelasmus streperus (Linnaeus)
MALE FEMALE

MALLARD
Anas boschas (Linnaeus)
MALE

BLACK DUCK
Anas obscura (Gmelin)
FEMALE MALE

All ⅕ nat. size

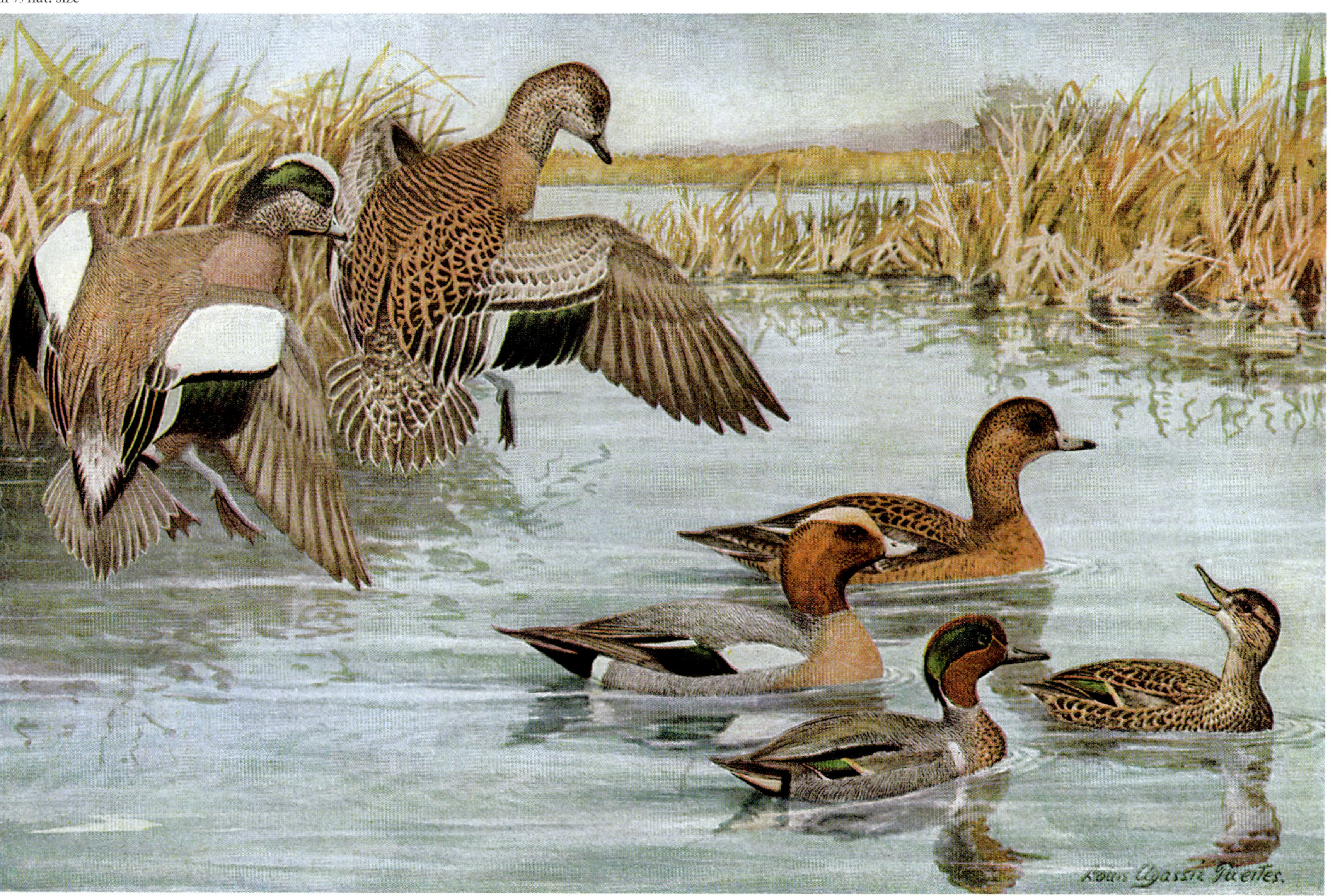

AMERICAN WIDGEON
Mareca americana (Gmelin)
MALE FEMALE

EUROPEAN WIDGEON
Mareca penelope (Linnaeus)
MALE FEMALE

GREEN-WINGED TEAL
Nettion carolinense (Gmelin)
MALE FEMALE

All ¼ nat. size

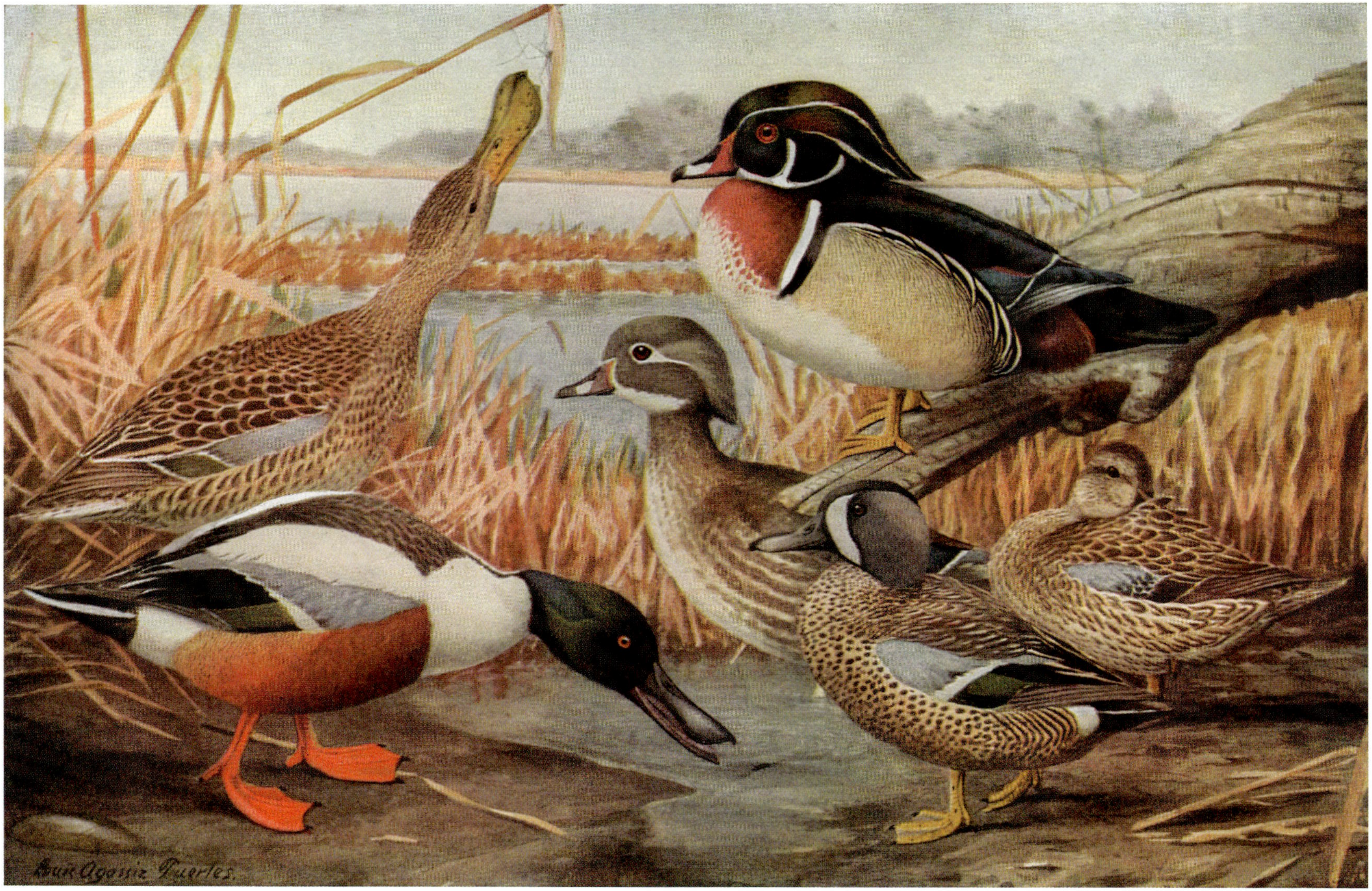

SHOVELER
Spatula clypeata (Linnaeus)
FEMALE MALE

WOOD DUCK
Aix sponsa (Linnaeus)
FEMALE MALE

BLUE-WINGED TEAL
Querquedula discors (Linnaeus)
MALE FEMALE

Both ⅕ nat. size

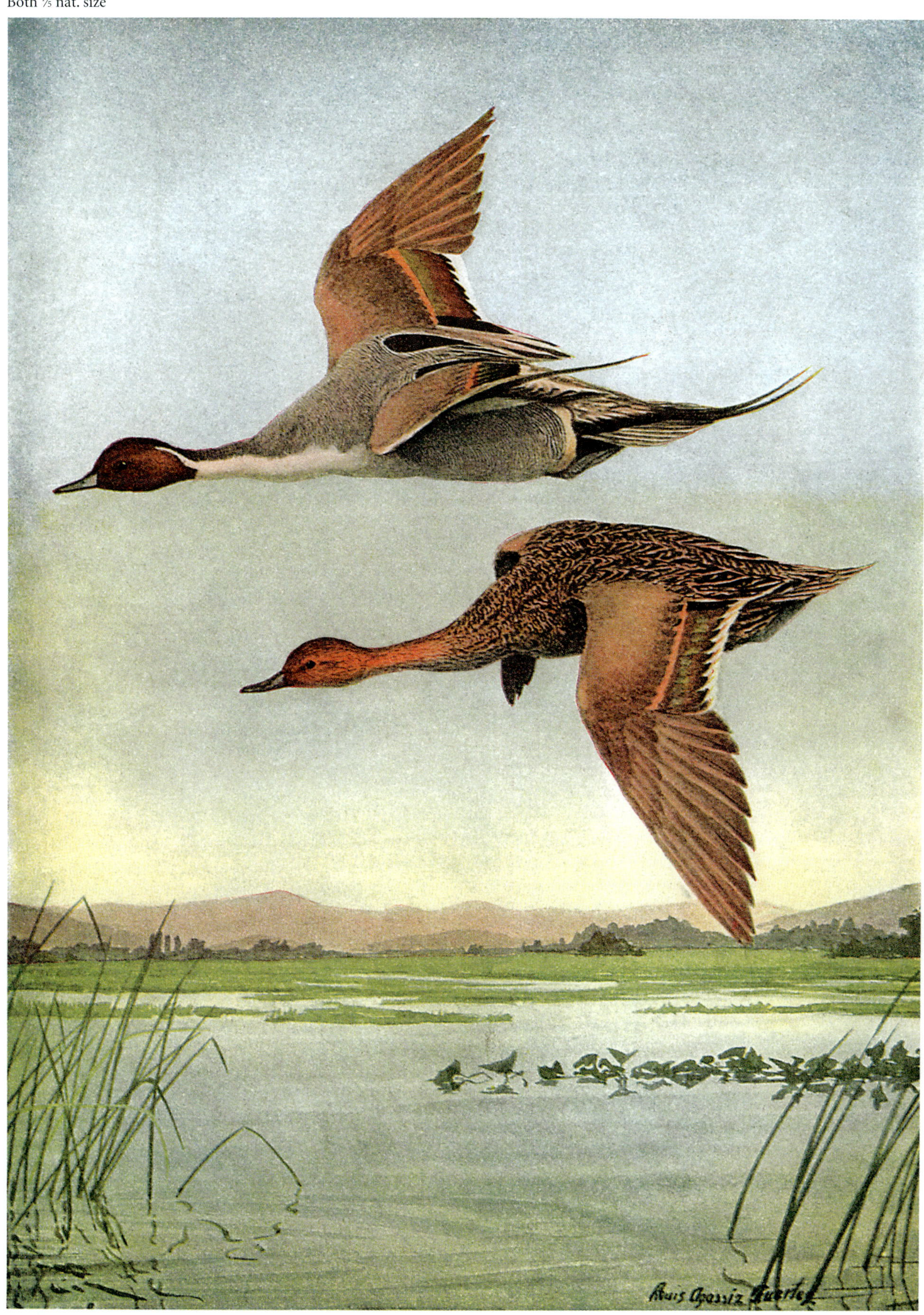

PINTAIL *Dafila acuta* (Linnaeus)
MALE FEMALE

All ¼ nat. size

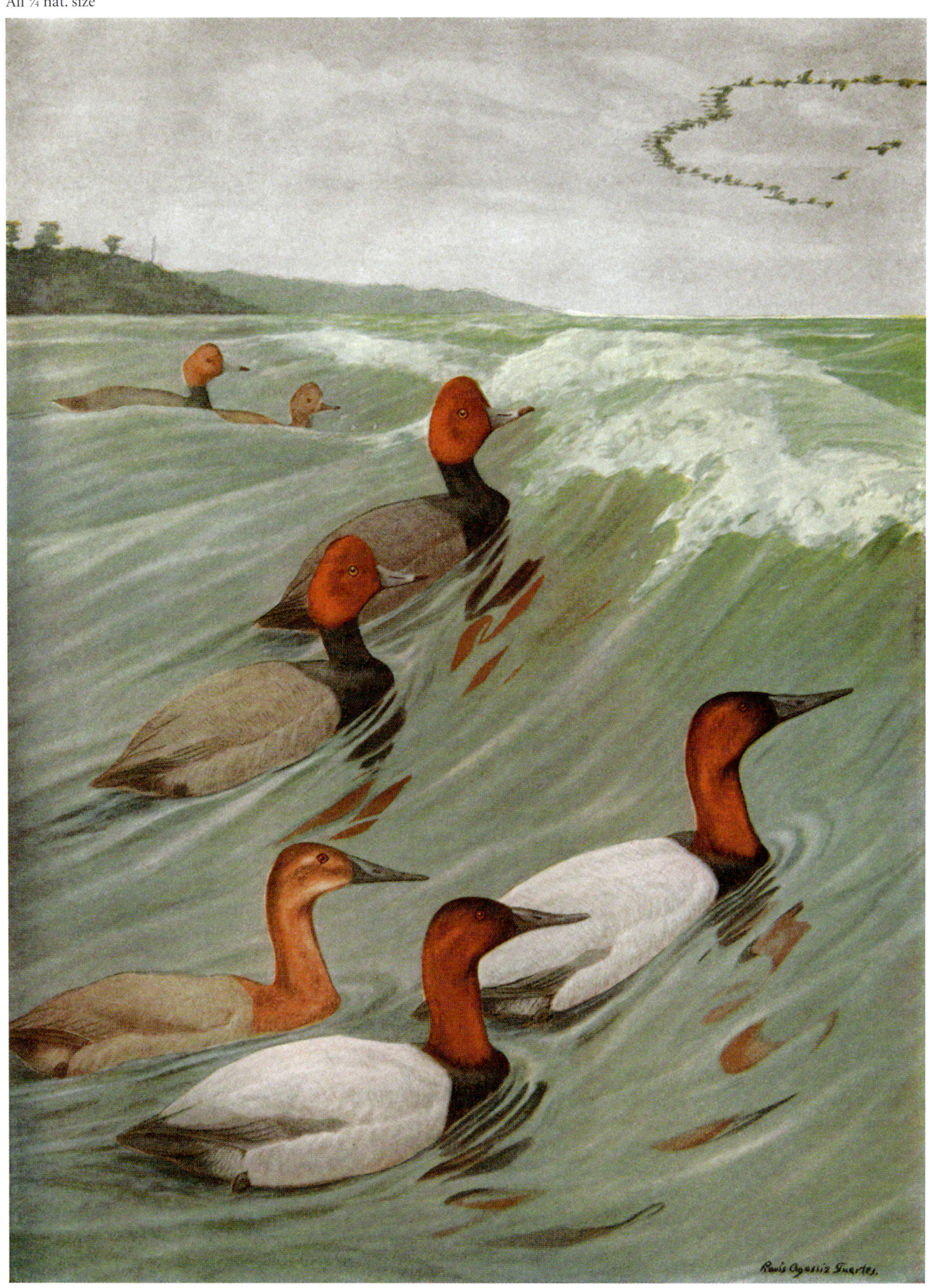

REDHEAD
Aythya americana (Eyton)
MALES

CANVASBACK
Aythya vallisneria (Wilson)
FEMALE
MALES

All ¼ nat. size

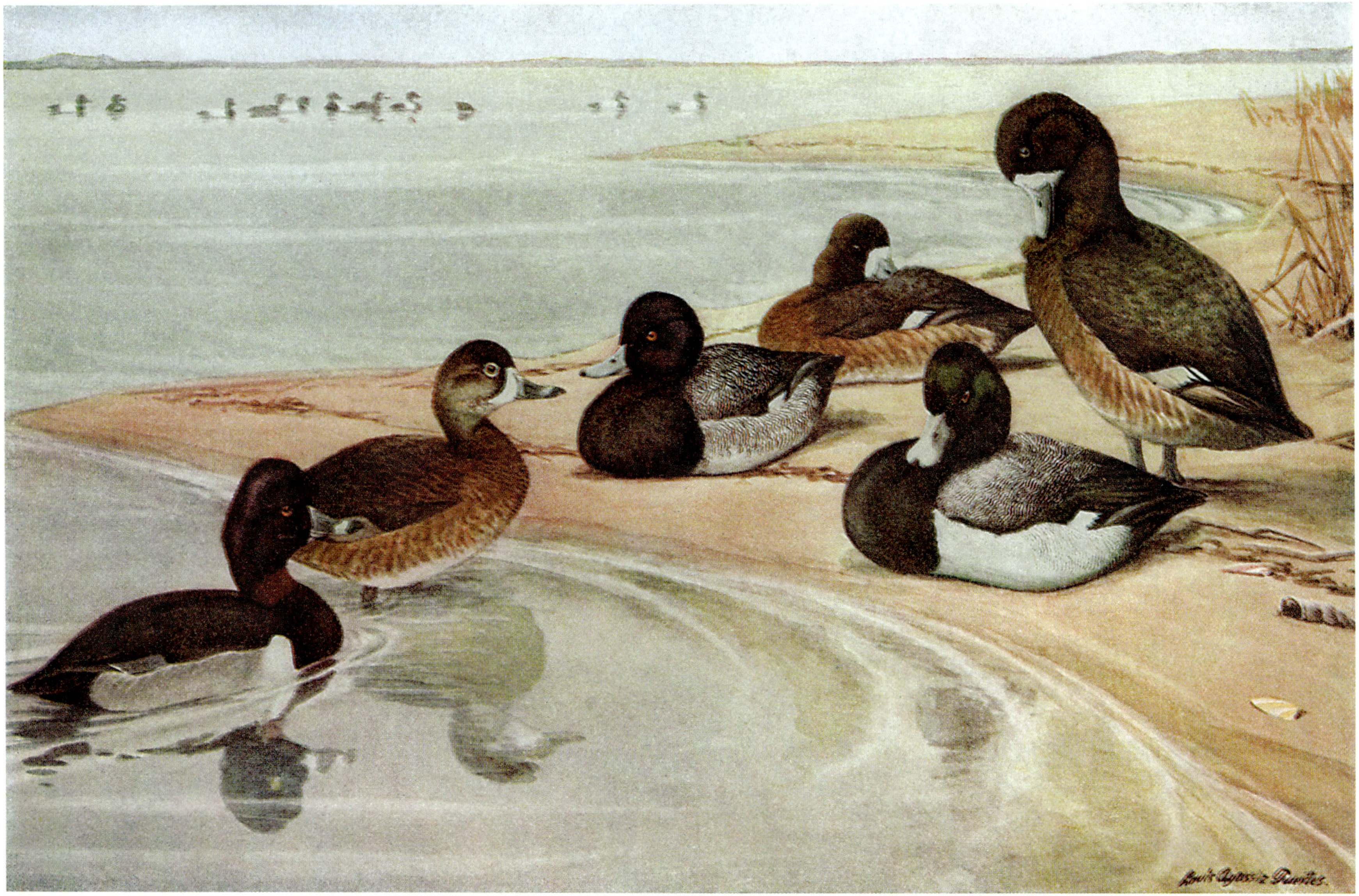

Louis Agassiz Fuertes

RING-NECKED DUCK
Aythya collaris (Donovan)
MALE FEMALE

LESSER SCAUP
Aythya affinis (Eyton)
MALE FEMALE

SCAUP
AYTHYA MARILA (LINNAEUS)
MALE FEMALE

PLATE 18

Both ⅓ nat. size

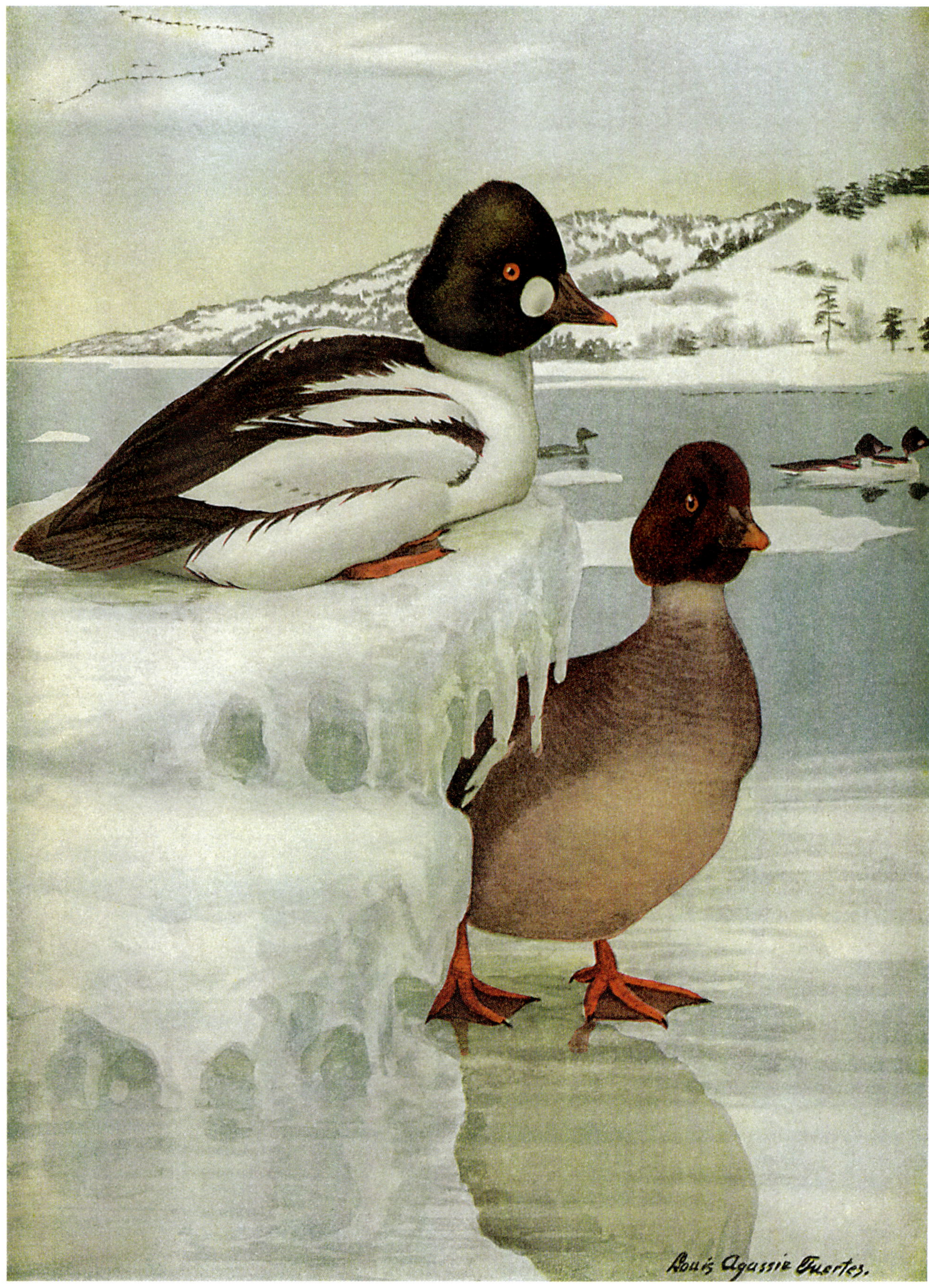

AMERICAN GOLDEN-EYE *Clangula clangula americana* (Bonaparte)
MALE FEMALE

All 1/5 nat. size

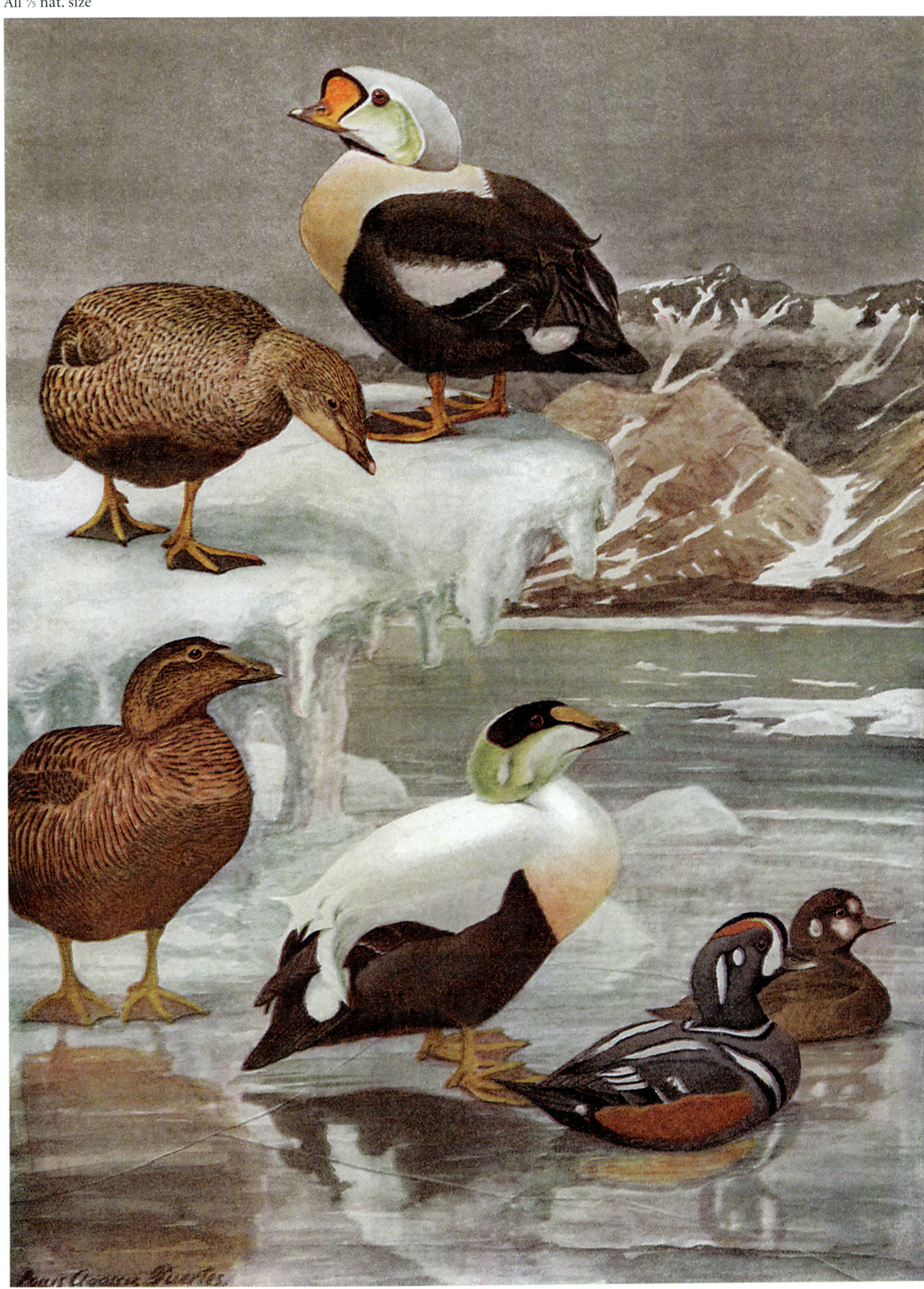

KING EIDER *Somateria spectabilis* (Linnaeus)
FEMALE MALE

AMERICAN EIDER *Somateria dresseri* (Sharpe)
FEMALE MALE

HARLEQUIN DUCK *Histrionicus histrionicus* (Linnaeus)
MALE FEMALE

All ⅕ nat. size

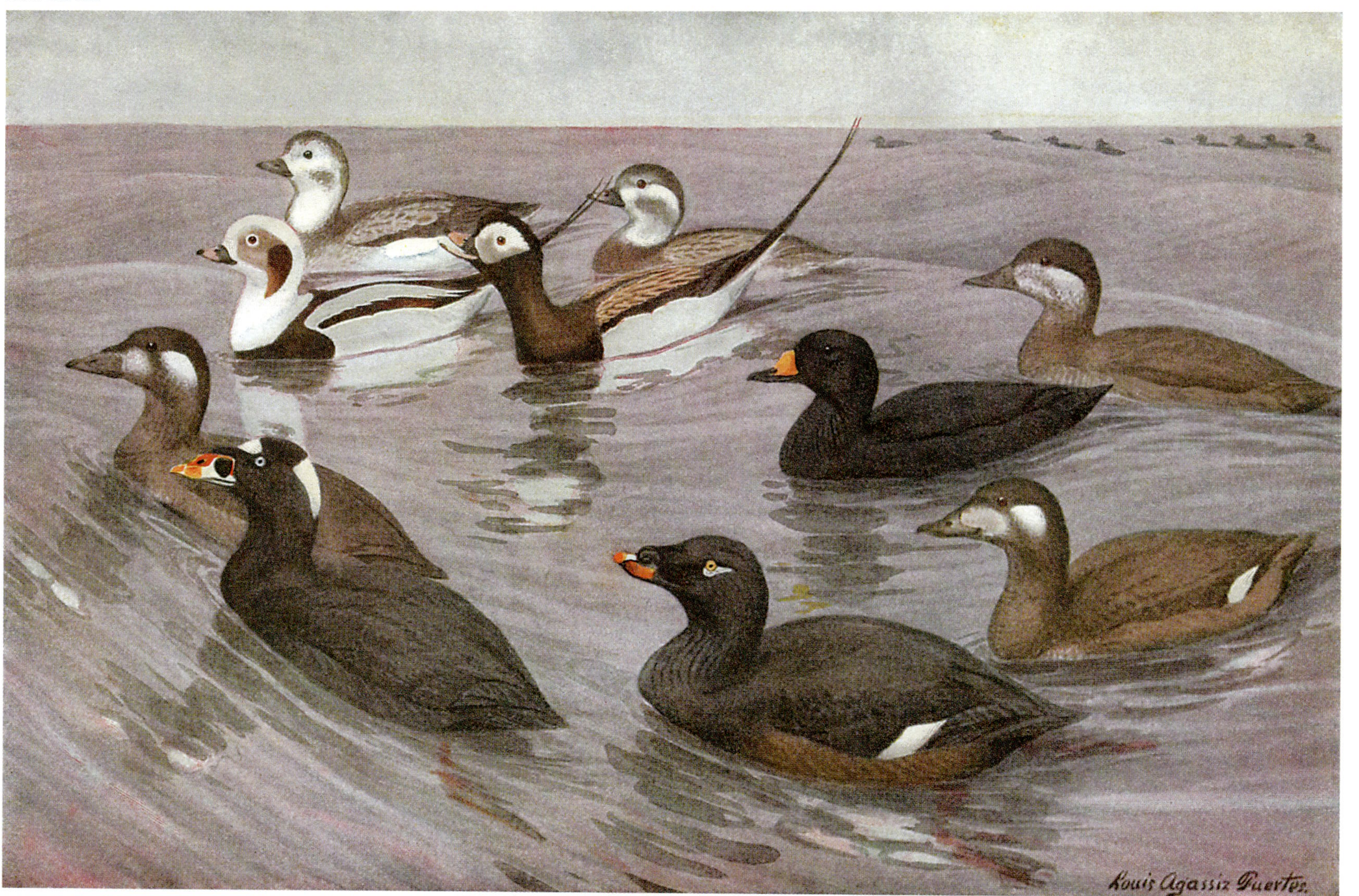

OLD-SQUAW
Harelda hyemalis (Linnaeus)
FEMALE } WINTER
MALE }
SUMMER { FEMALE
{ MALE

SURF SCOTER
Oiedemia perspicillata (Linnaeus)
FEMALE MALE

AMERICAN SCOTER
Oiedemia americana (Swainson)
MALE FEMALE

WHITE-WINGED SCOTER
Oidemia deglandi (Bonaparte)
MALE FEMALE

All ⅛ nat. size

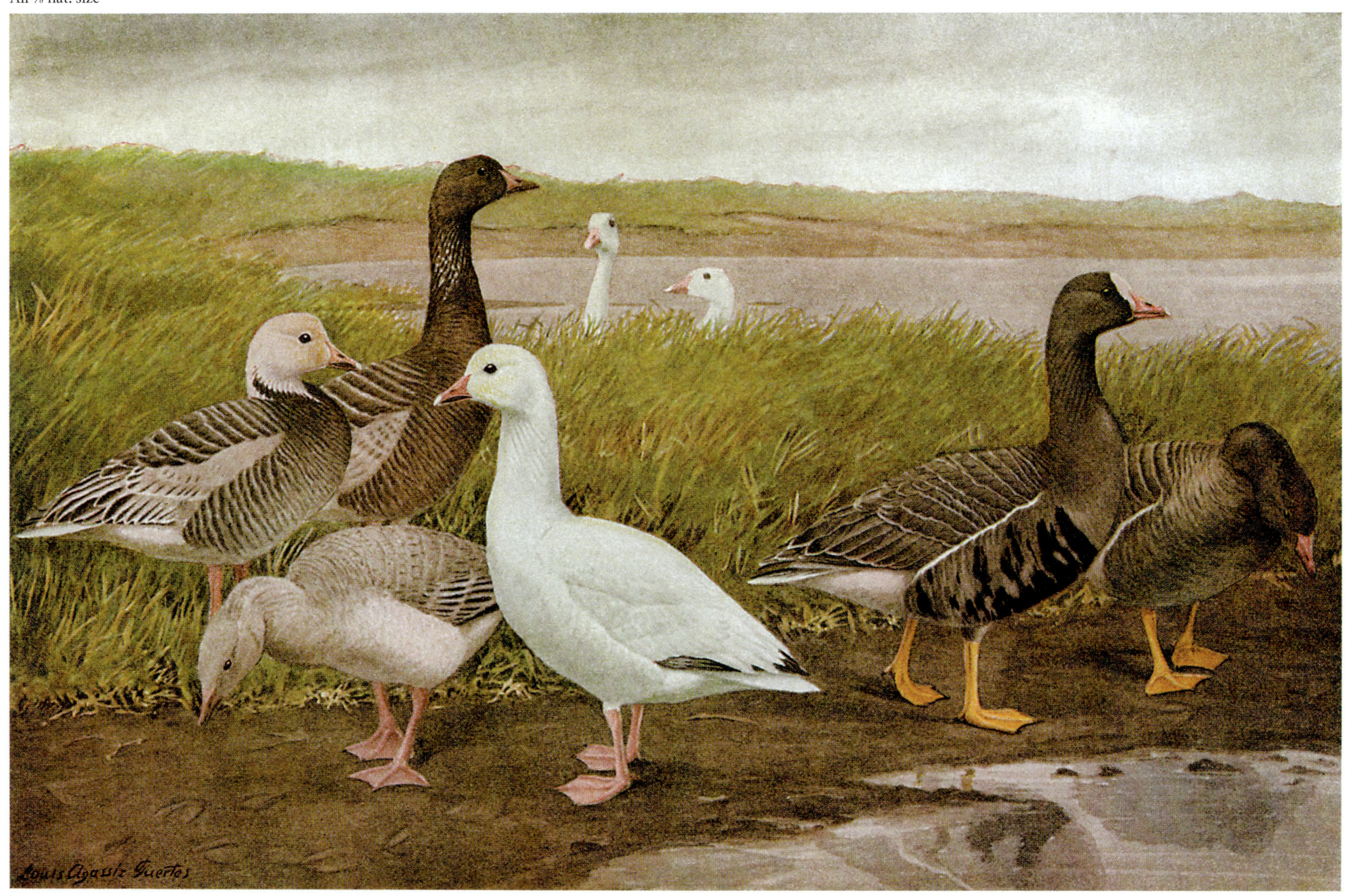

BLUE GOOSE
Chen caerulescens (Linnaeus)
ADULT IMMATURE

SNOW GOOSE
Chen hyperborea nivalis (Forster)
IMMATURE ADULT

AMERICAN WHITE-FRONTED GOOSE
Anser albifrons gambeli (Hartlaub)
ADULT IMMATURE

All ½ nat. size

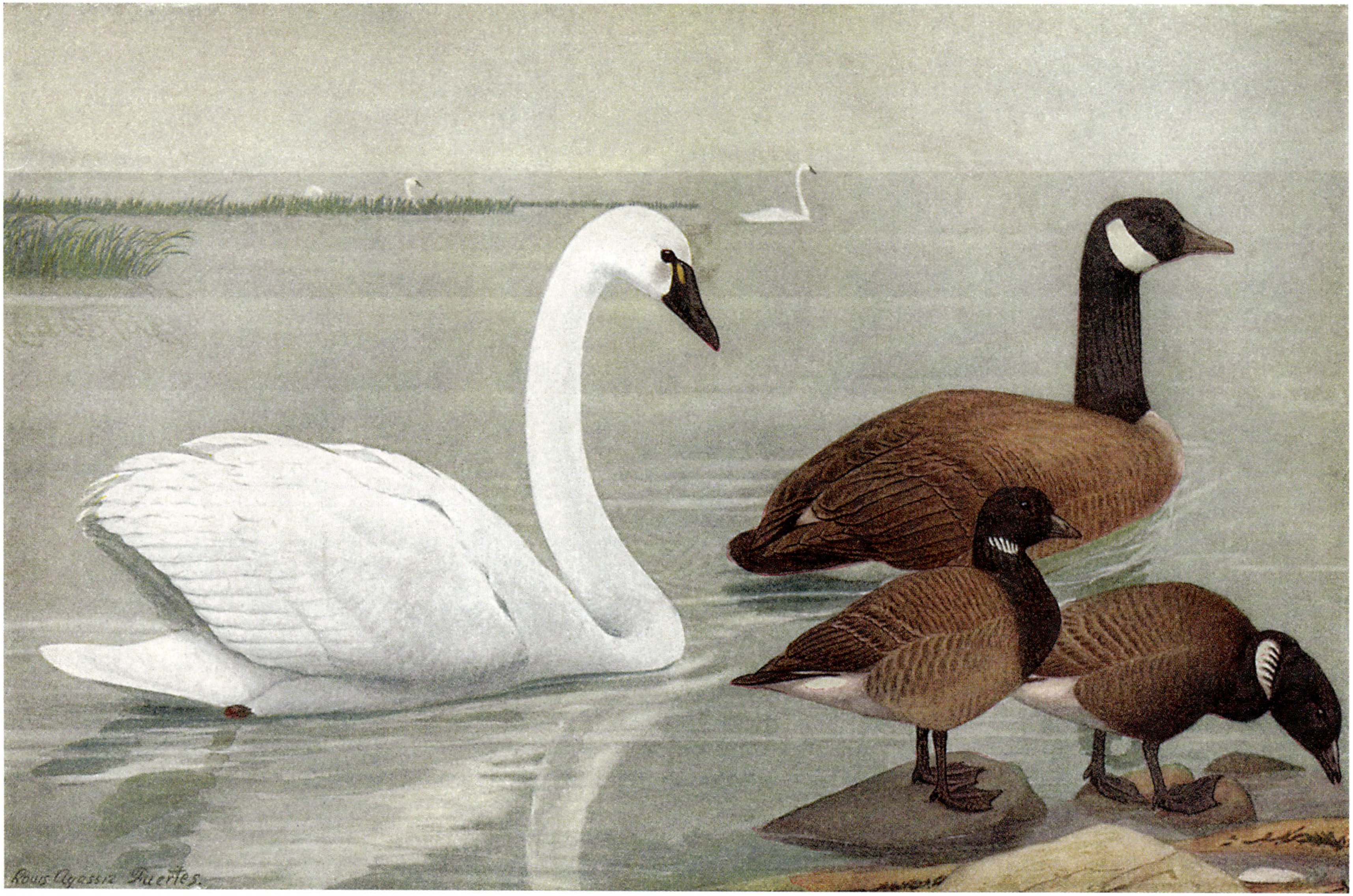

WHISTLING SWAN
Olor columbianus (Ord)

CANADA GOOSE
Branta canadensis (Linnaeus)

BRANT
Branta bernicla glaucogastra (Brehm)

BLACK BRANT
Branta nigricans (Lawrence)

All ¼ nat. size

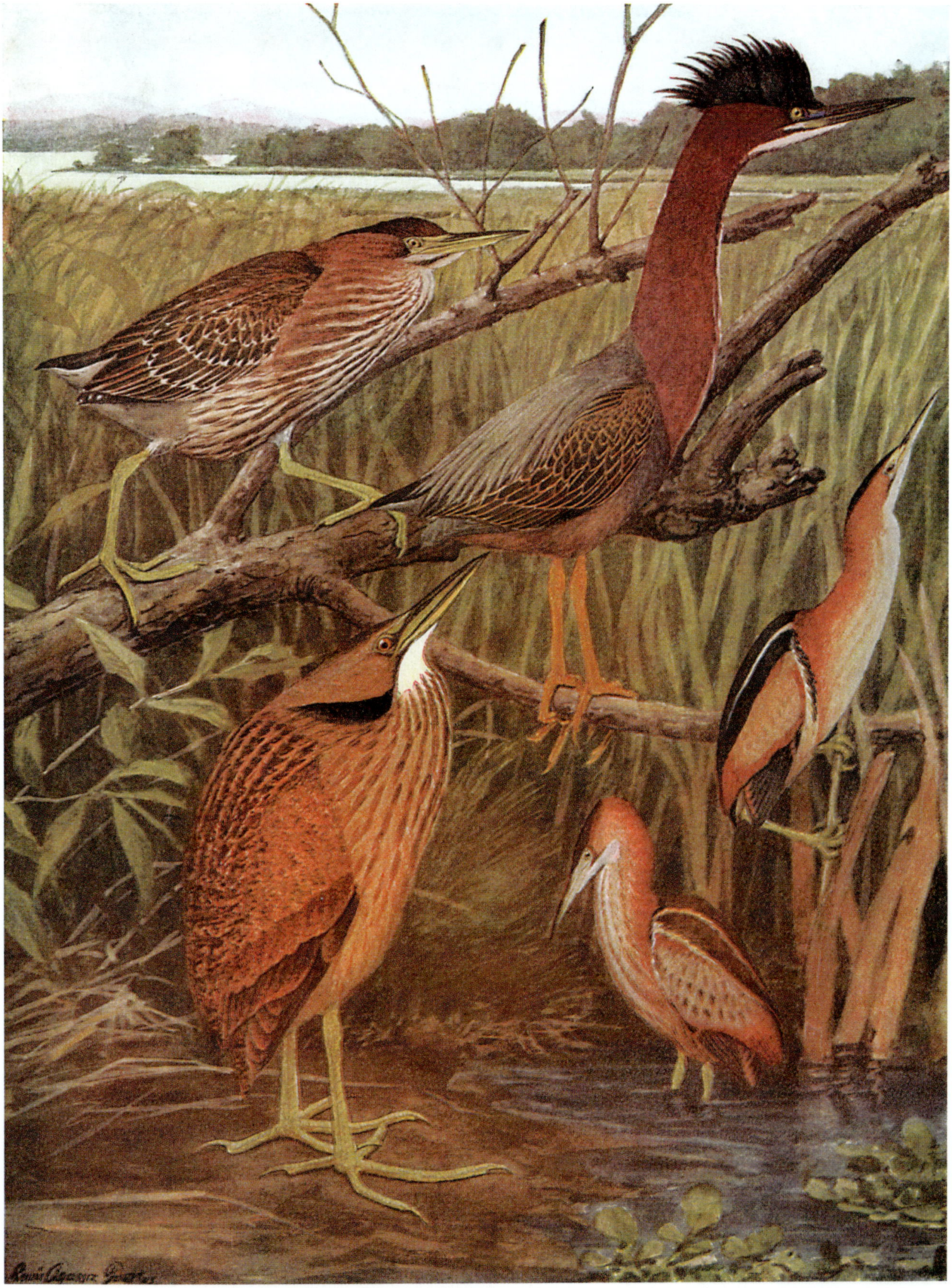

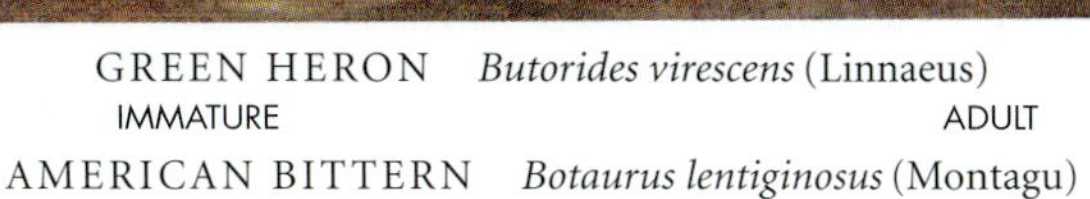

GREEN HERON *Butorides virescens* (Linnaeus)
IMMATURE ADULT

LEAST BITTERN *Ixobrychus exilis* (Gmelin)
FEMALE MALE

AMERICAN BITTERN *Botaurus lentiginosus* (Montagu)

All ½ nat. size

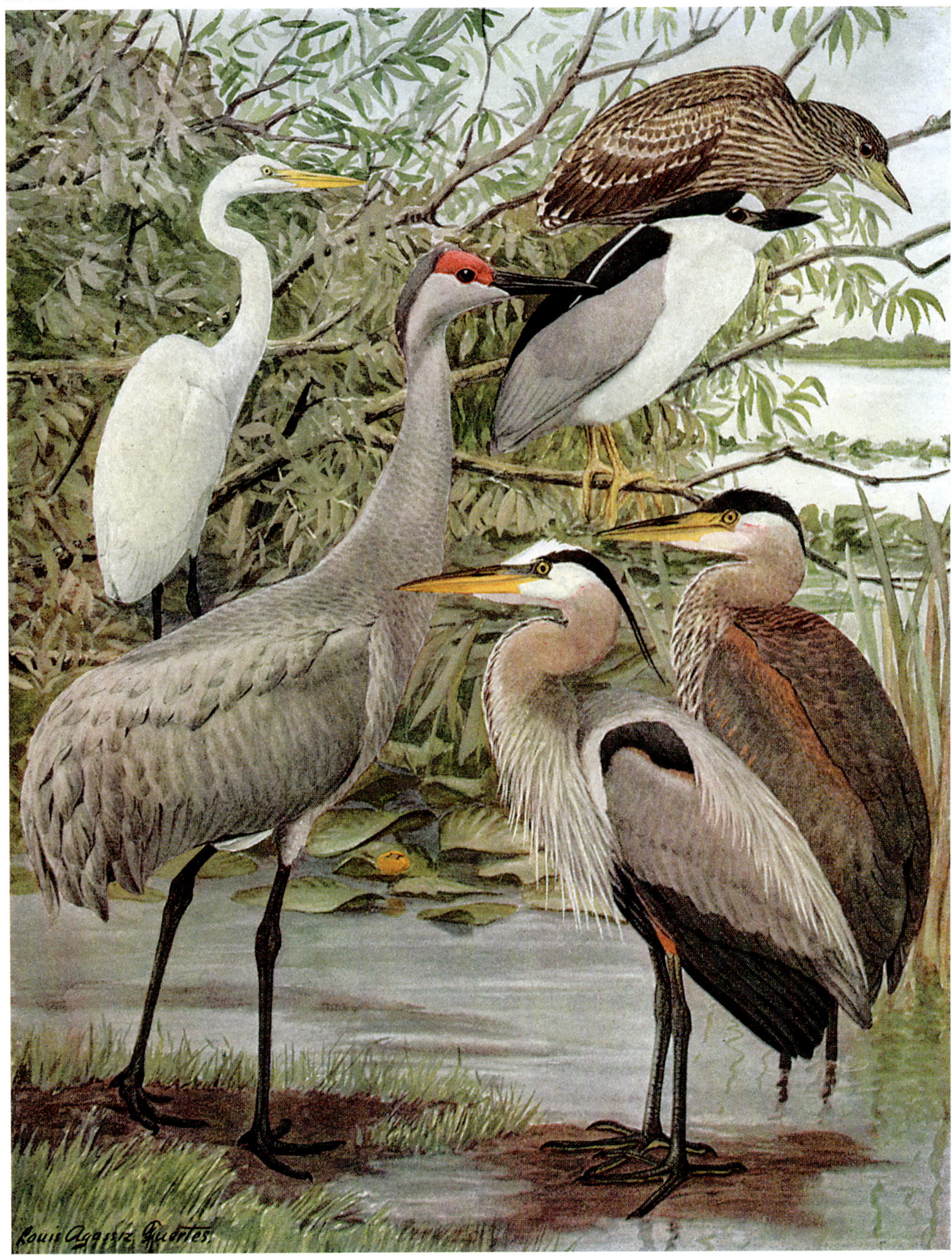

AMERICAN EGRET
Herodias egretta (Gmelin)

SANDHILL CRANE
Grus mexicana (Müller)

BLACK-CROWNED NIGHT HERON
Nycticorax nycticorax naevius (Boddaert)
ADULT IMMATURE

GREAT BLUE HERON
Ardea herodias herodias (Linnaeus)
ADULT IN SUMMER IMMATURE

All ½ nat. size

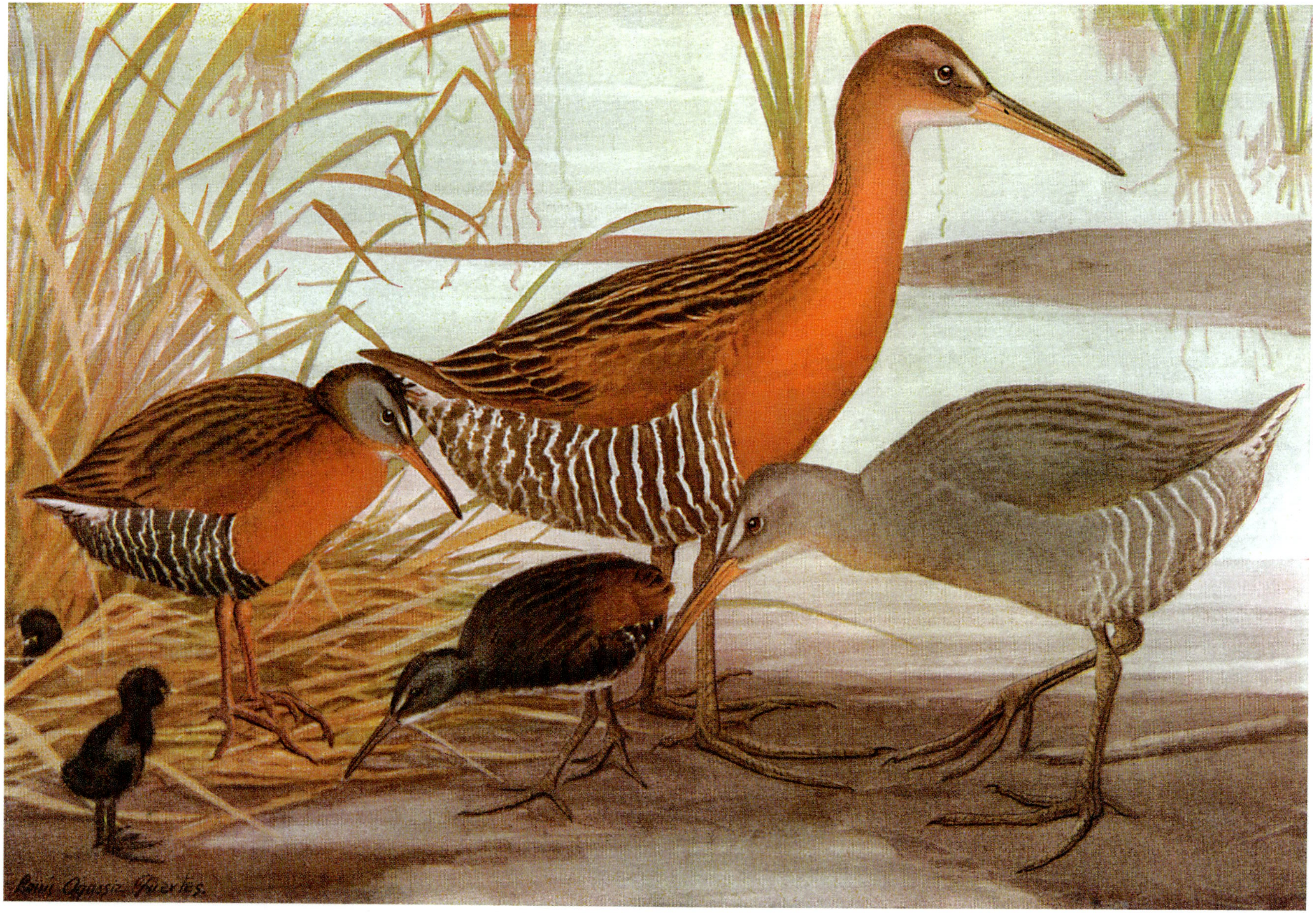

VIRGINIA RAIL
Rallus virginianus (Linnaeus)
DOWNY YOUNG ADULT

IMMATURE

KING RAIL
Rallus elegans (Audubon)

CLAPPER RAIL
Rallus longirostris crepitans (Gmelin)

All ¾ nat. size

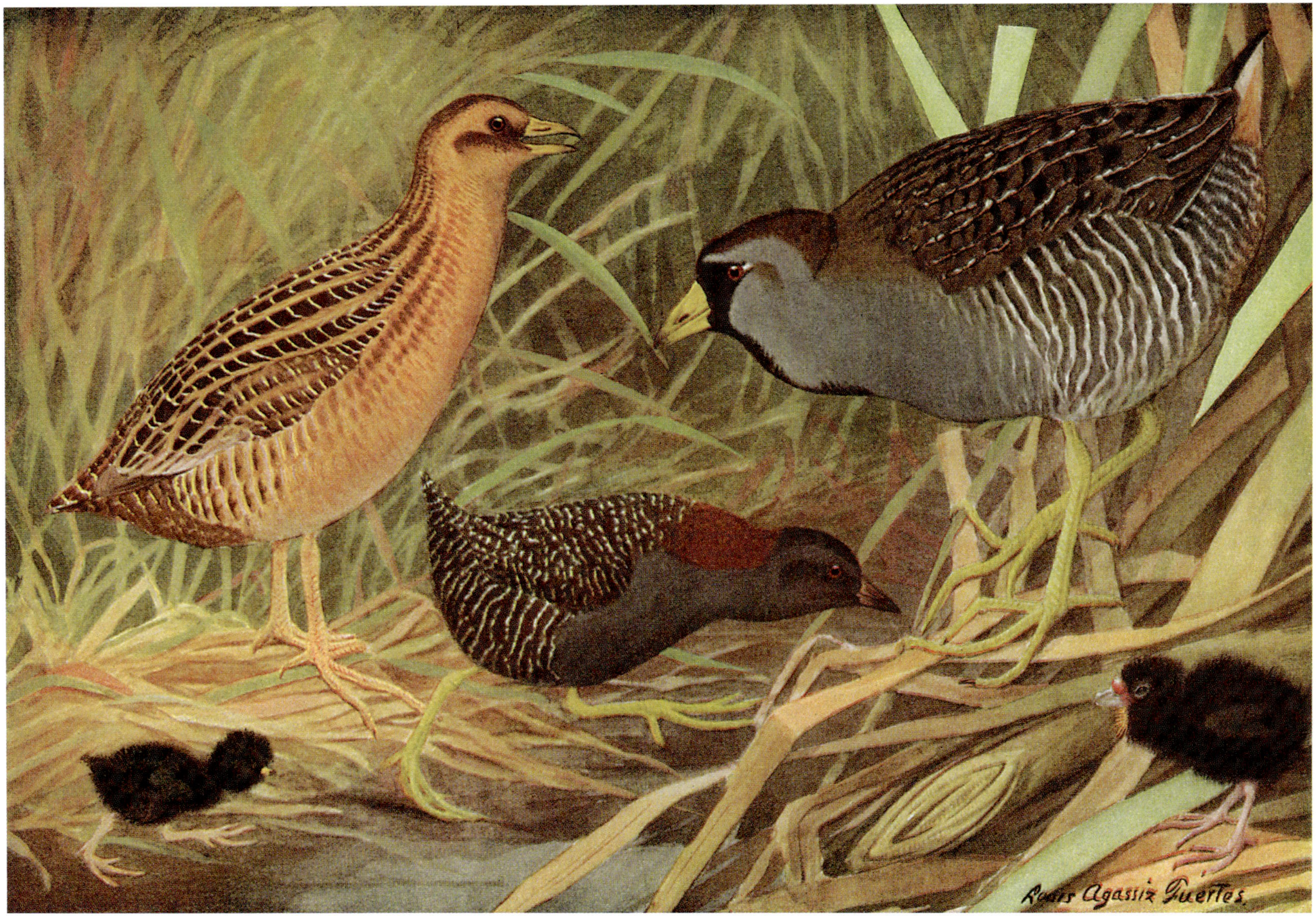

Louis Agassiz Fuertes

YELLOW RAIL
Coturnicops noveboracensis (Gmelin)
ADULT
DOWNY YOUNG of Little Black Rail

LITTLE BLACK RAIL
Crecciscus jamaicensis (Gmelin)
ADULT

CAROLINA RAIL OR SORA
Porzana carolina (Linnaeus)
ADULT

DOWNY YOUNG

All ⅔ nat. size

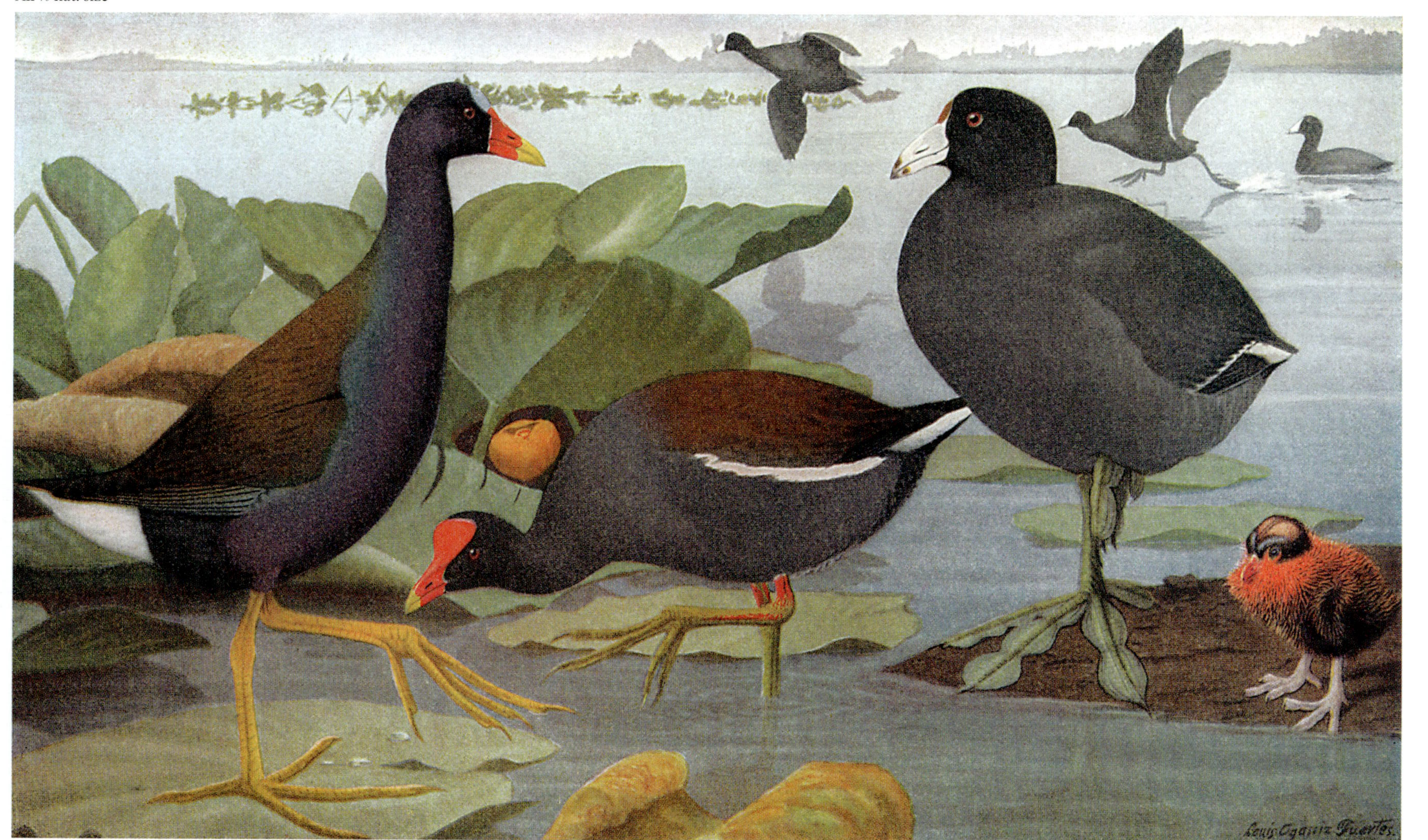

PURPLE GALLINULE
Ionornis martinica (Linnaeus)

FLORIDA GALLINULE
Gallinula galeata (Lichtenstein)

AMERICAN COOT
Fulica americana (Gmelin)
ADULT DOWNY YOUNG

All ¾ nat. size

RED PHALAROPE *Phalaropus fulicarius* (Linnaeus)

FEMALE MALE AUTUMN AND WINTER PLUMAGE

All $^{3}/_{5}$ nat. size

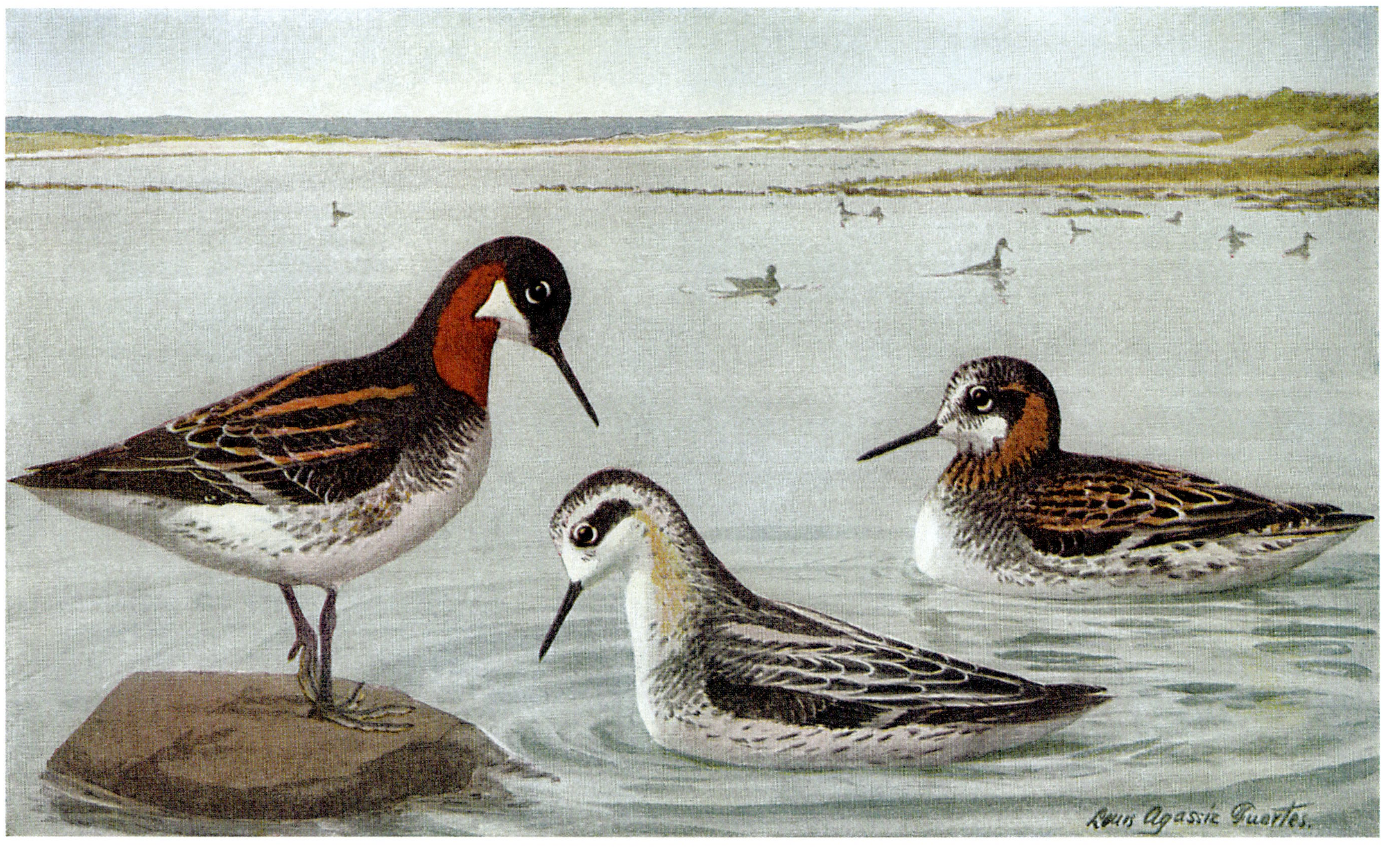

NORTHERN PHALAROPE *Lobipes lobatus* (Linnaeus)

FEMALE

AUTUMN AND WINTER PLUMAGE

MALE

All ⅔ nat. size

Louis Agassiz Fuertes.

WILSON'S PHALAROPE *Sieganopus tricolor* (Vieillot)

AUTUMN AND WINTER PLUMAGE FEMALE MALE

7/8 nat. size

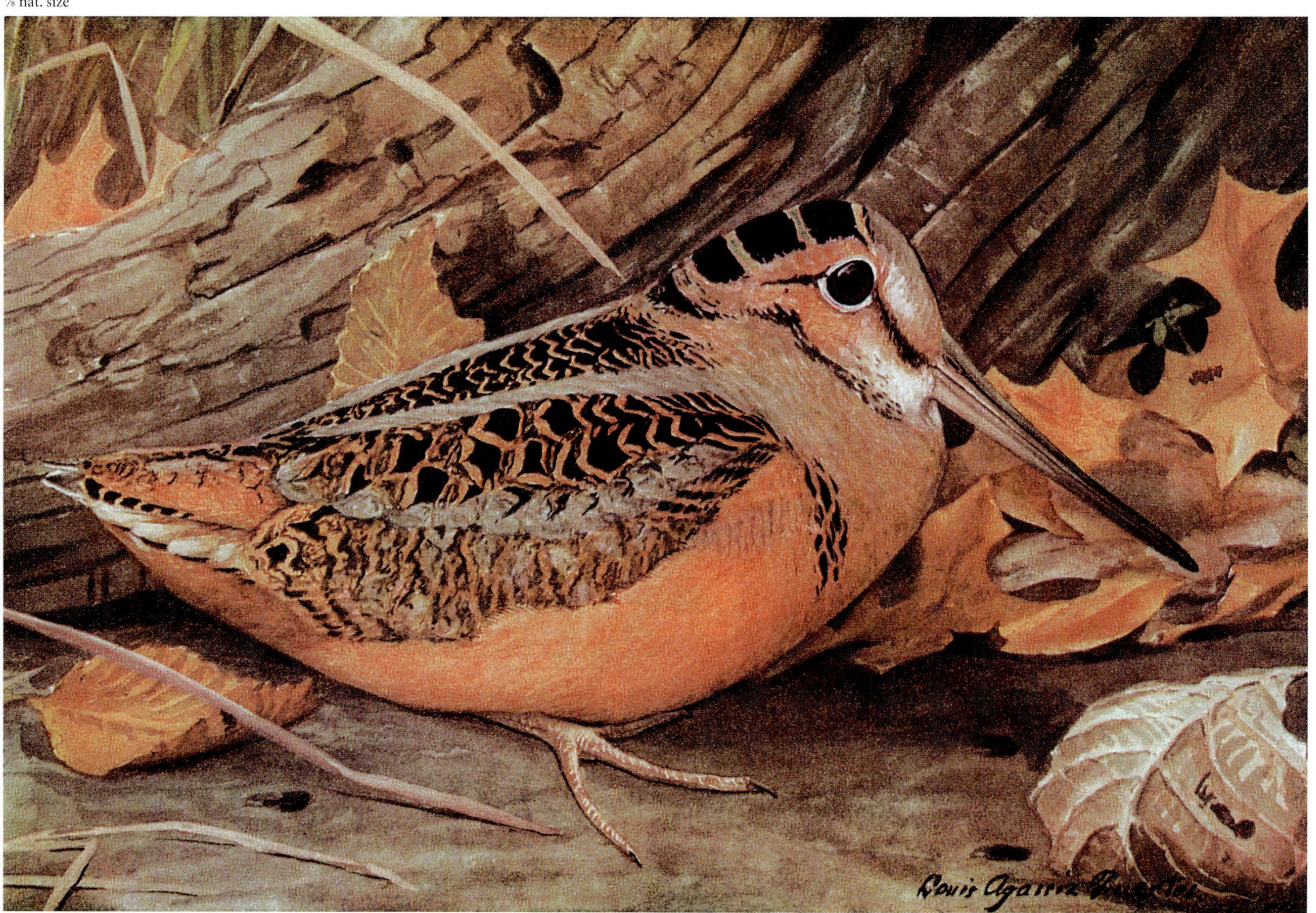

AMERICAN WOODCOCK *Philohela minor* (Gmelin)

⅞ nat. size

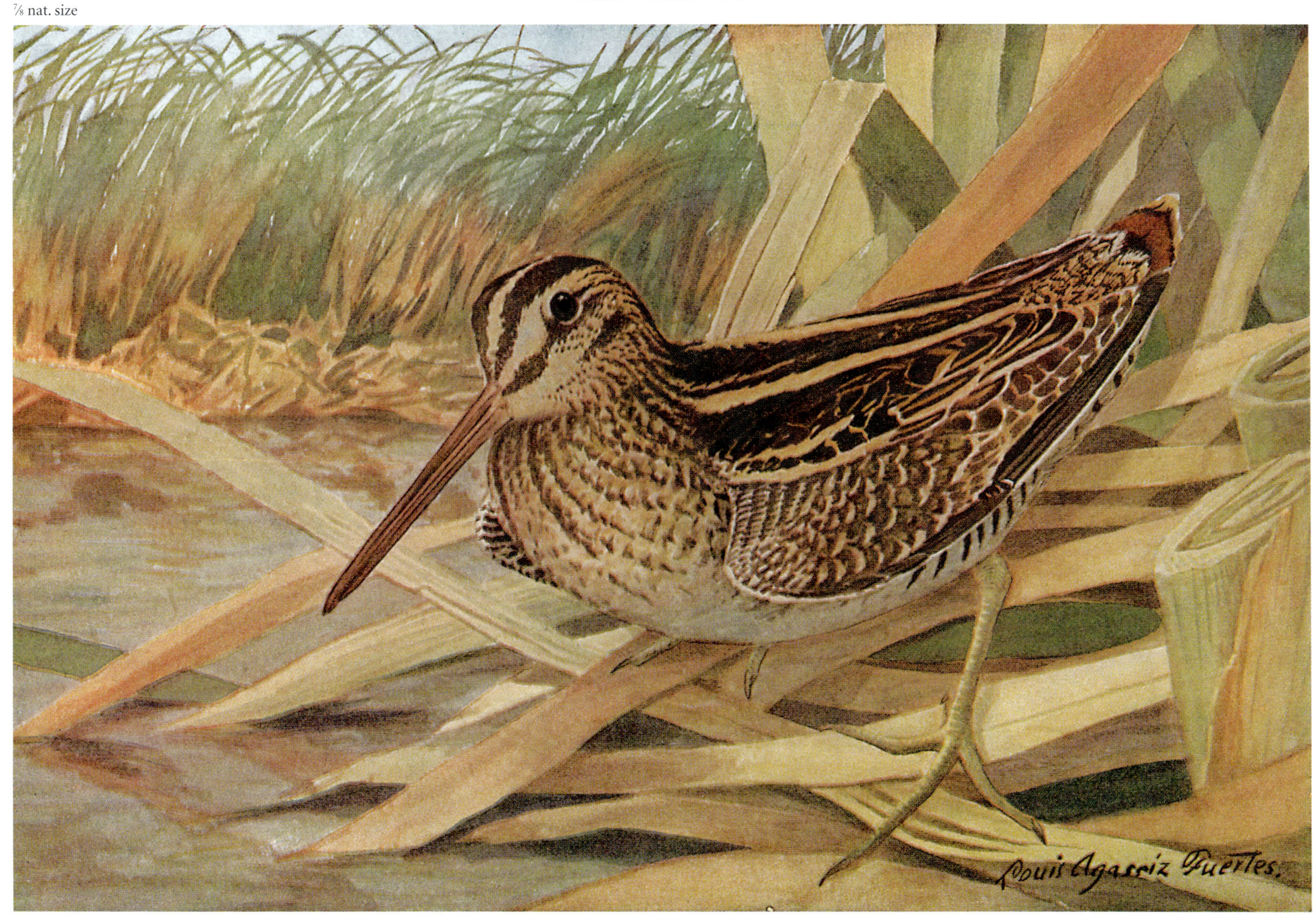

WILSON'S SNIPE *Gallinago delicata* (Ord)

All ½ nat. size

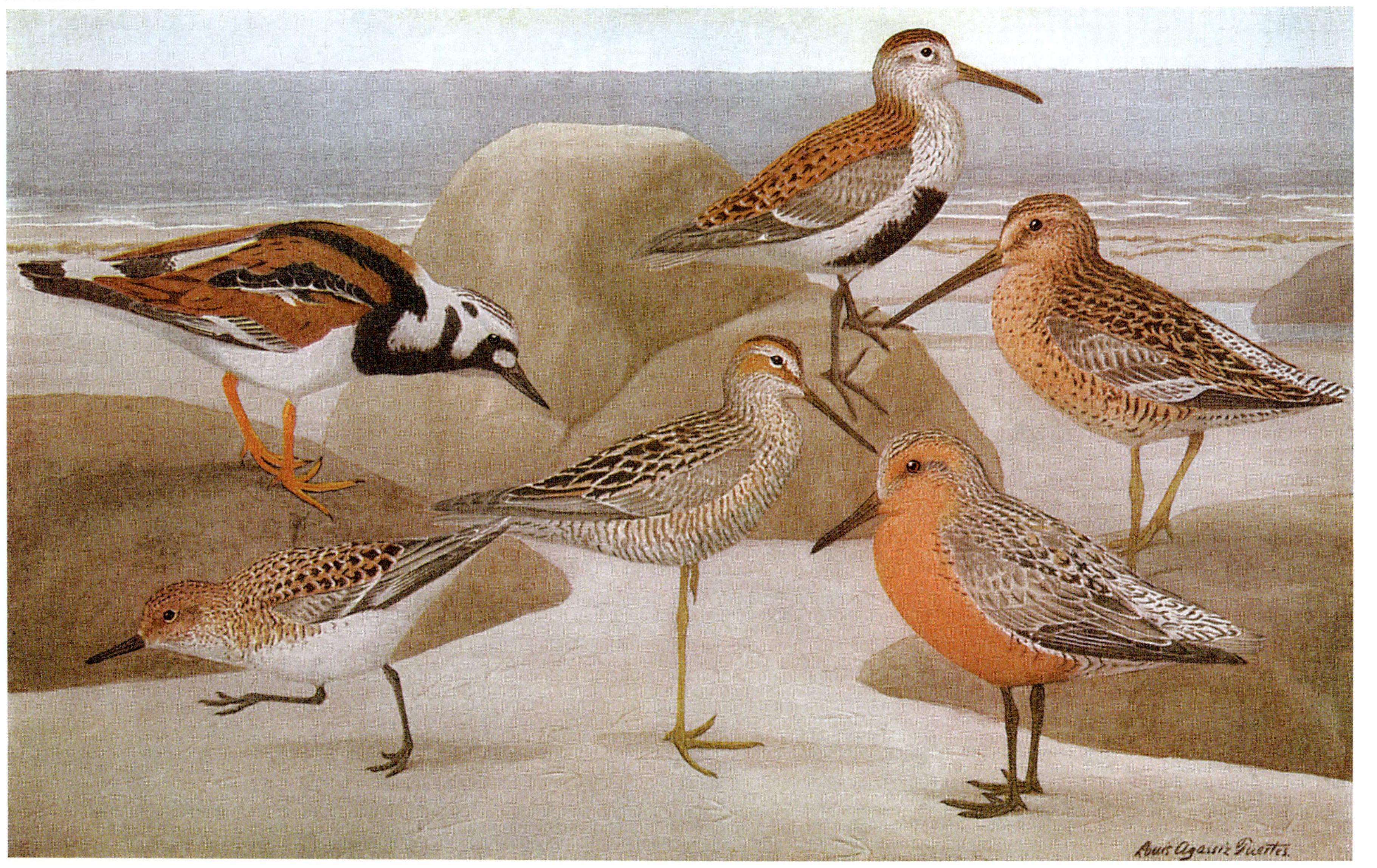

TURNSTONE
Arenaria morinella (Linnaeus)
SANDERLING
Calidris alba (Pallas)

RED-BACKED SANDPIPER
Peliana alpine sakhalina (Vieillot)
STILT SANDPIPER
Micropalma himantopus (Bonaparte)
BREEDING PLUMAGES

DOWITCHER
Macrohamphus griseus (Gmelin)
KNOT
Tringa canutus (Linnaeus)

All ½ nat. size

PURPLE SANDPIPER
Arquatella maritima maritima (Brünnich)

SANDERLING
Calidris leucophaea (Pallas)

STILT SANDPIPER
Micropalama himantopus (Bonaparte)

RED-BACKED SANDPIPER
Pelidna alpina sakhalina (Vieillot)

KNOT
Tringa canutus (Linnaeus)

DOWITCHER
Macrorhamphus griseus griseus (Gmelin)

AUTUMN AND WINTER PLUMAGES

Louis Agassiz Fuertes

All ½ nat. size

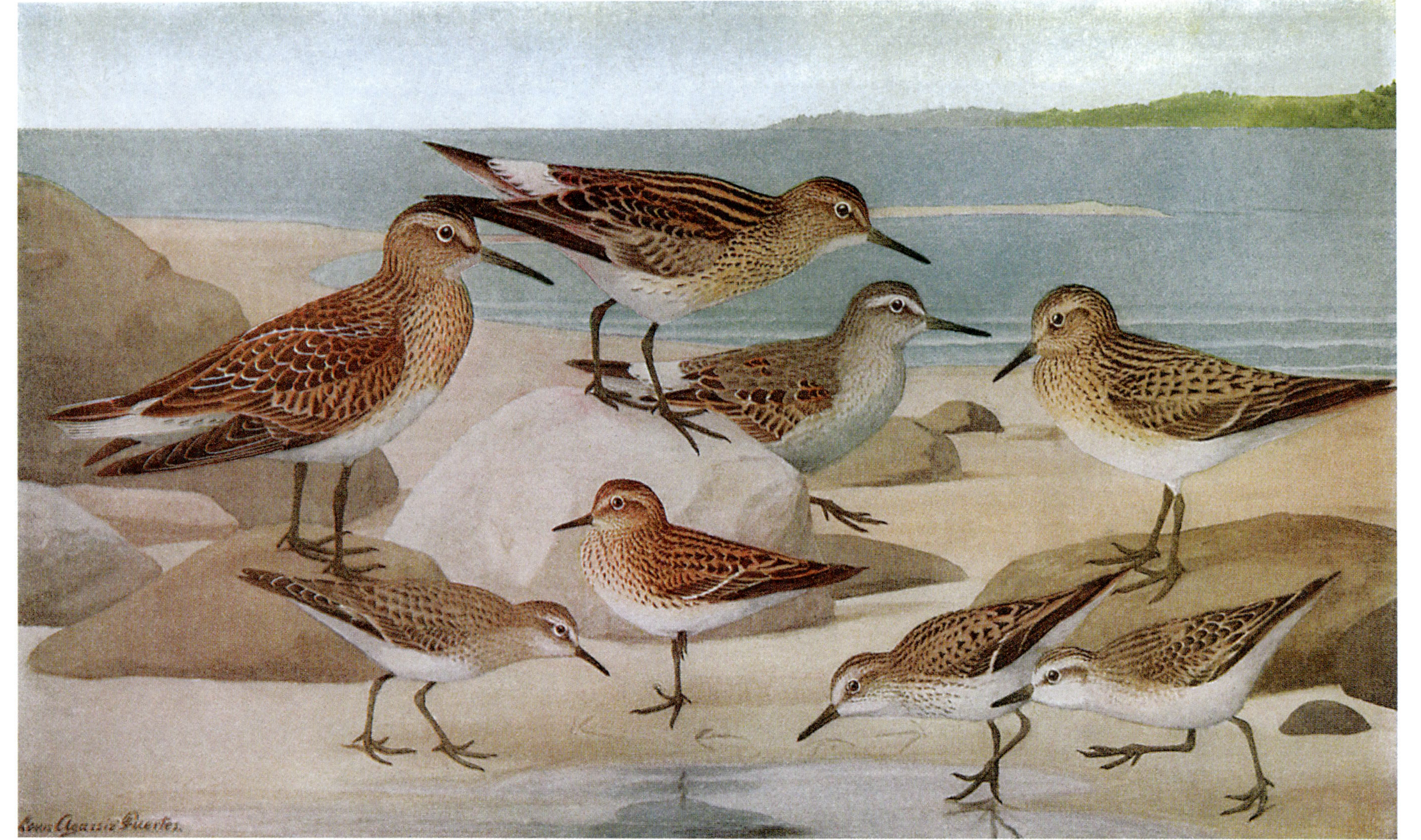

PECTORAL SANDPIPER
Actodromas maculata (Vieillot)

WHITE-RUMPED SANDPIPER
Actodromas fuscicollis (Vieillot)
SPRING AUTUMN

LEAST SANDPIPER
Actodromas minutilla (Vieillot)
AUTUMN SPRING

BAIRD SANDPIPER
Actodromas bairdi (Coues)

SEMIPALMATED SANDPIPER
Ereunetes pusillus (Linnaeus)
SPRING AUTUMN

All ½ nat. size

SOLITARY SANDPIPER
Helodromas solitarius (Wilson)

GREATER YELLOWLEGS
Totanus melanoleucus (Gmelin)

SPOTTED SANDPIPER
Actitis macularia (Linnaeus)
IMMATURE ADULT
SUMMER PLUMAGES

LESSER YELLOWLEGS
Totanus flavipes (Gmelin)

All ⅔ nat. size

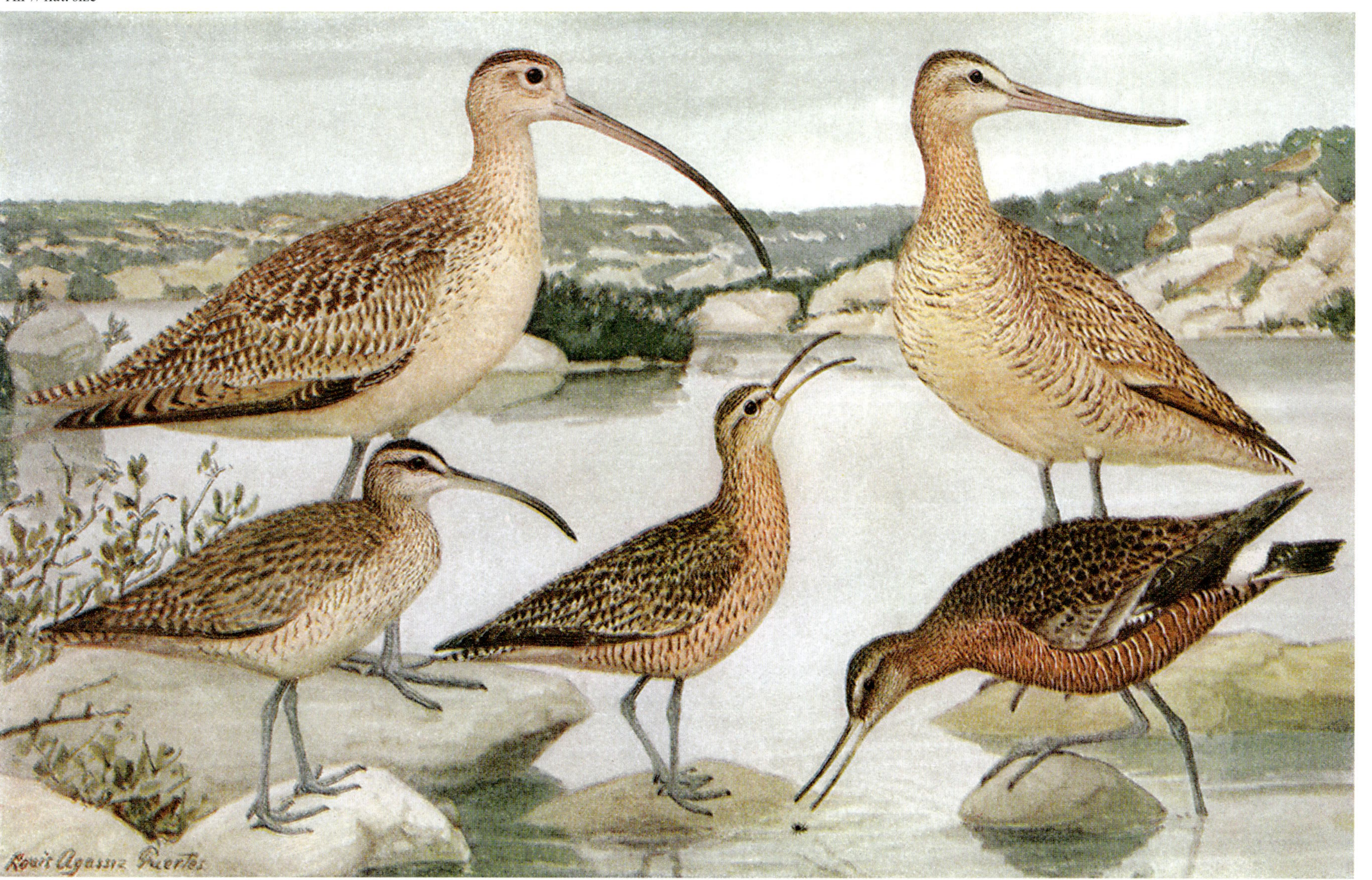

LONG-BILLED CURLEW
Numenius longirostris (Wilson)

HUDSONIAN CURLEW
Numenius hudsonicus (Latham)

ESKIMO CURLEW
Numenius borealis (Forster)

MARBLED GODWIT
Limosa fedoa (Linnaeus)

HUDSONIAN GODWIT SPRING
Limosa haemastica (Linnaeus)

All ⅖ nat. size

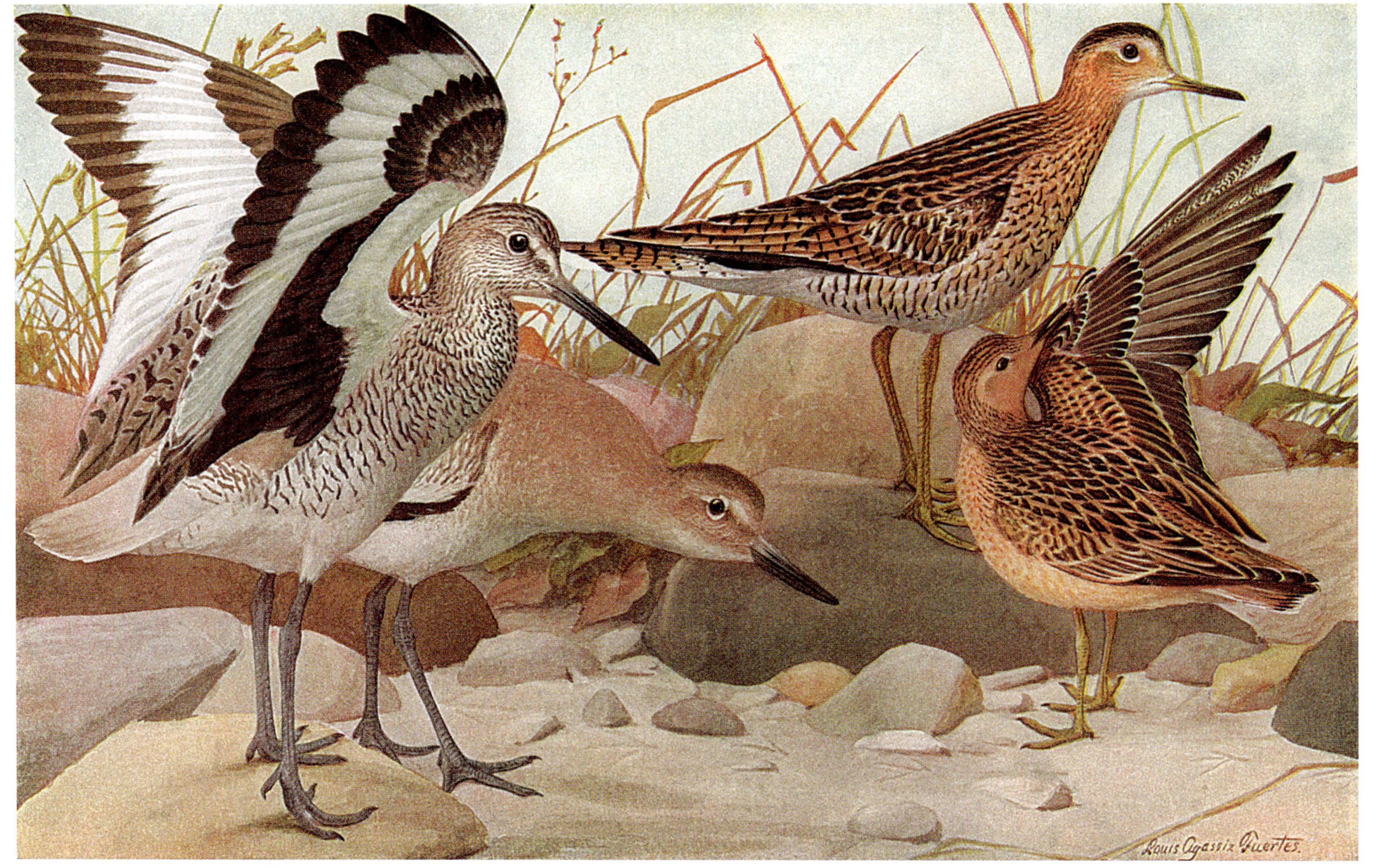

WILLET
Catoptrophorus semipalmata (Gmelin)
SPRING AUTUMN

BARTRAMIAN SANDPIPER OR UPLAND PLOVER
Bartramia longicauda (Bechstein)

BUFF-BREASTED SANDPIPER
Tryngytes subruficollis (Vieillot)

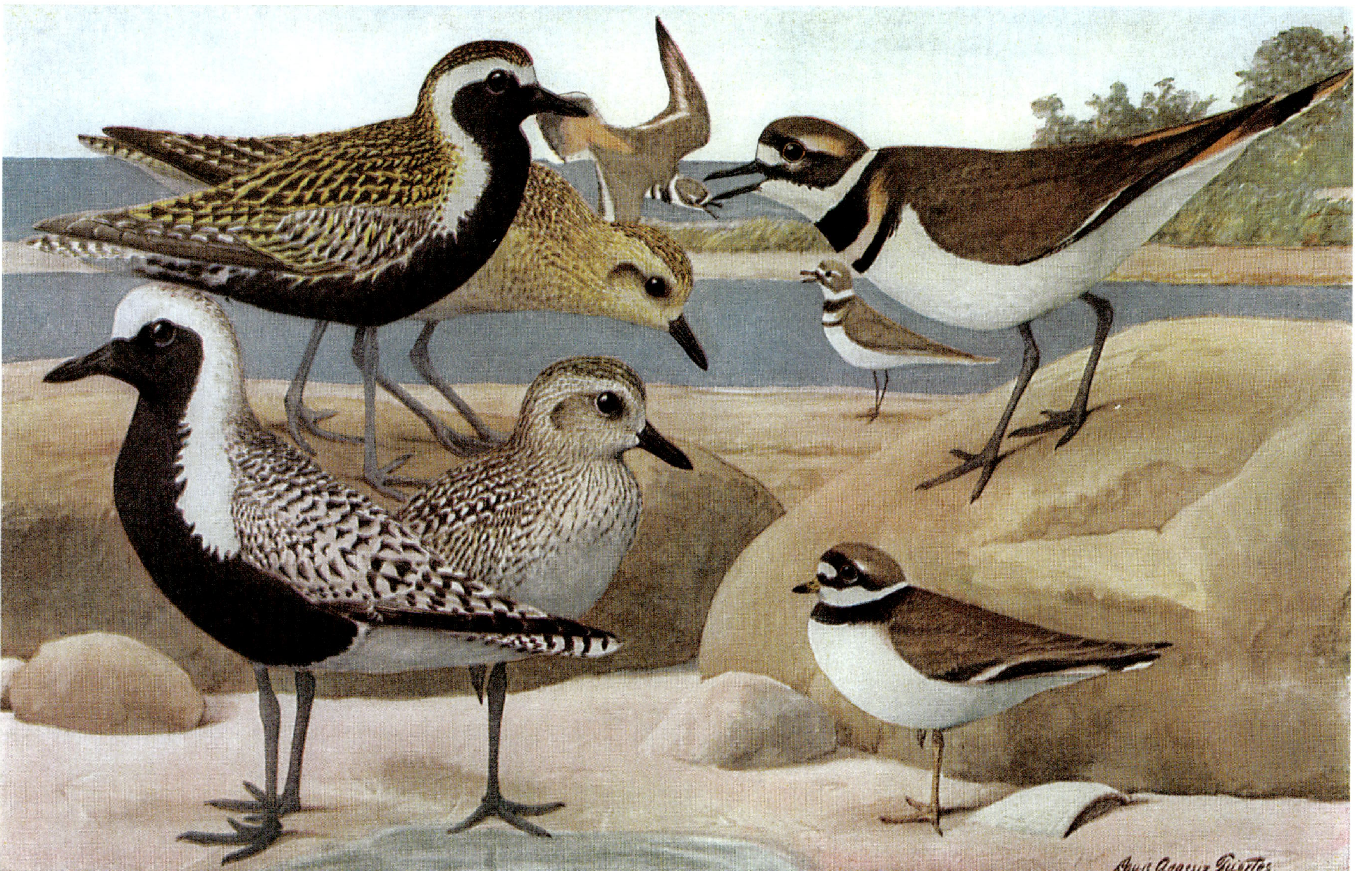

AMERICAN GOLDEN PLOVER
Charadrius dominicus (Müller)
SPRING AUTUMN
BLACK-BELLIED PLOVER
Squatarola squatarola (Linnaeus)
SPRING AUTUMN

KILLDEER PLOVER
Oxyechus vociferus (Linnaeus)
SEMIPALMATED PLOVER
Aegialitis semipalmata (Bonaparte)

Both ½ nat. size

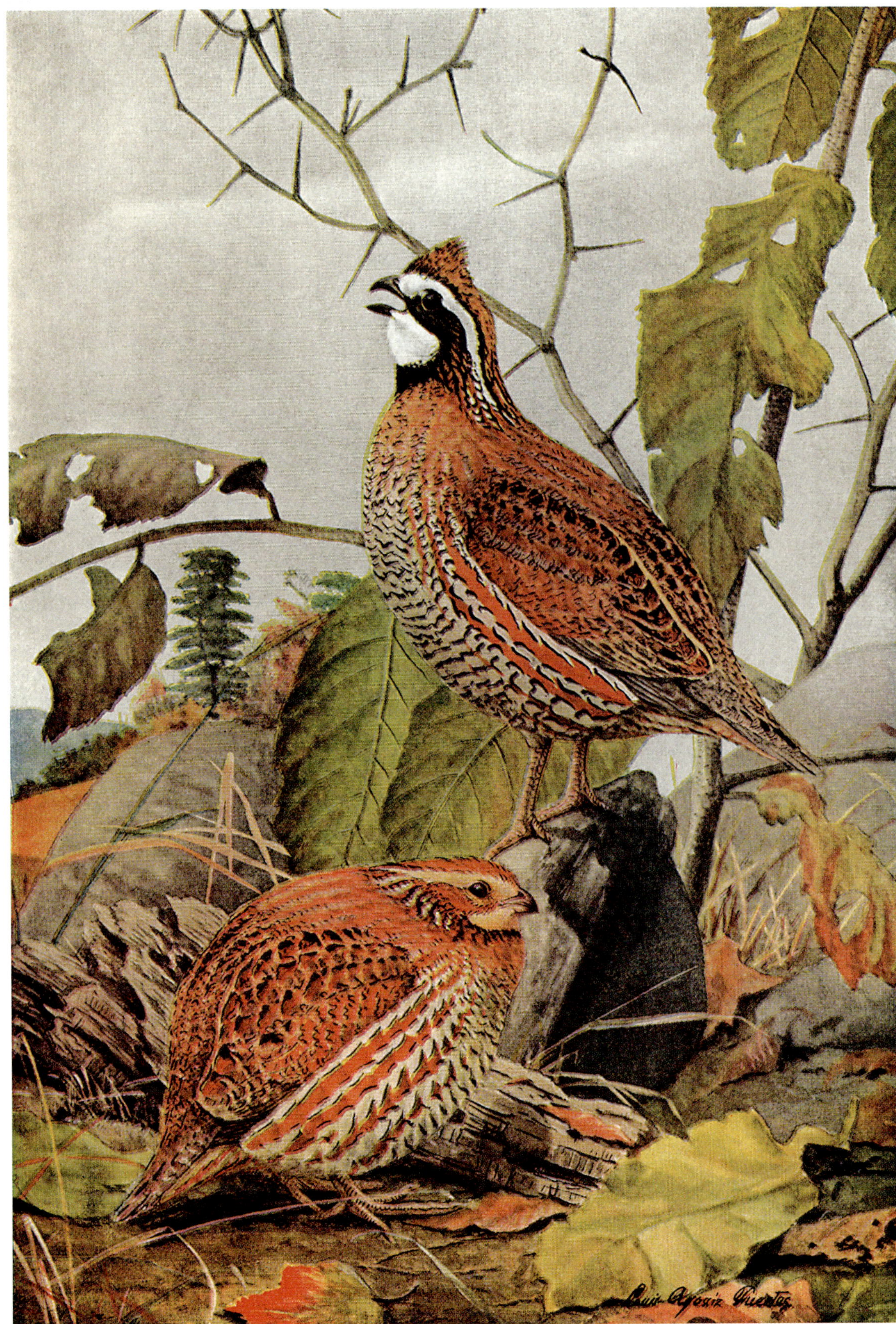

BOBWHITE OR QUAIL *Colinus virginianus* (Linnaeus)
MALE AND FEMALE

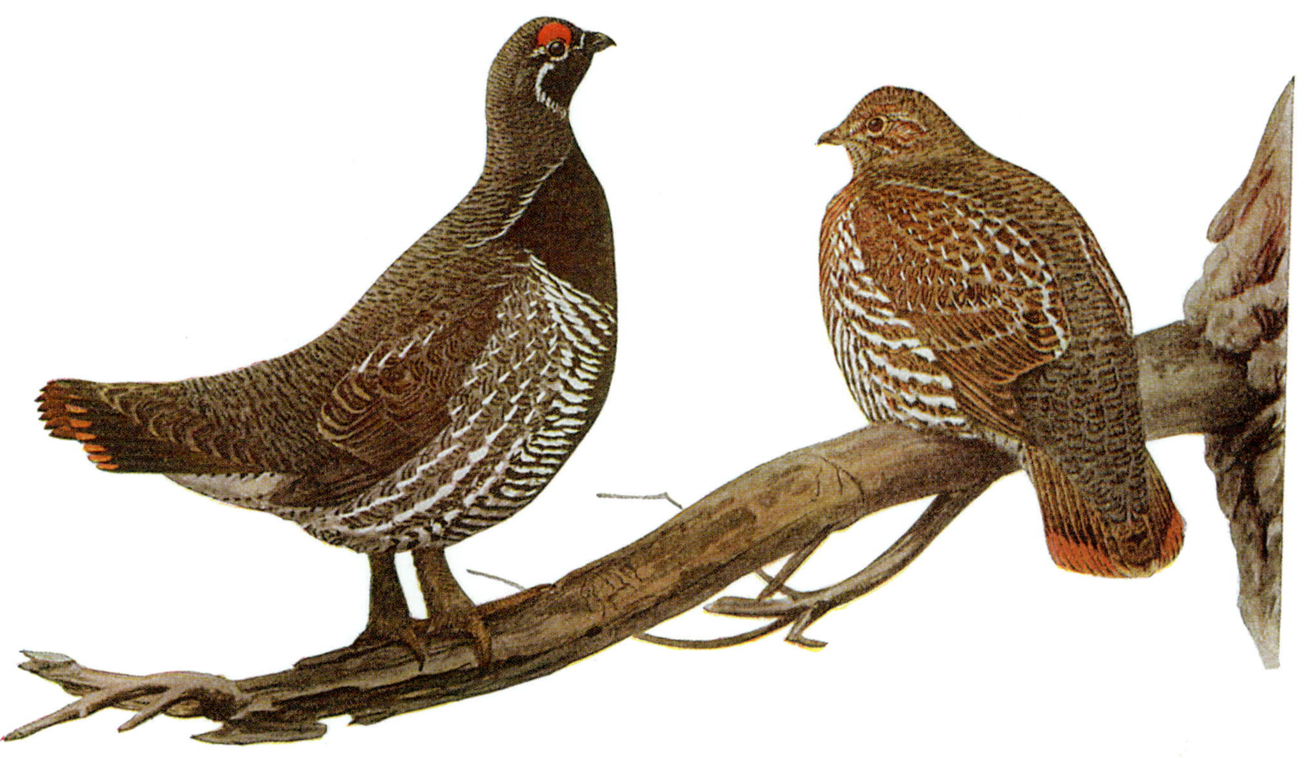

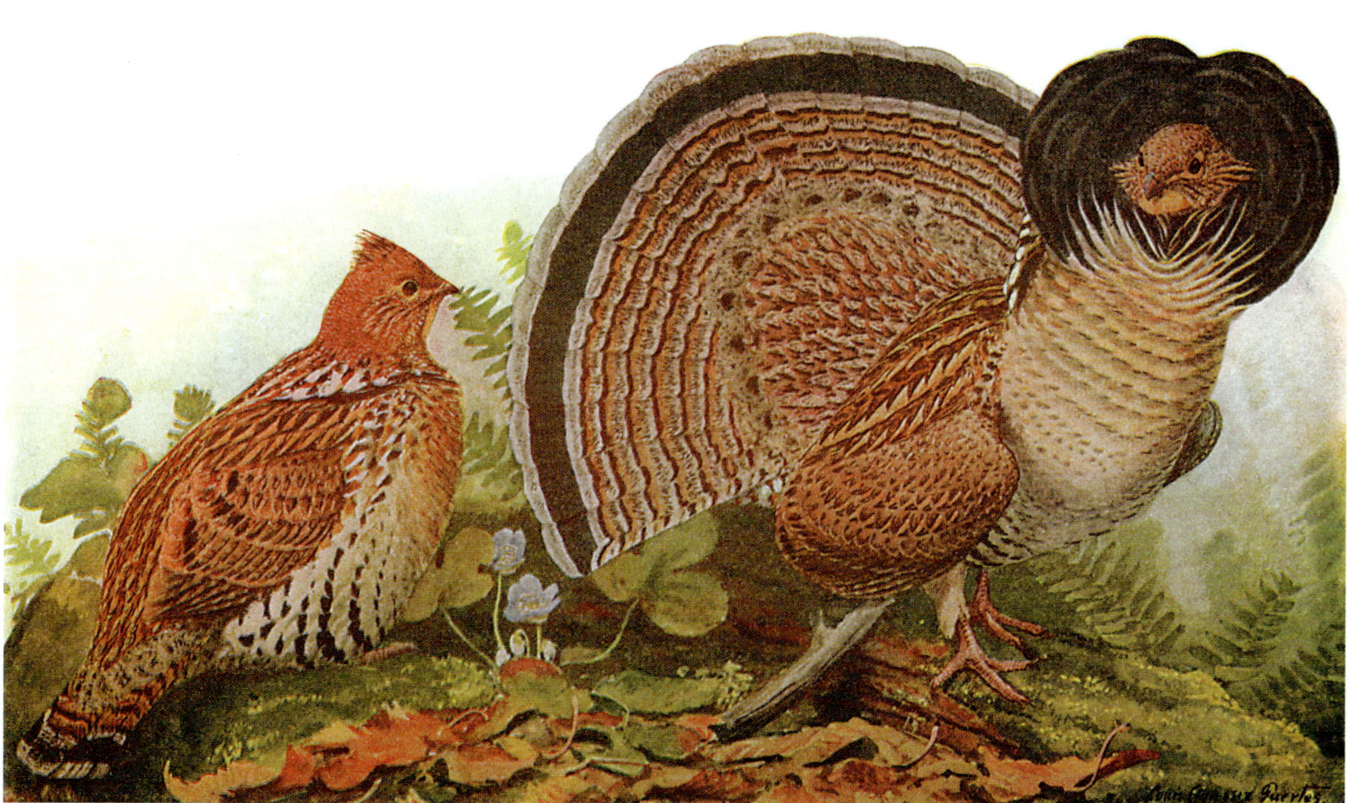

CANADA OR SPRUCE GROUSE *Canachites canadensis canace* (Linnaeus)
MALE AND FEMALE
Both ⅖ nat. size

RUFFED GROUSE *Bonansa umbellus umbellus* (Linnaeus)
FEMALE MALE, STRUTTING
Both ¼ nat. size

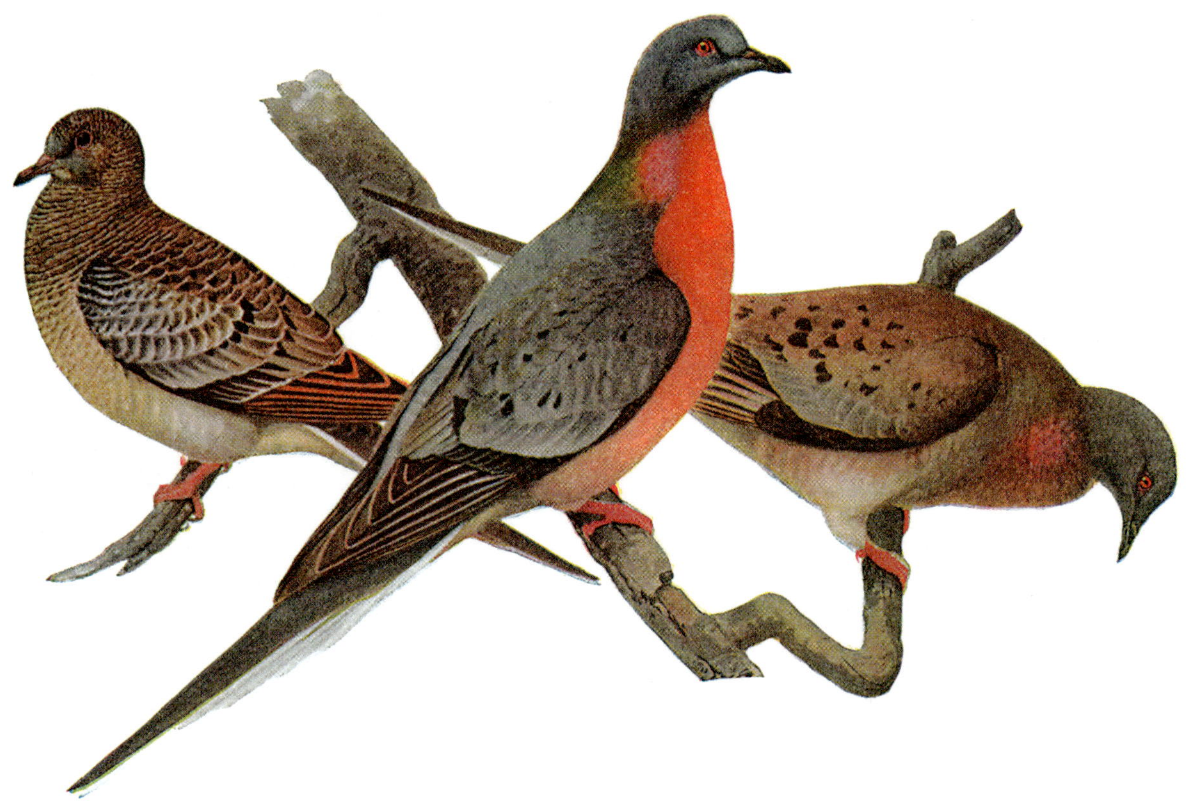

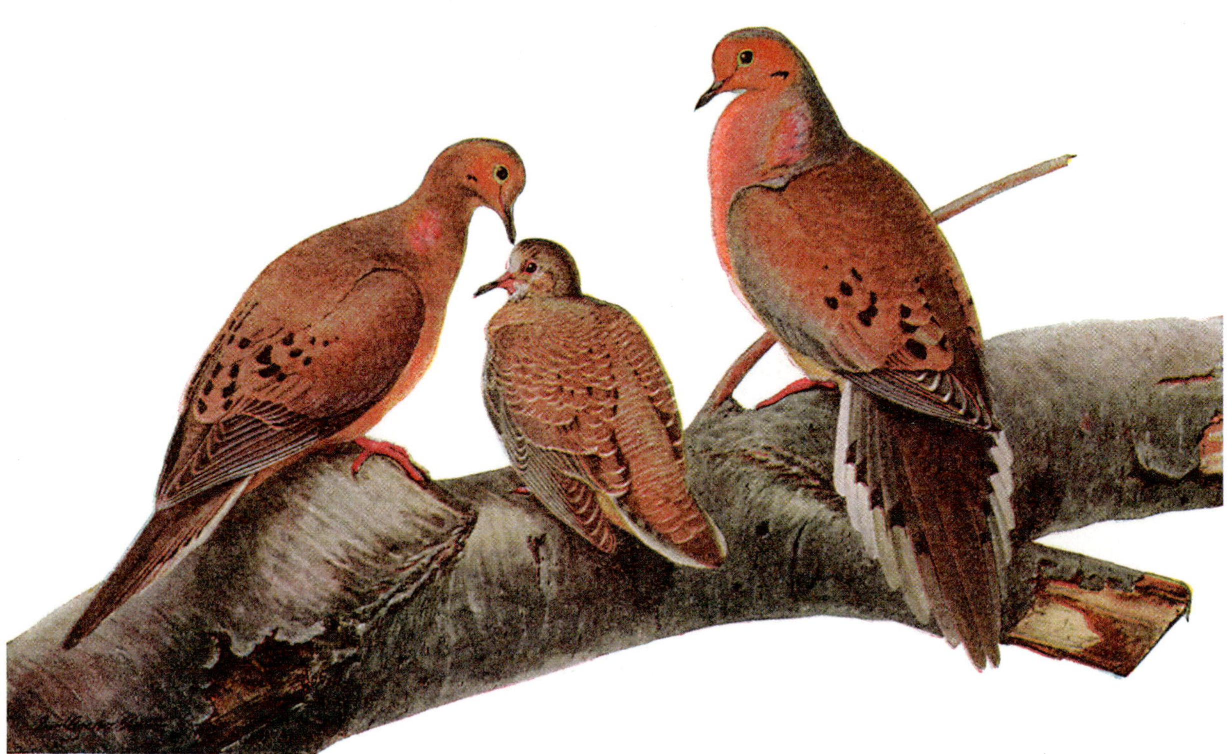

PASSENGER PIGEON *Ectopistes migratorius* (Linnaeus)

YOUNG MALE FEMALE

All ⅓ nat. size

MOURNING DOVE *Zenaidura macroura carolinensis* (Linnaeus)

FEMALE YOUNG MALE

All ⅓ nat. size

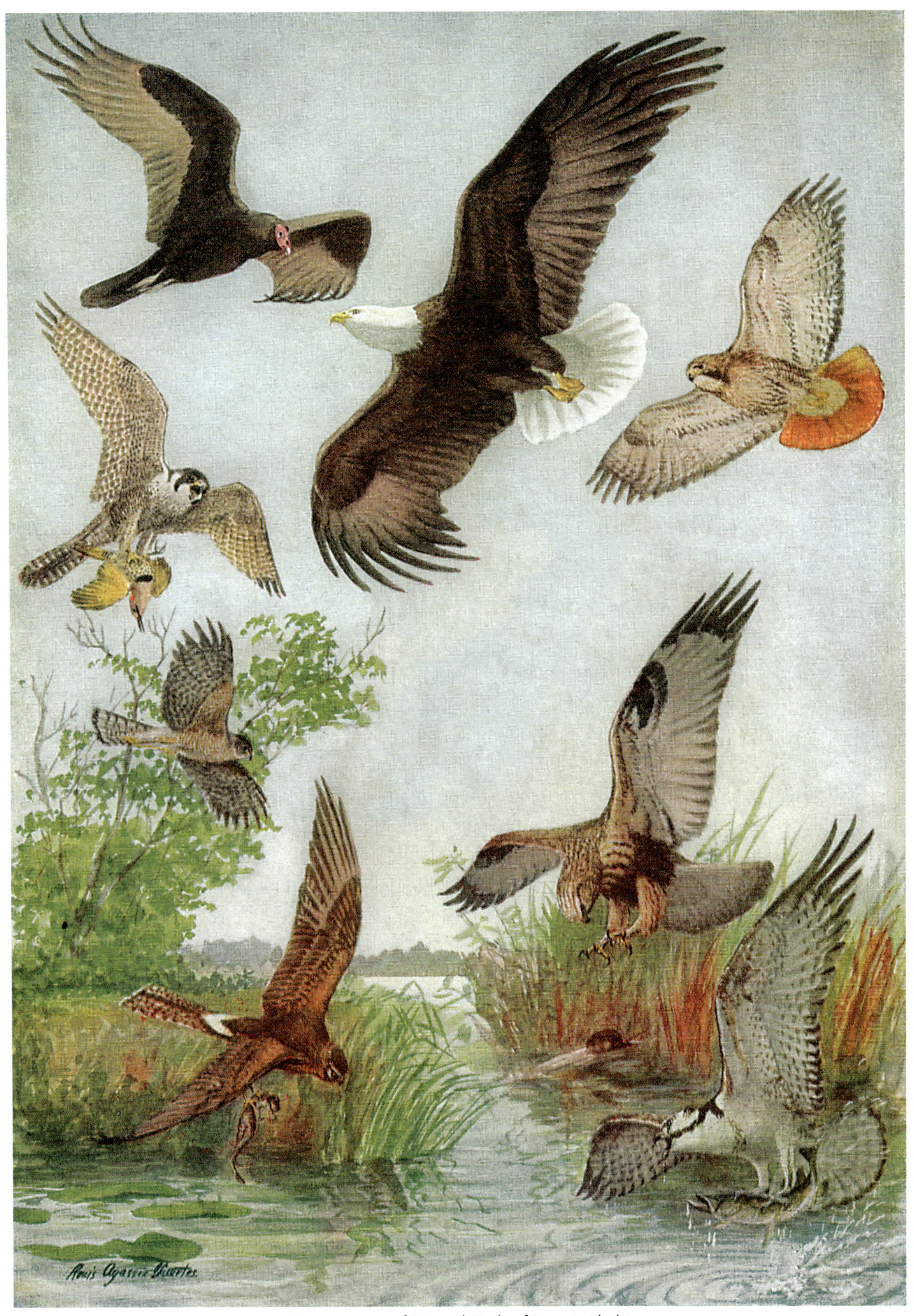

Appearance of Diurnal Birds of Prey in Flight

TURKEY VULTURE
FALCON (DUCK HAWK)
ACCIPITER (COOPER'S HAWK)
MARSH HAWK FEMALE

BALD EAGLE

BUTEO (RED-TAILED HAWK)
ARCHIBUTEO (ROUGH-LEGGED HAWK)
FISH HAWK

Both ⅓ nat. size

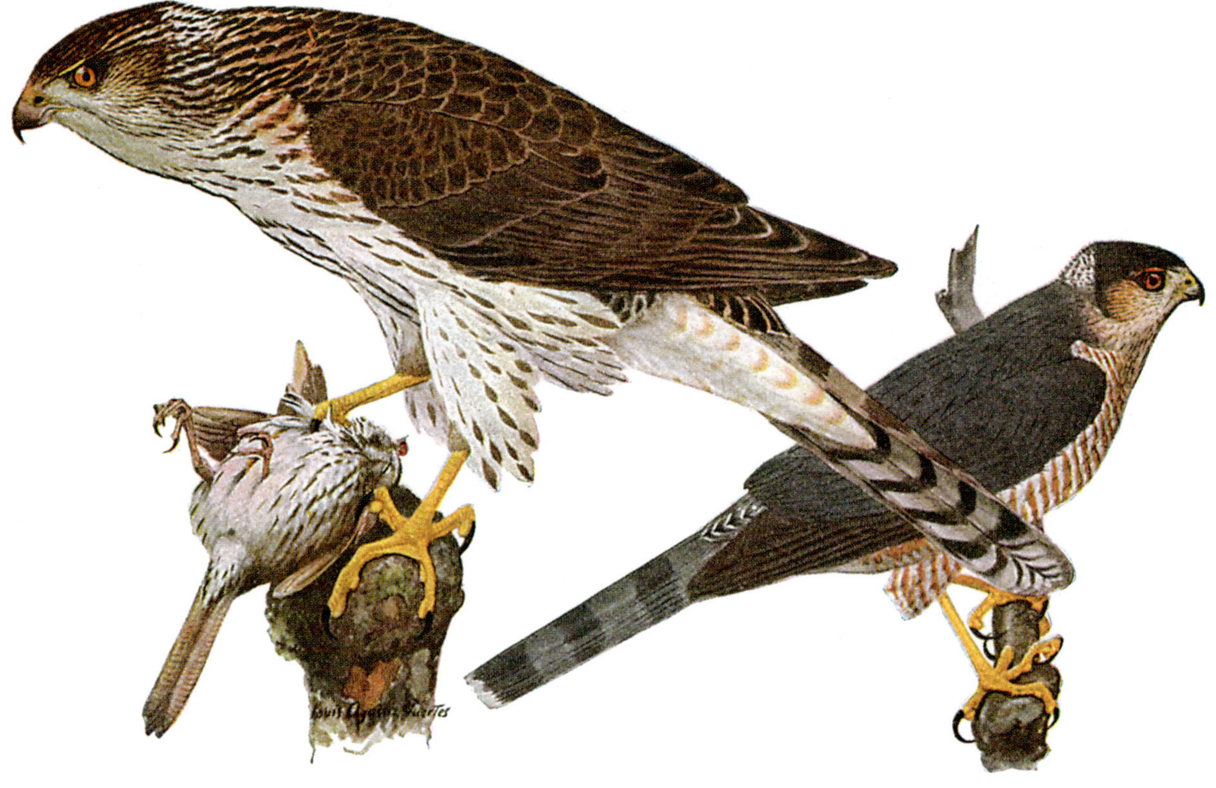

COOPER'S HAWK
Accipiter cooperi (Bonaparte)
IMMATURE FEMALE

SHARP-SHINNED HAWK
Accipiter velox (Wilson)
ADULT MALE

Both ⅓ nat. size

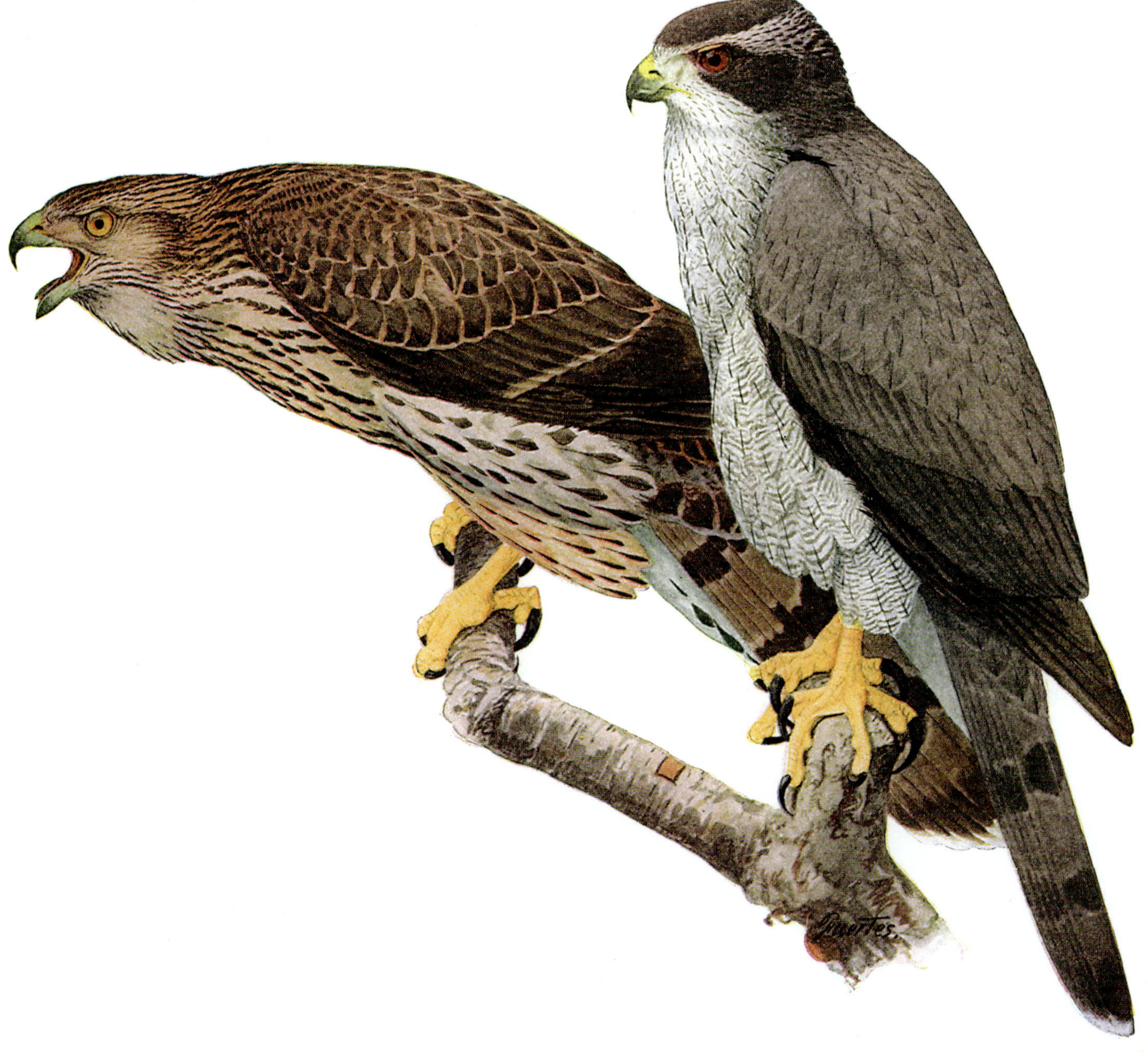

GOSHAWK
Astur atricapillus atricapillus (Wilson)

IMMATURE ADULT

Both ¼ nat. size

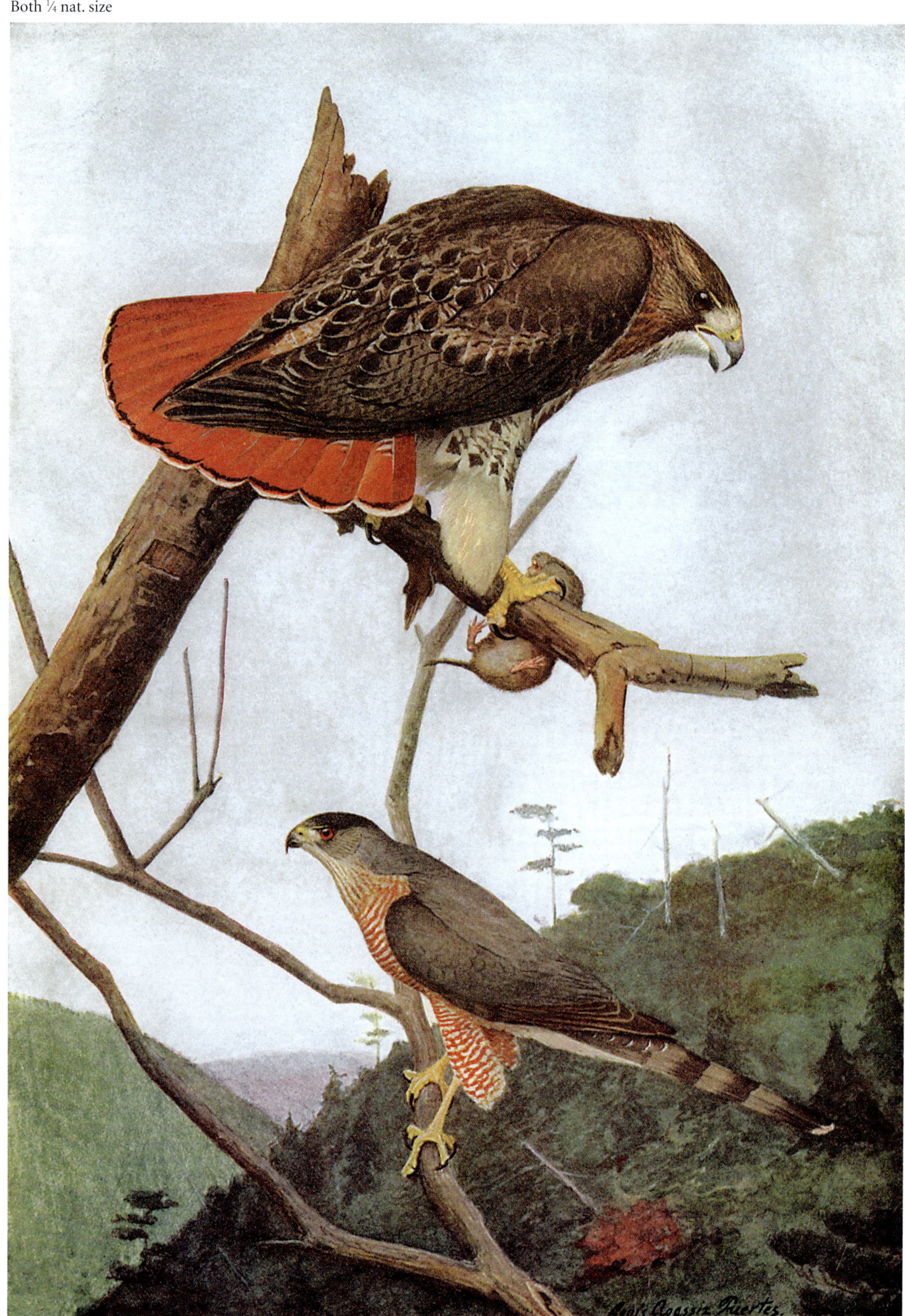

RED-TAILED HAWK *Buteo borealis borealis* (Gmelin)
ADULT

COOPER'S HAWK *Accipiter cooperi* (Bonaparte)
ADULT FEMALE

All ⅓ nat. size

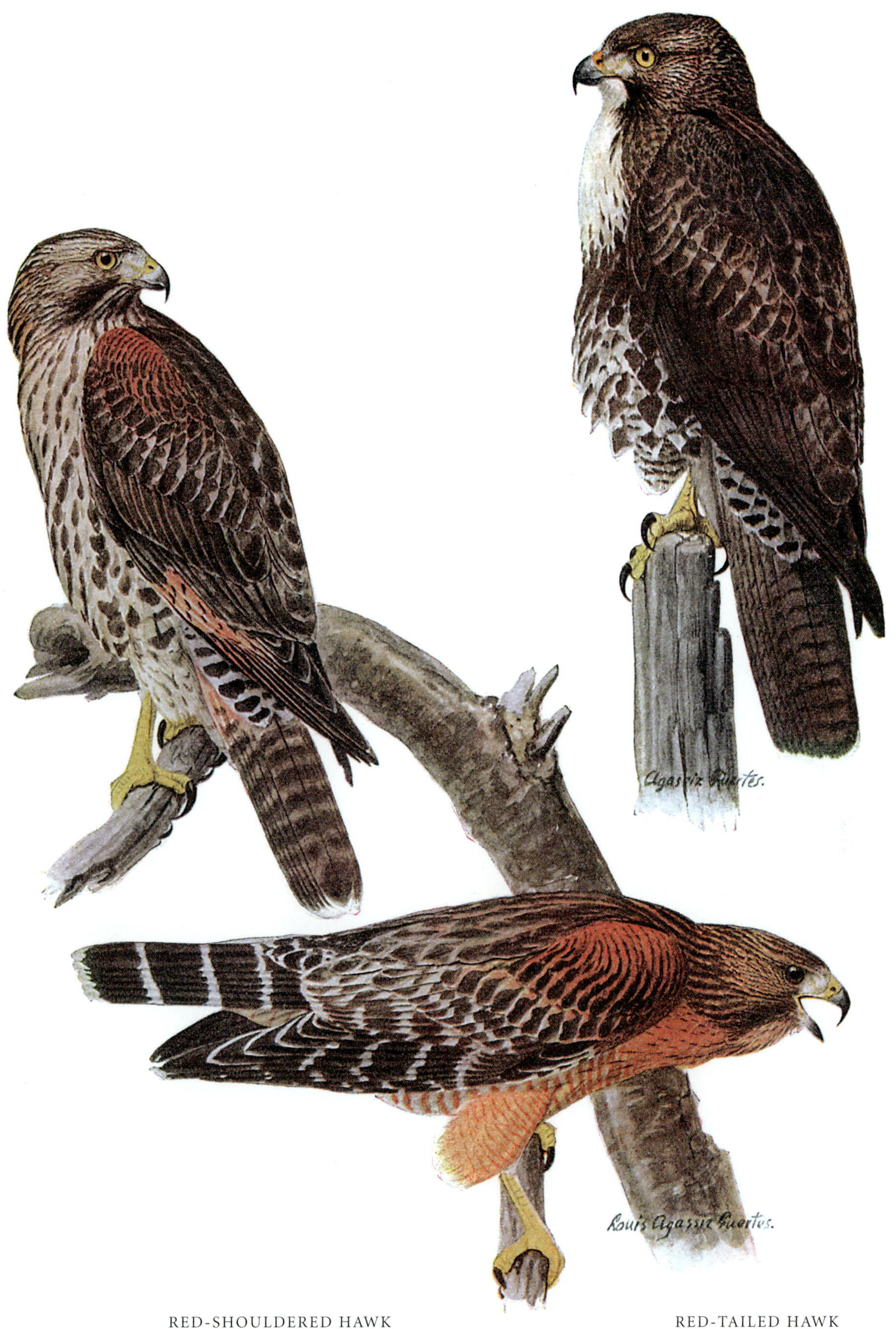

RED-SHOULDERED HAWK
Buteo lineatus lineatus (Gmelin)

RED-TAILED HAWK
Buteo borealis borealis (Gmelin)

IMMATURE ADULT IMMATURE

All ¼ nat. size

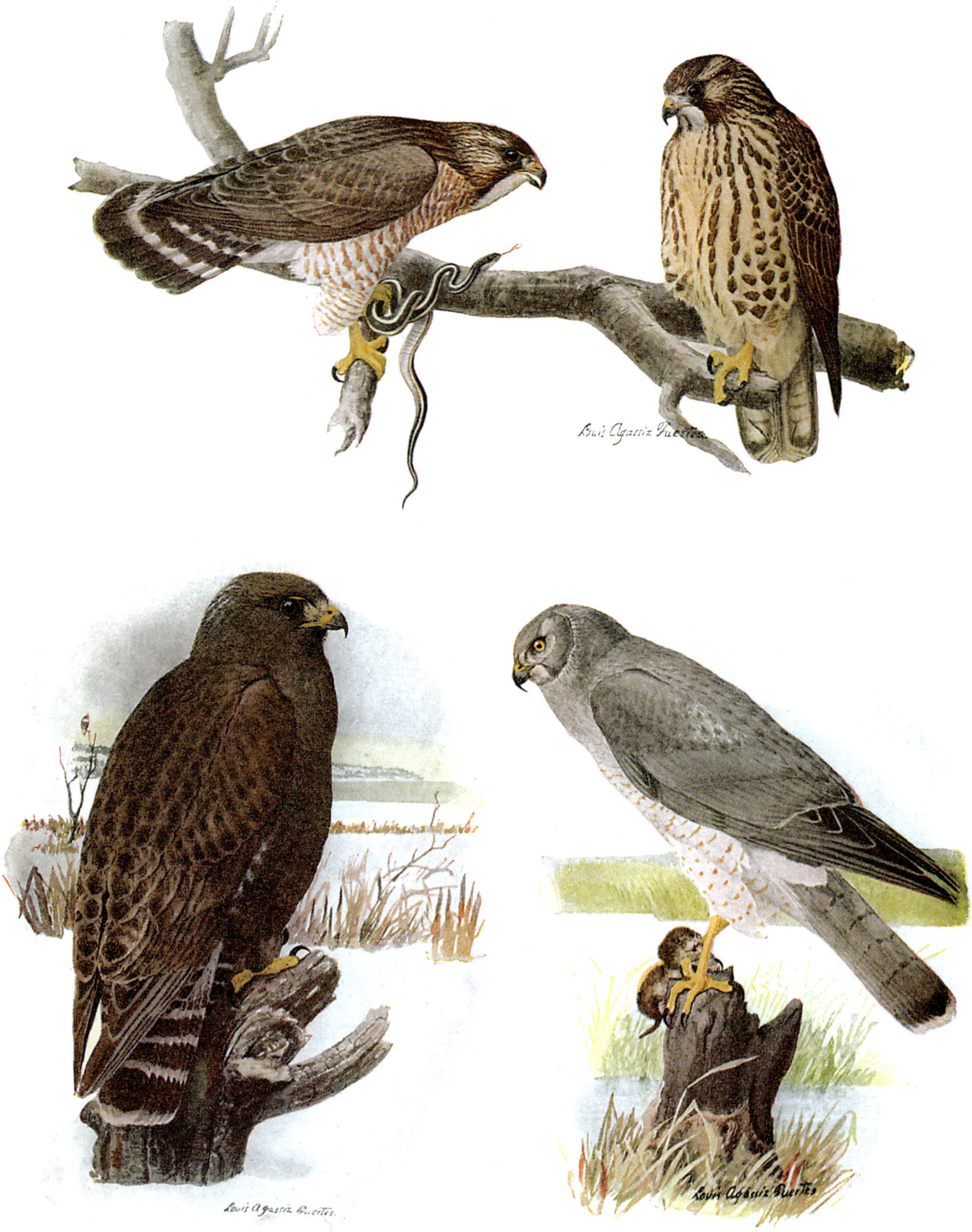

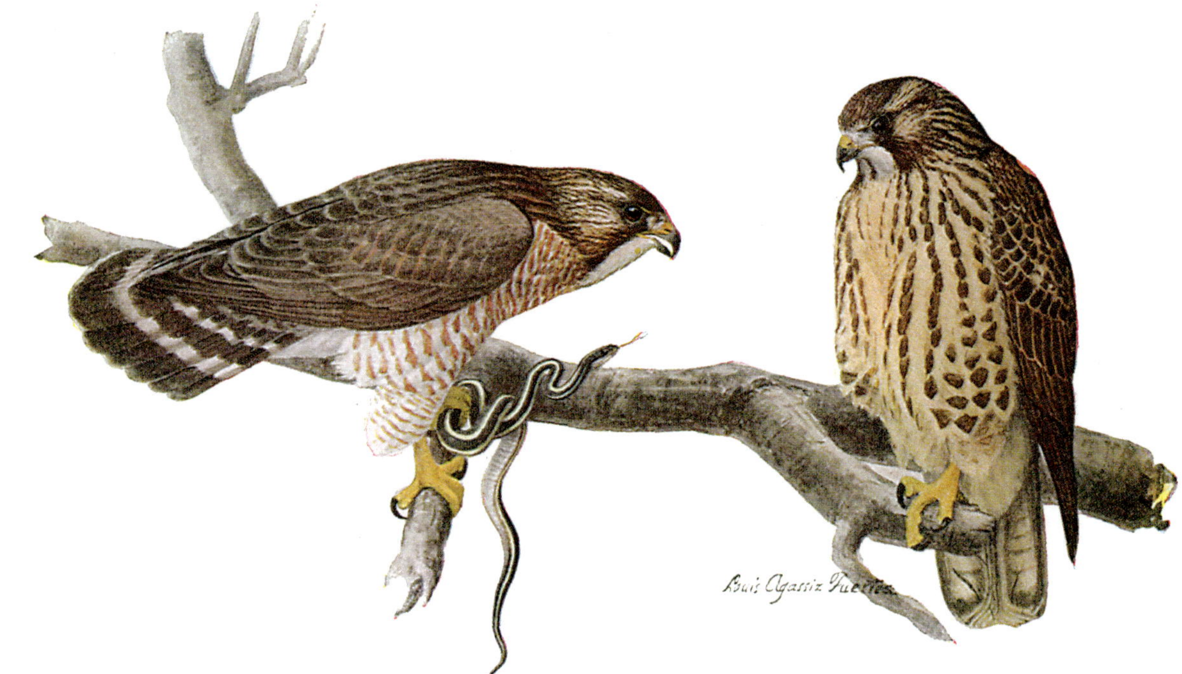

BROAD-WINGED HAWK *Buteo platypterus* (Vieillot)

ADULT IMMATURE

ROUGH-LEGGED HAWK
Archibuteo lagopus sancti-johannis (Gmelin)
BLACK PHASE

MARSH HAWK
Circus hudsonius (Linnaeus)
MALE

Both ⅙ nat. size

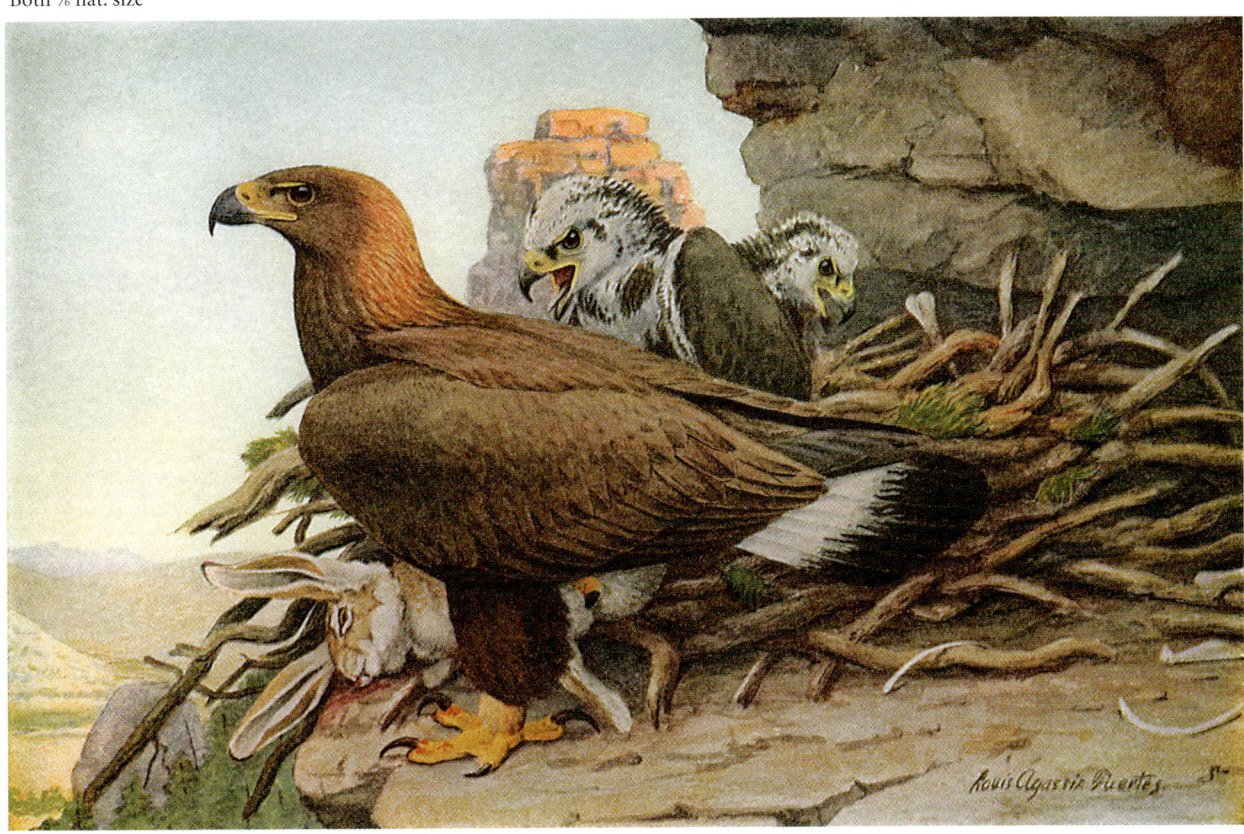

GOLDEN EAGLE *Aquila chrysaetos* (Linnaeus)

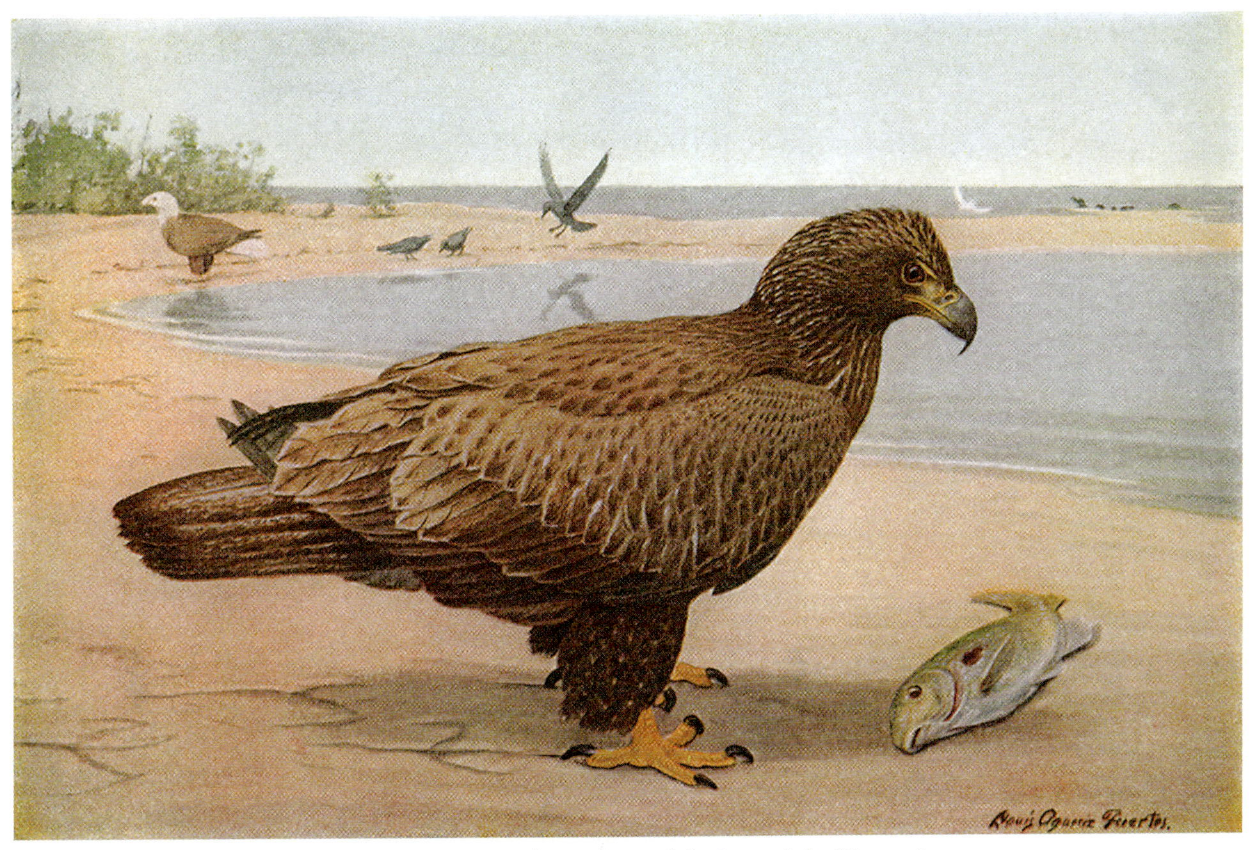

BALD EAGLE *Haliaeetus leucocephalus leucocephalus* (Linnaeus)
IMMATURE

All ¼ nat. size

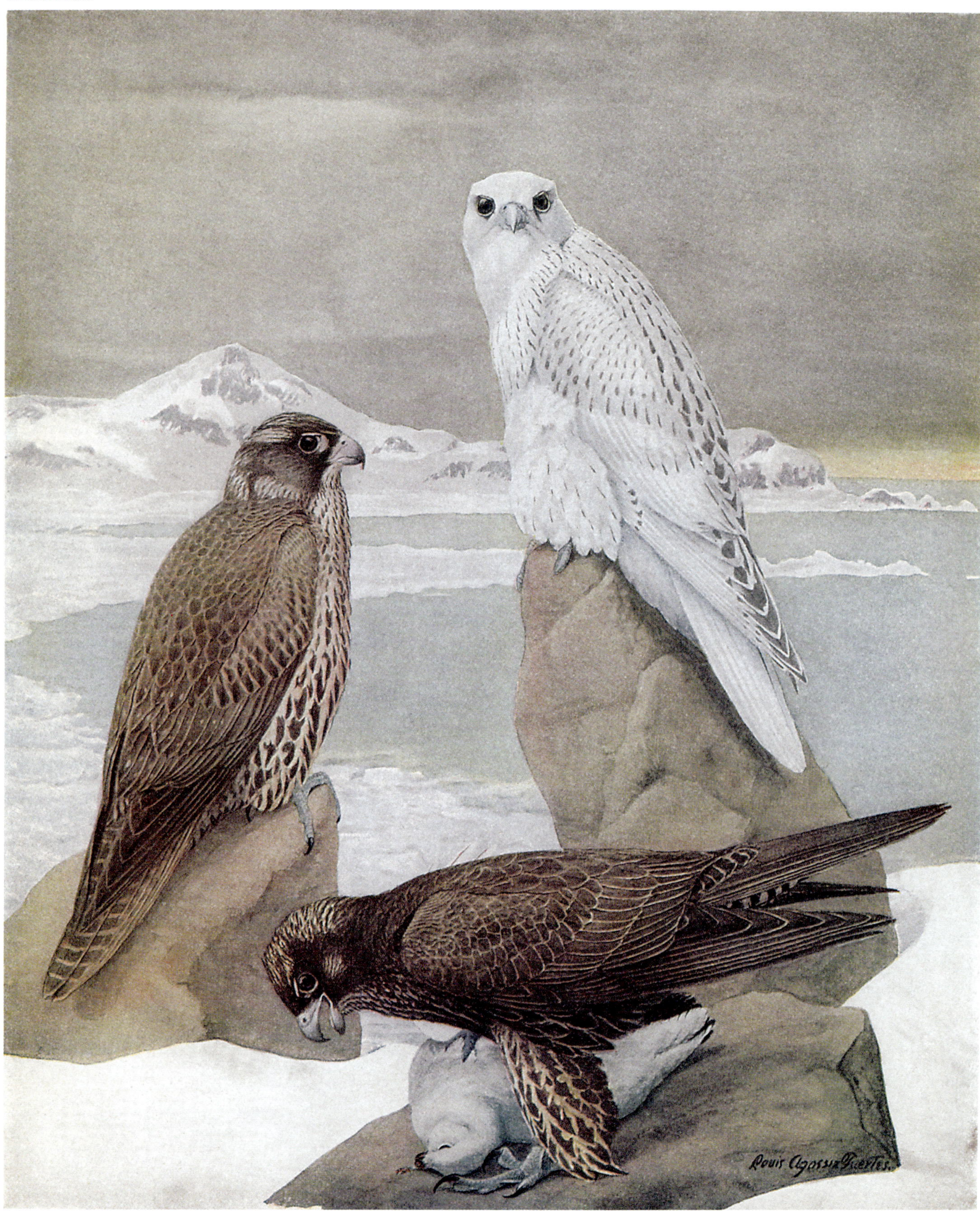

GYRFALCON
Falco rusticolus gyrfalco (Linnaeus)

WHITE GYRFALCON
Falco islandus (Brünnich)

BLACK GYRFALCON *Falco rusticolus obsoletus* (Gmelin)

All ⅓ nat. size

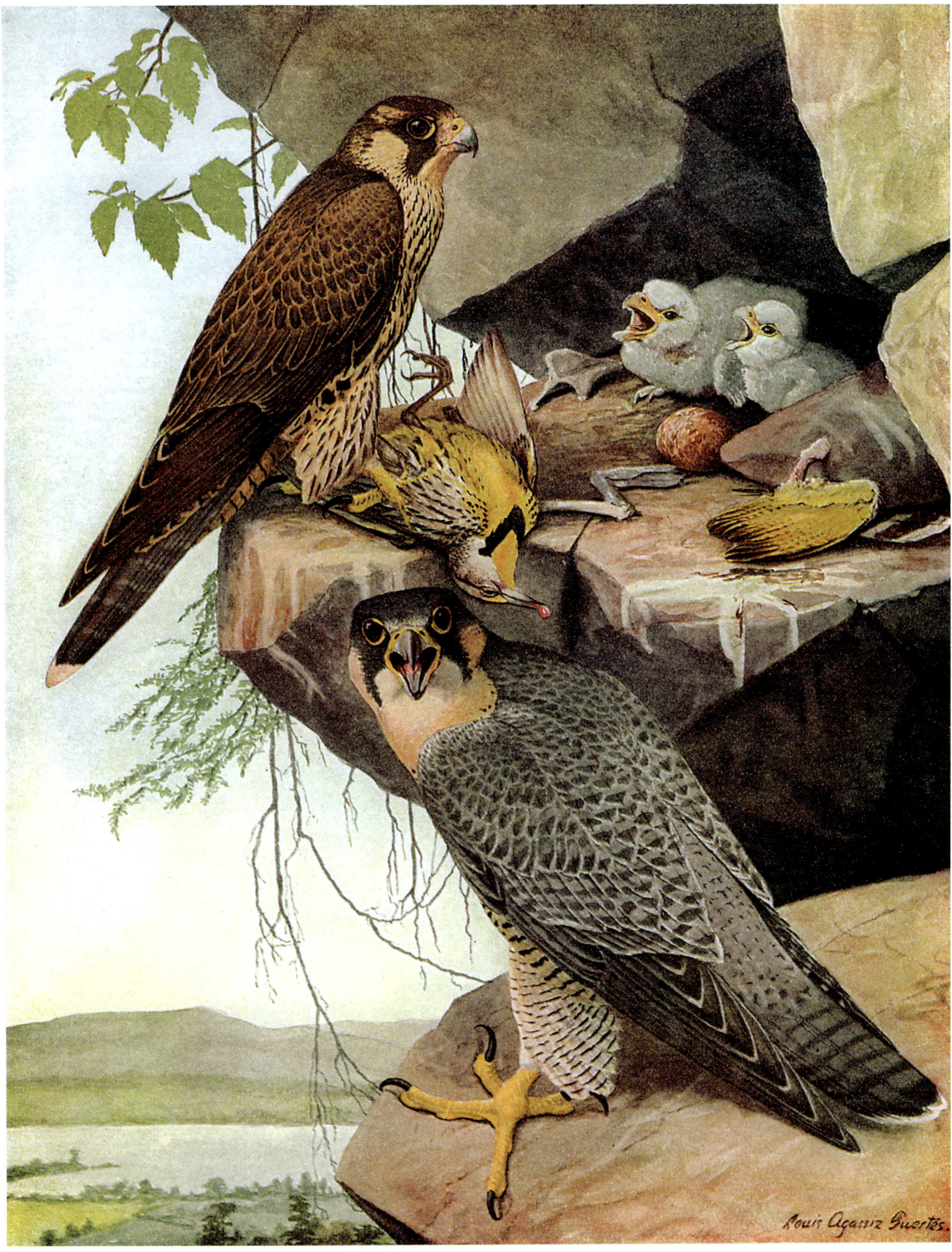

DUCK HAWK *Falco peregrinus anatum* (Bonaparte)

FIRST YEAR MALE ADULT FEMALE CHICKS AND EGG

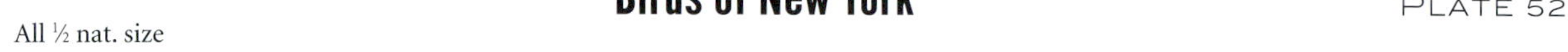

All ½ nat. size

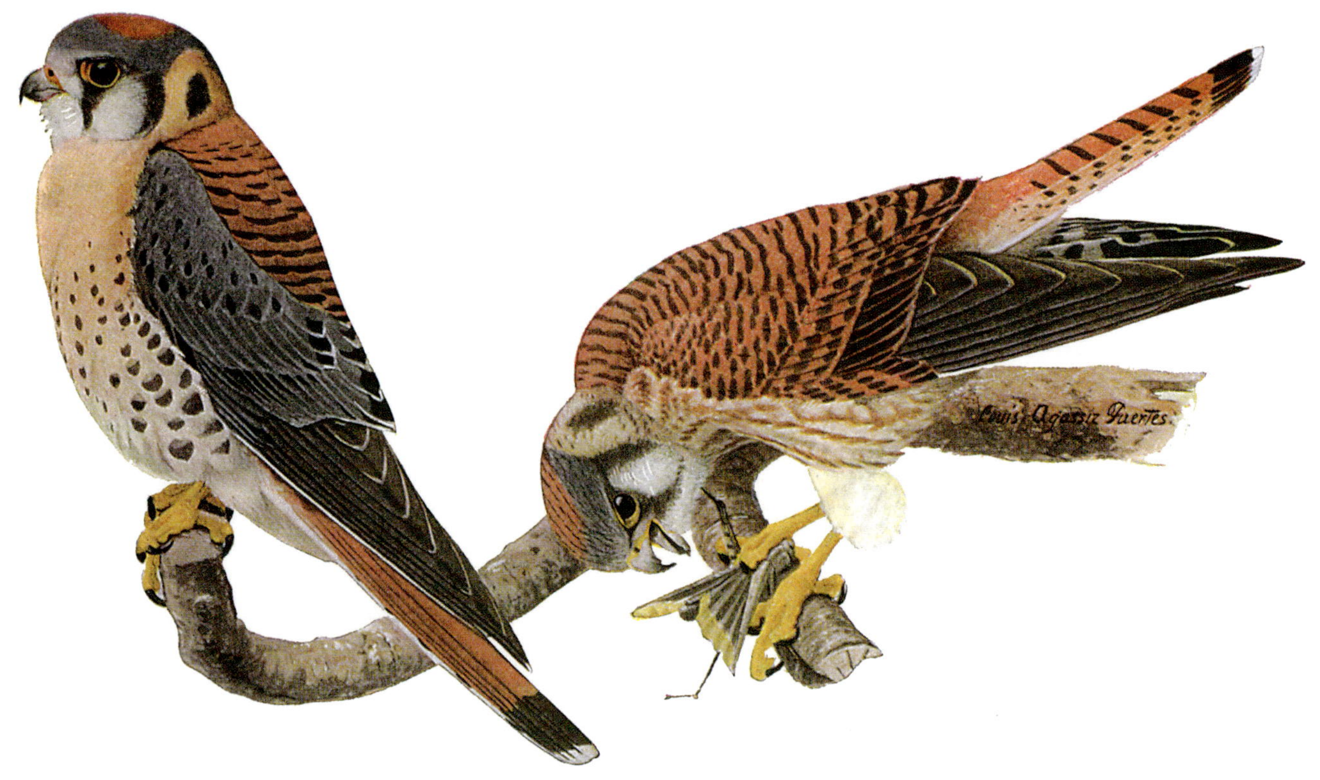

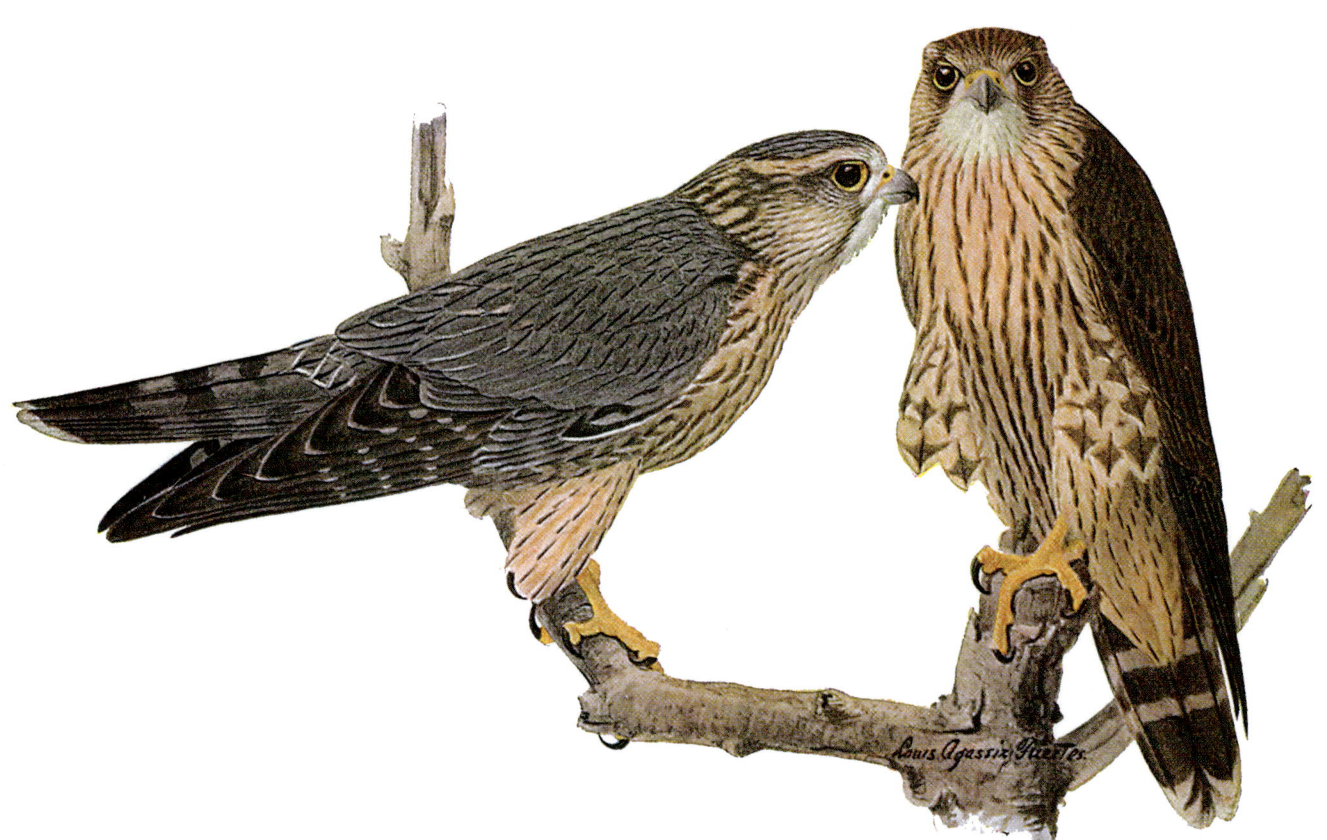

SPARROW HAWK *Falco sparverius sparverius* (Linnaeus)

MALE FEMALE

PIGEON HAWK *Falco columbarius columbarius* (Linnaeus)

ADULT IMMATURE

Both ⅓ nat. size

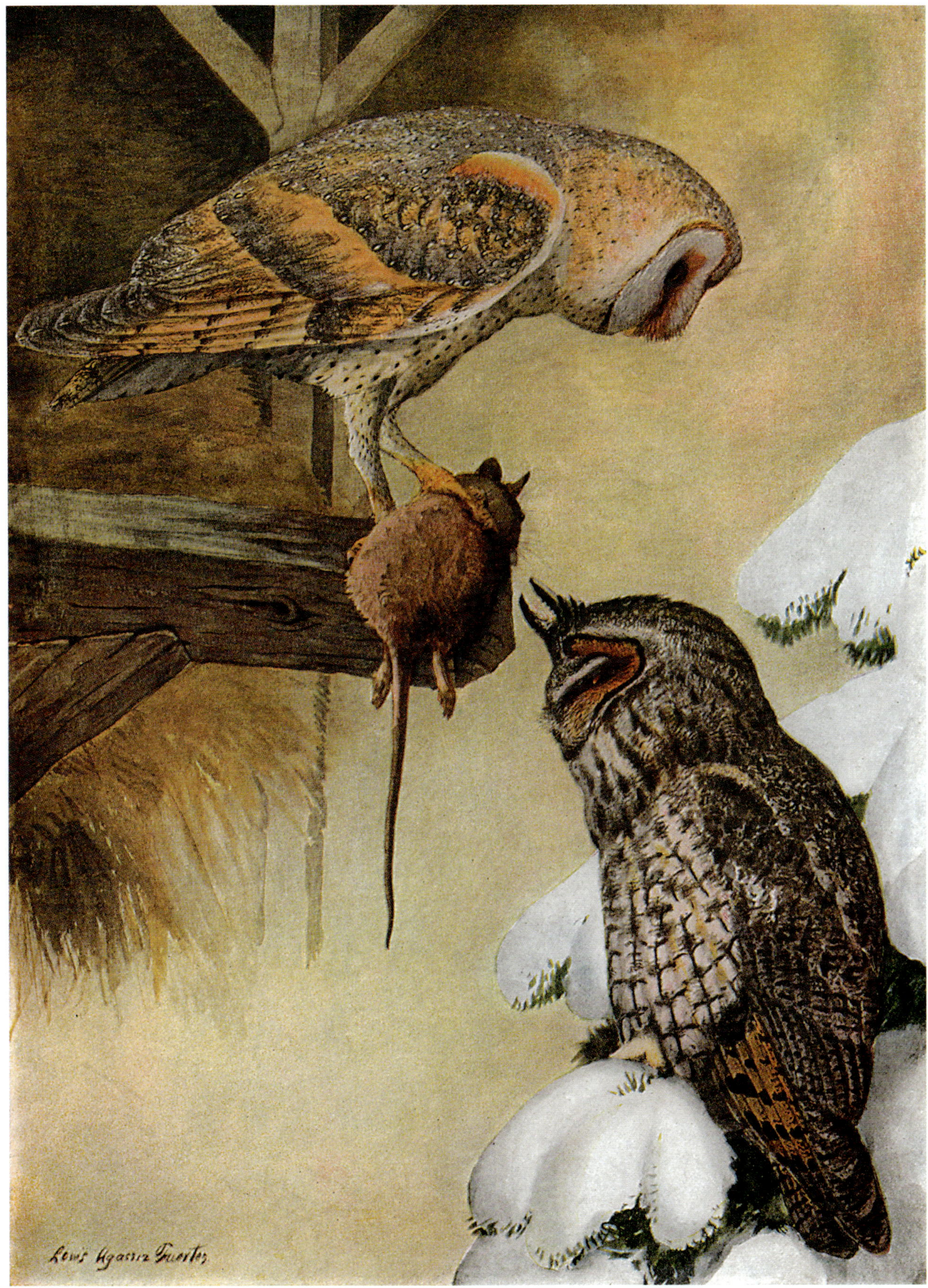

BARN OWL
Aluco pratincola (Bonaparte)

LONG-EARED OWL
Asio wilsonianus (Lesson)

All ⅕ nat. size

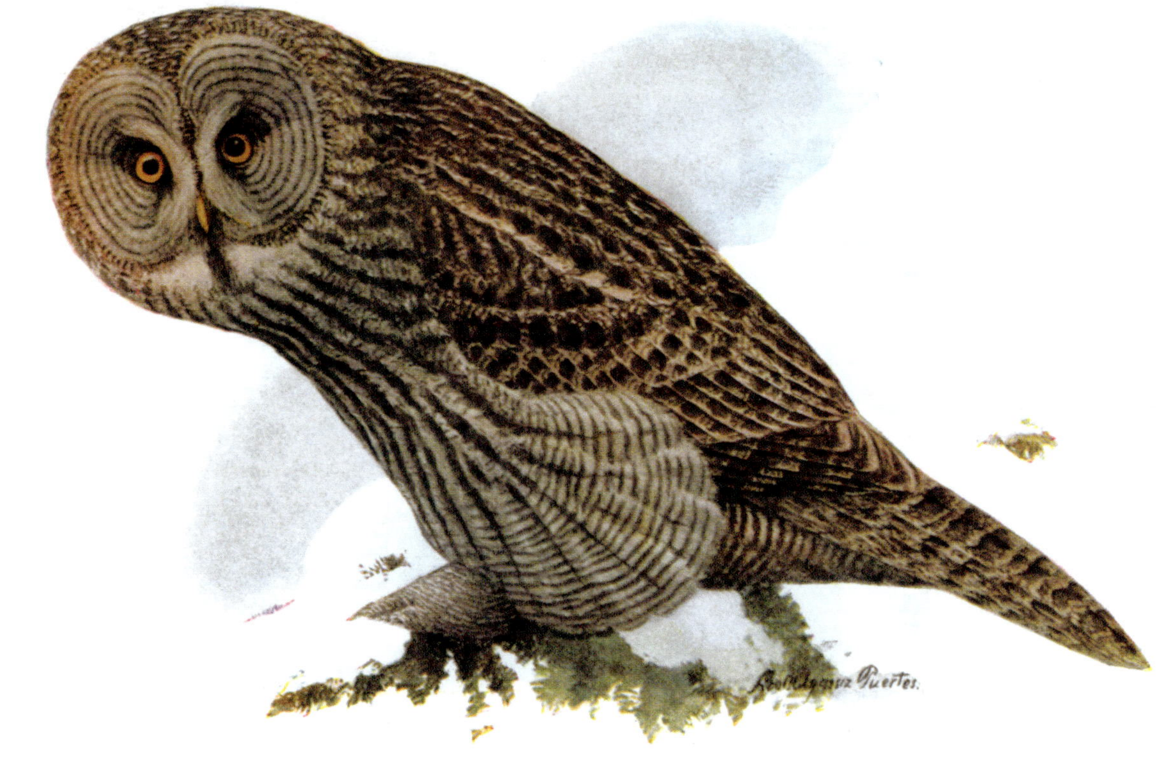

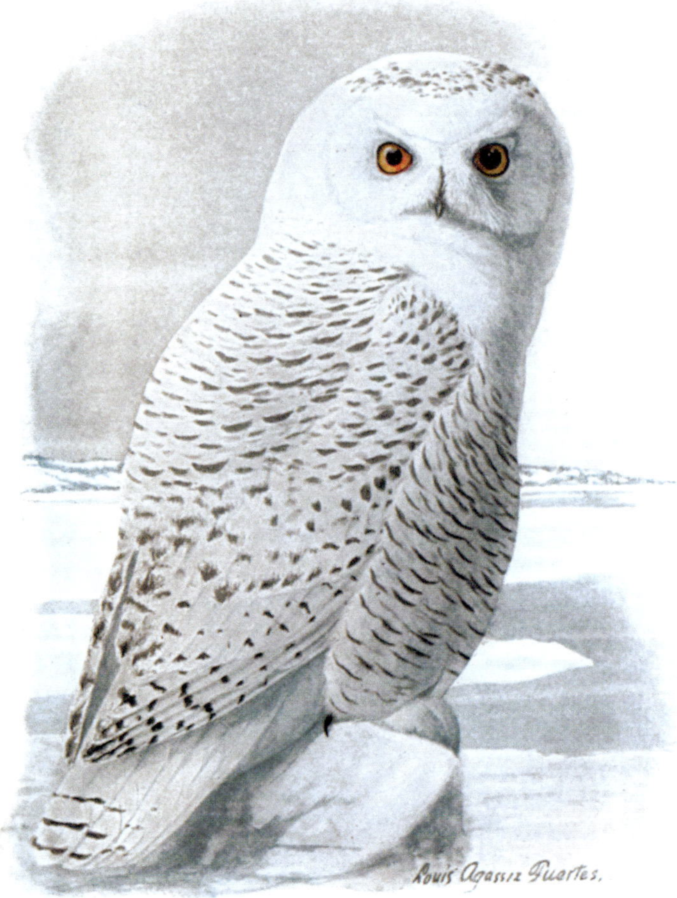

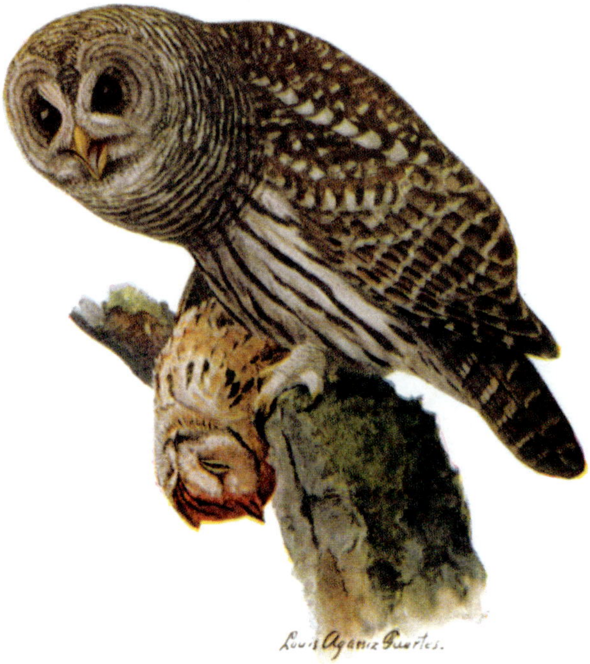

GREAT GRAY OWL *Scotiaptex nebulosa nebulosa* (J. R. Forster)

SNOWY OWL *Nyctea nyctea* (Linnaeus)

BARRED OWL *Strix varia varia* (Barton)

All ½ nat. size

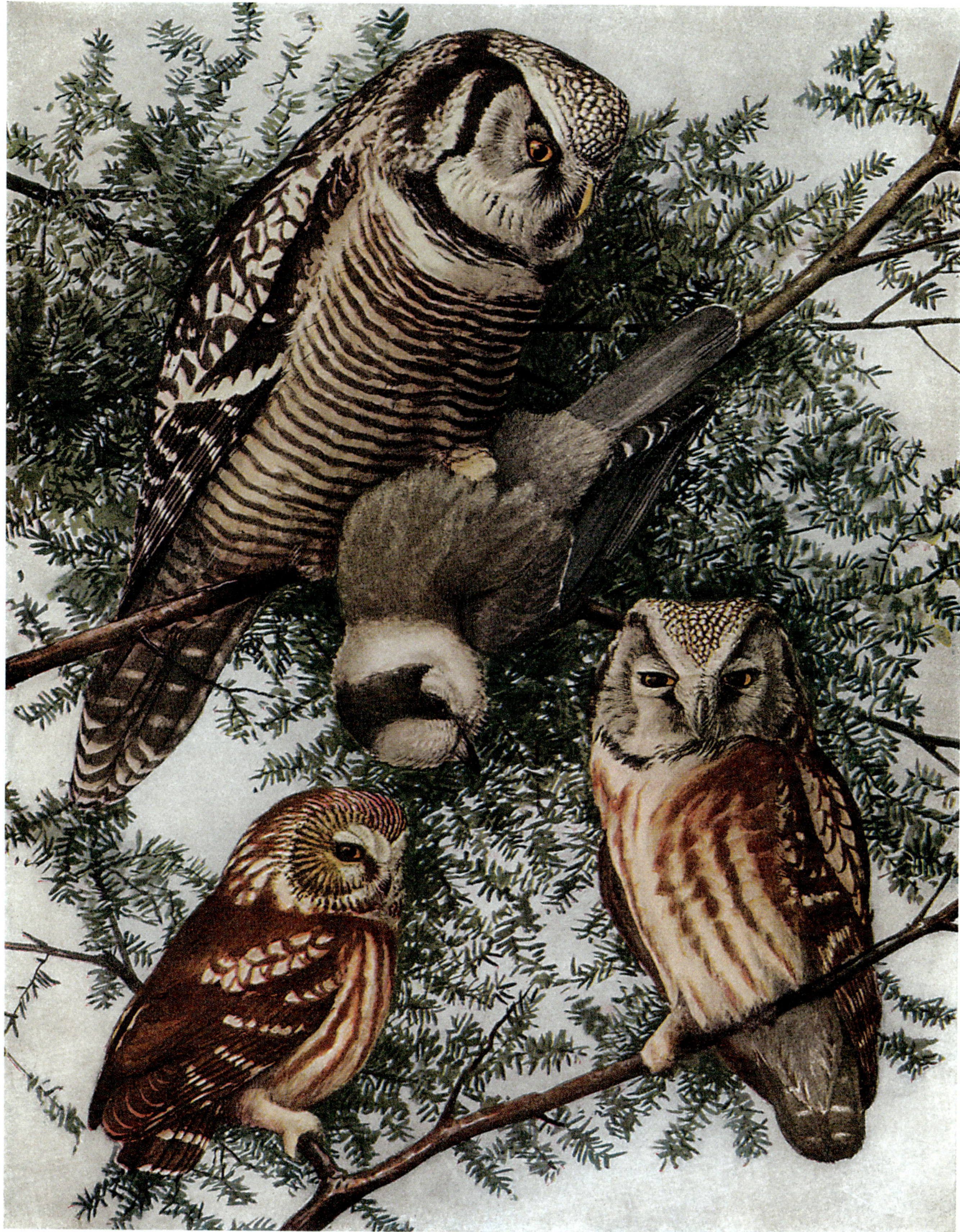

HAWK OWL *Surnia ulula caparoch* (Müller)

SAW-WHET OWL
Cryptoglaux acadica acadica (Gmelin)

RICHARDSON'S OWL
Cryptoglaux funerea richardsoni (Bonaparte)

All ⅓ nat. size

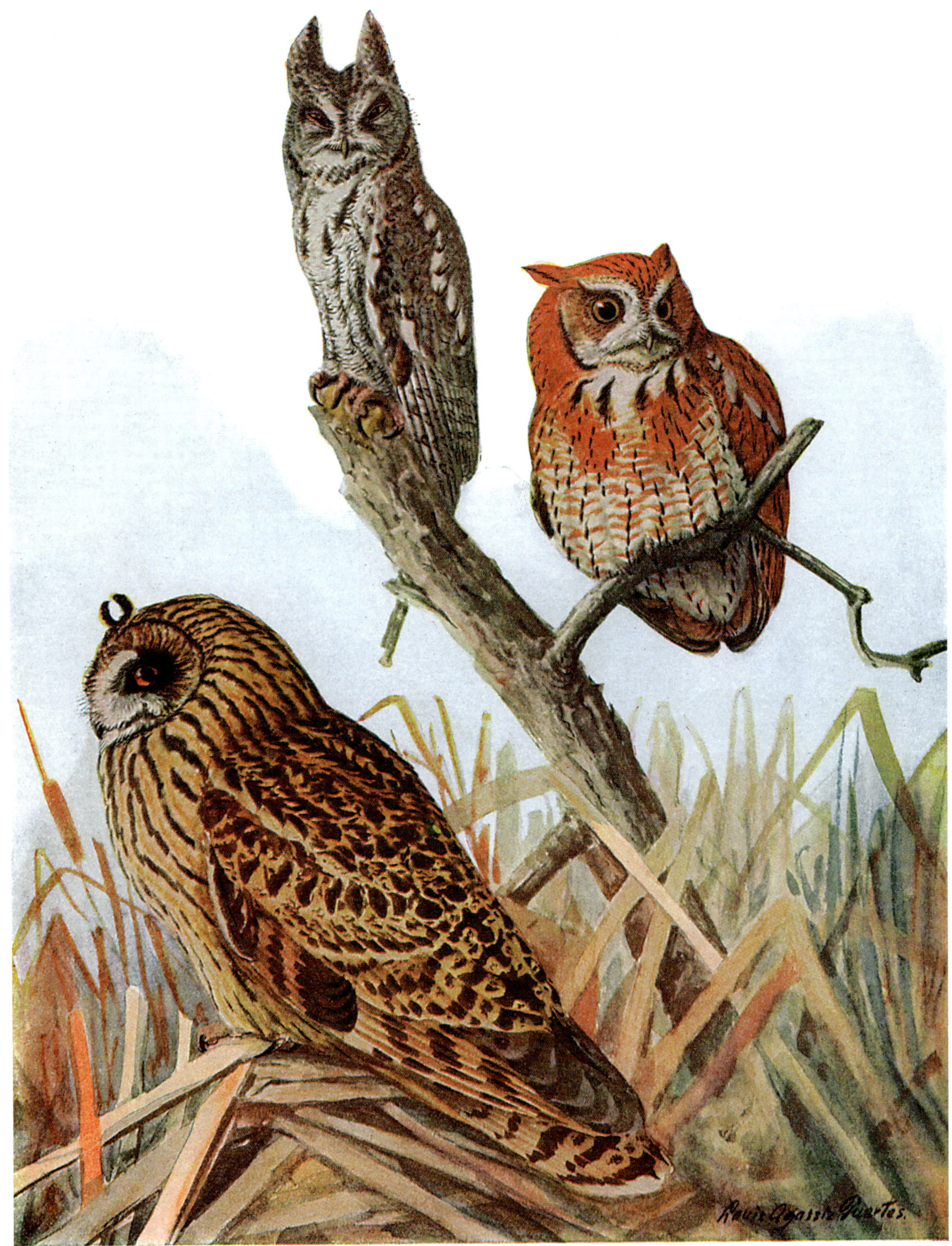

SCREECH OWL *Otus asio asio* (Linnaeus)
GRAY AND RED PHASES

SHORT-EARED OWL *Asio flammeus* (Pontoppidan)

3/8 nat. size

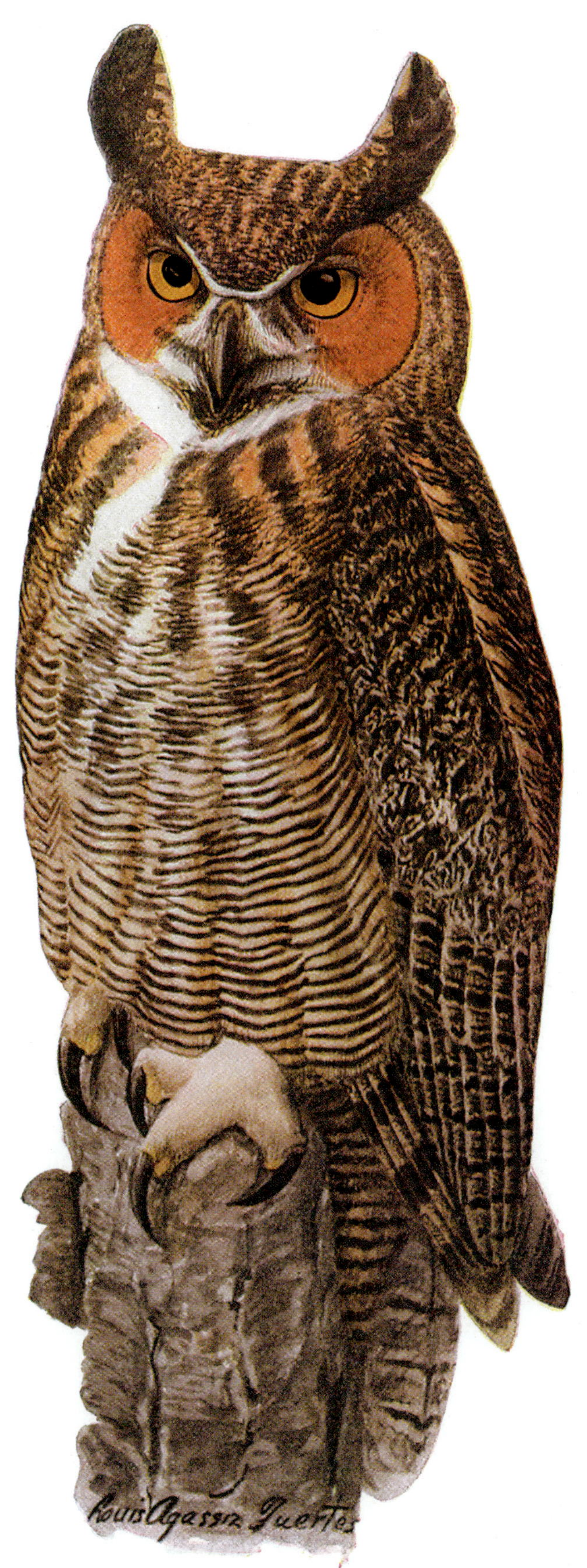

GREAT HORNED OWL
Bubo virginianus virginianus (Gmelin)

All ½ nat. size

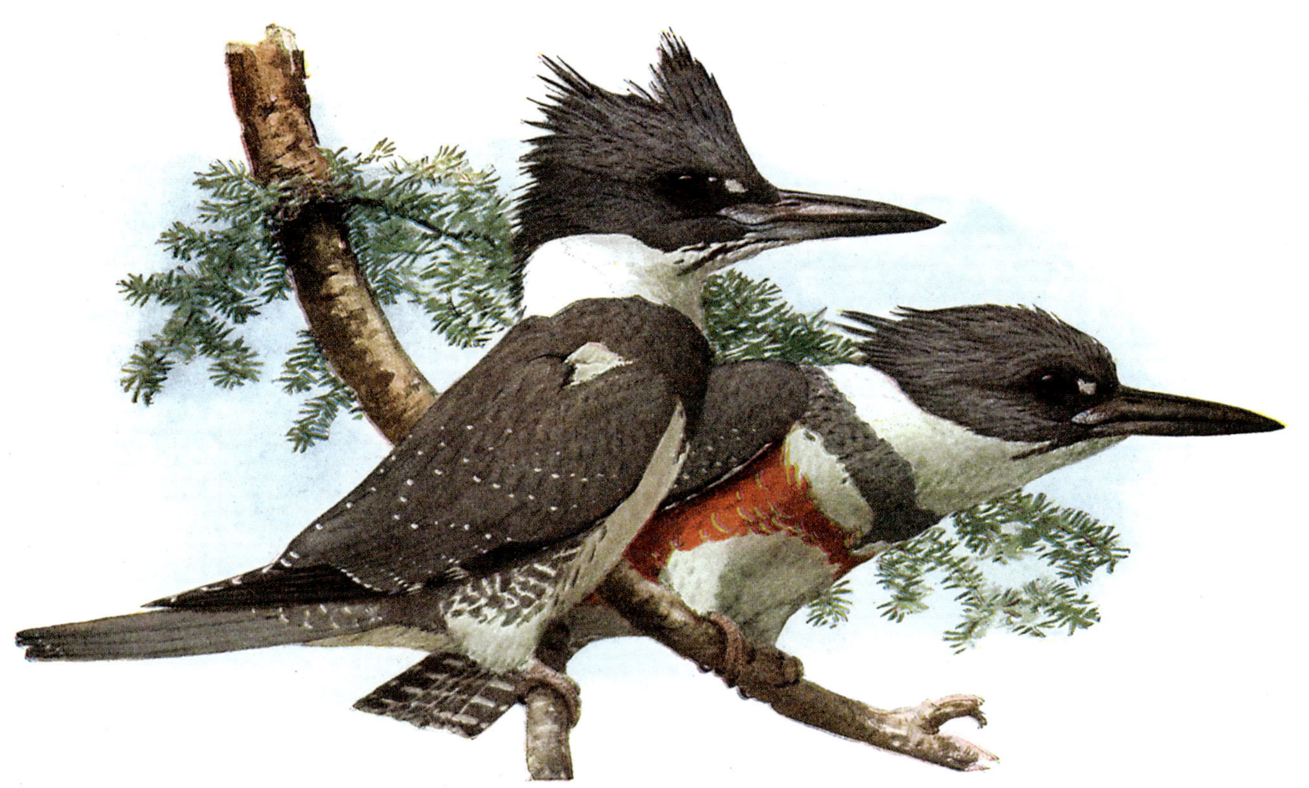

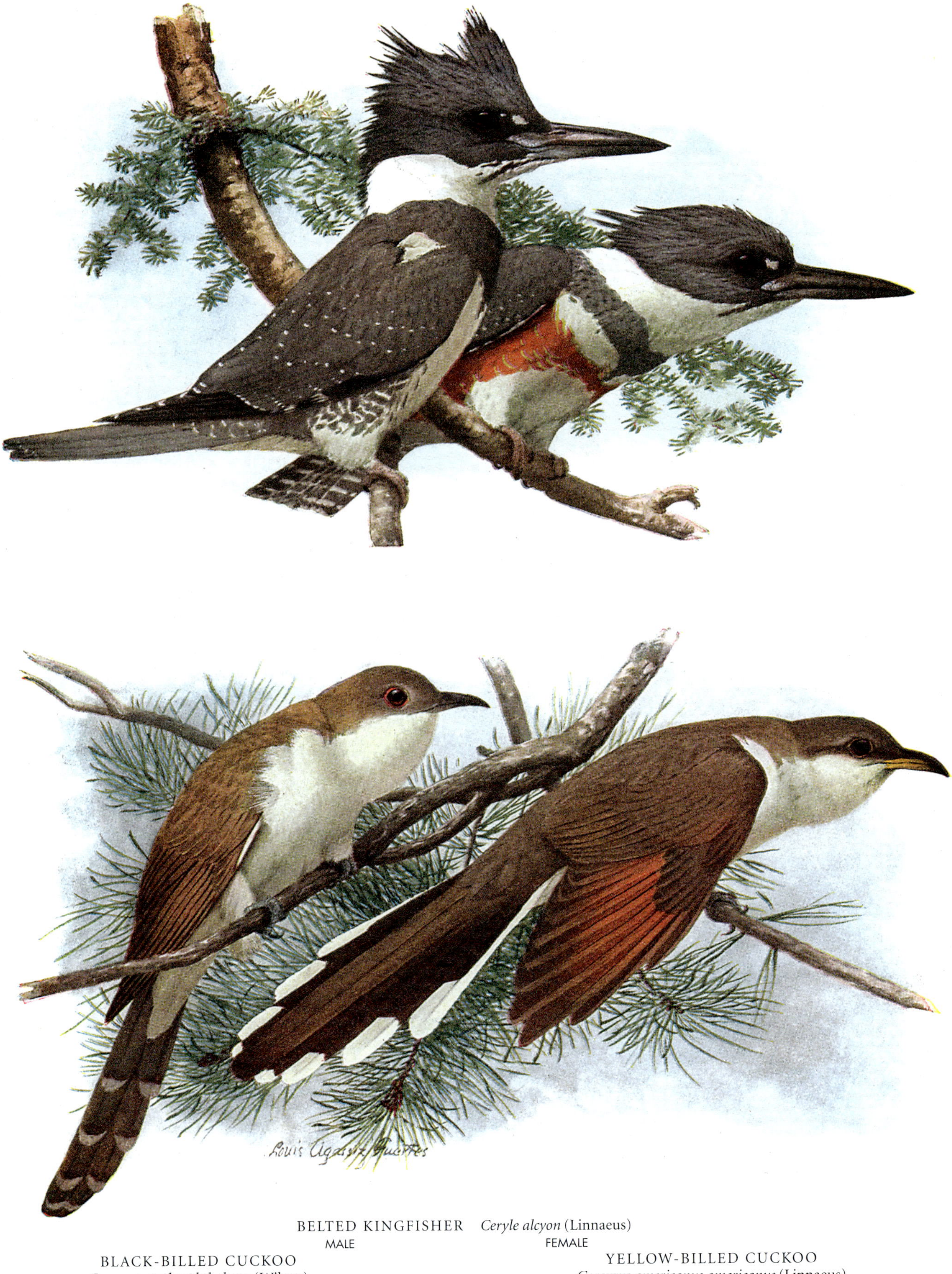

BELTED KINGFISHER *Ceryle alcyon* (Linnaeus)

MALE FEMALE

BLACK-BILLED CUCKOO
Coccyzus erythrophthalmus (Wilson)

YELLOW-BILLED CUCKOO
Coccyzus americanus americanus (Linnaeus)

All ¾ nat. size

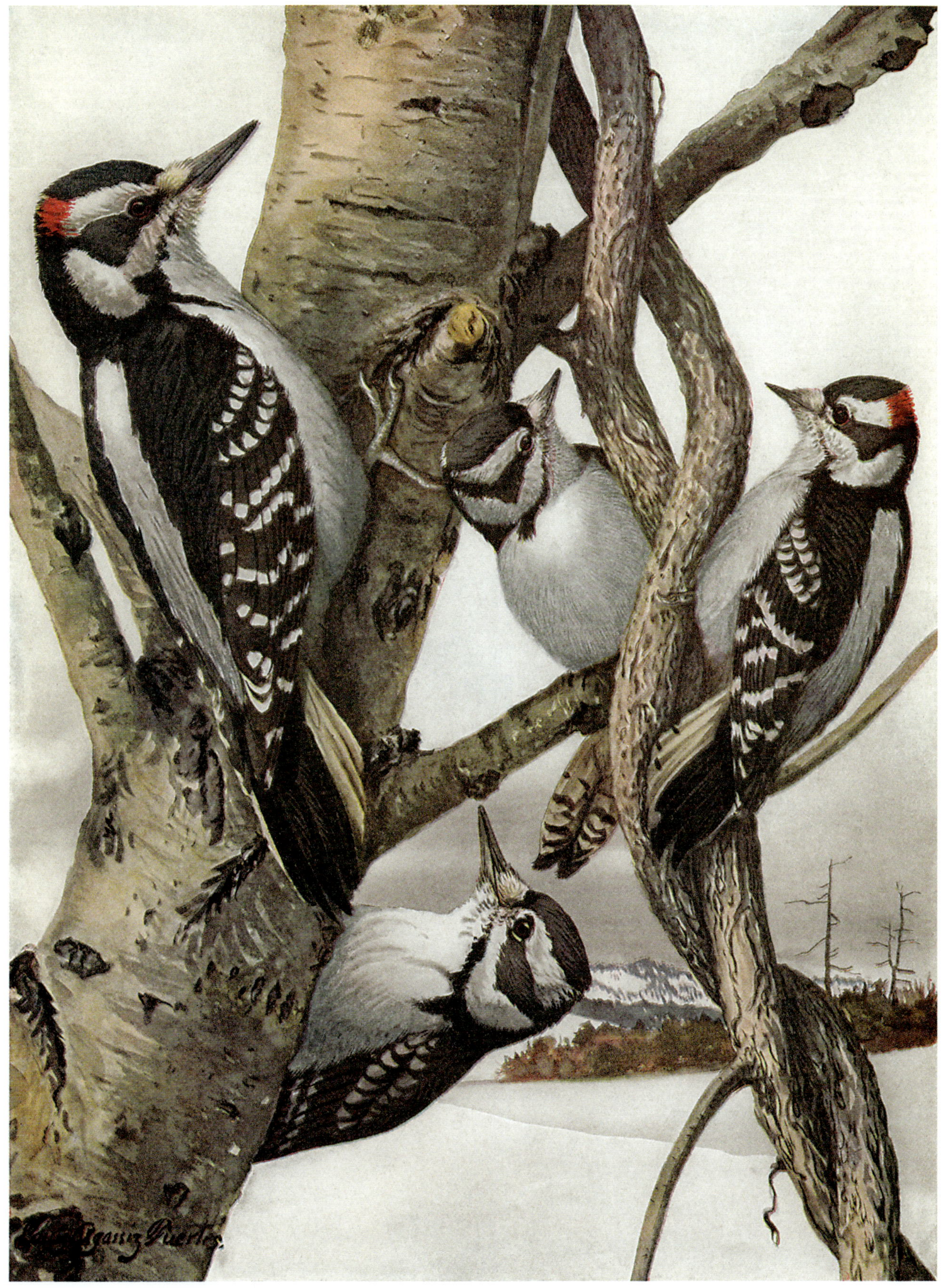

HAIRY WOODPECKER
Dryobates villosus villosus (Linnaeus)
MALE FEMALE

DOWNY WOODPECKER
Dryobates pubescens medianus (Swainson)
FEMALE MALE

Both ⅘ nat. size

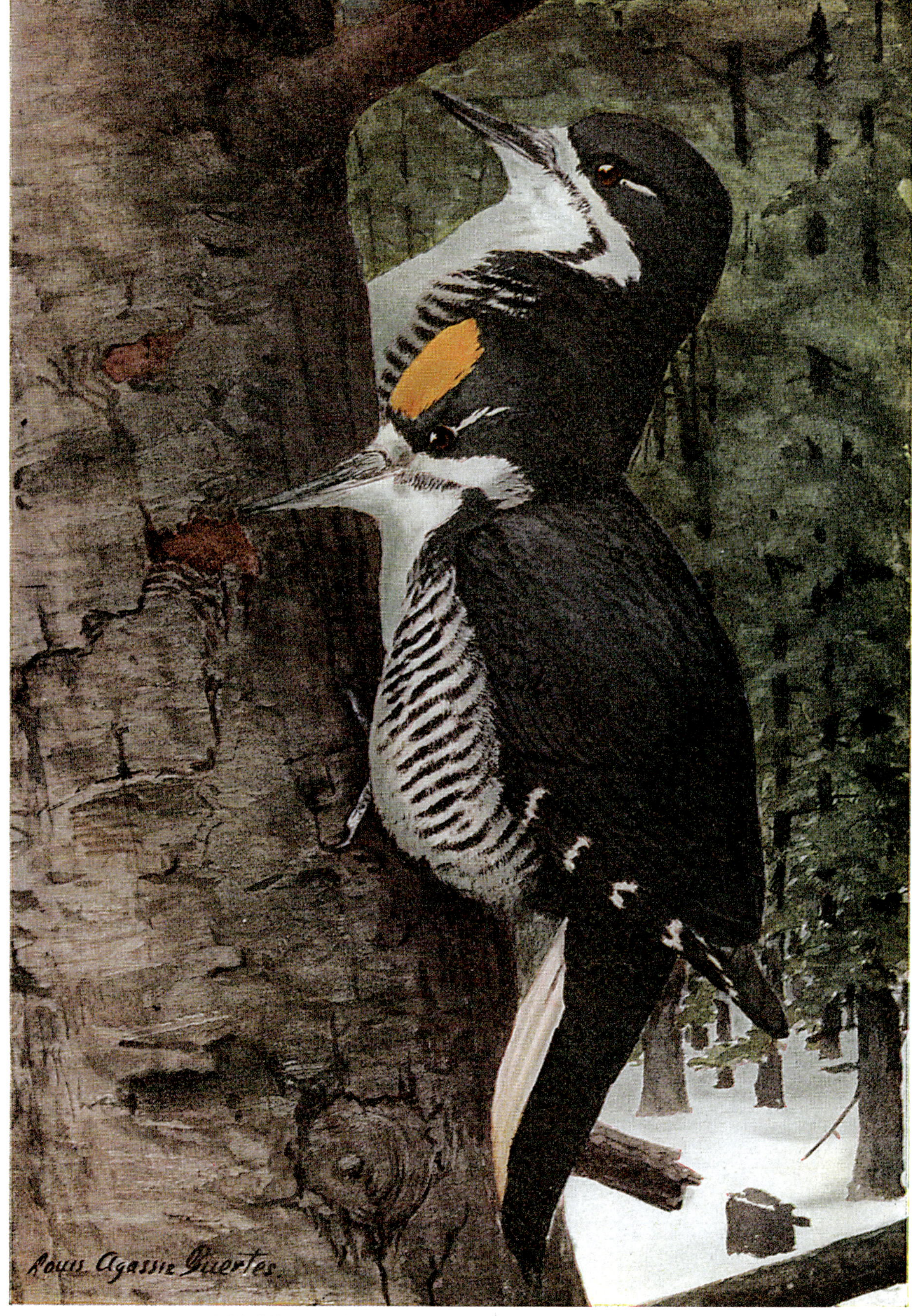

ARCTIC THREE-TOED WOODPECKER *Picoides arcticus* (Swainson)
FEMALE
MALE

Both ⅞ nat. size

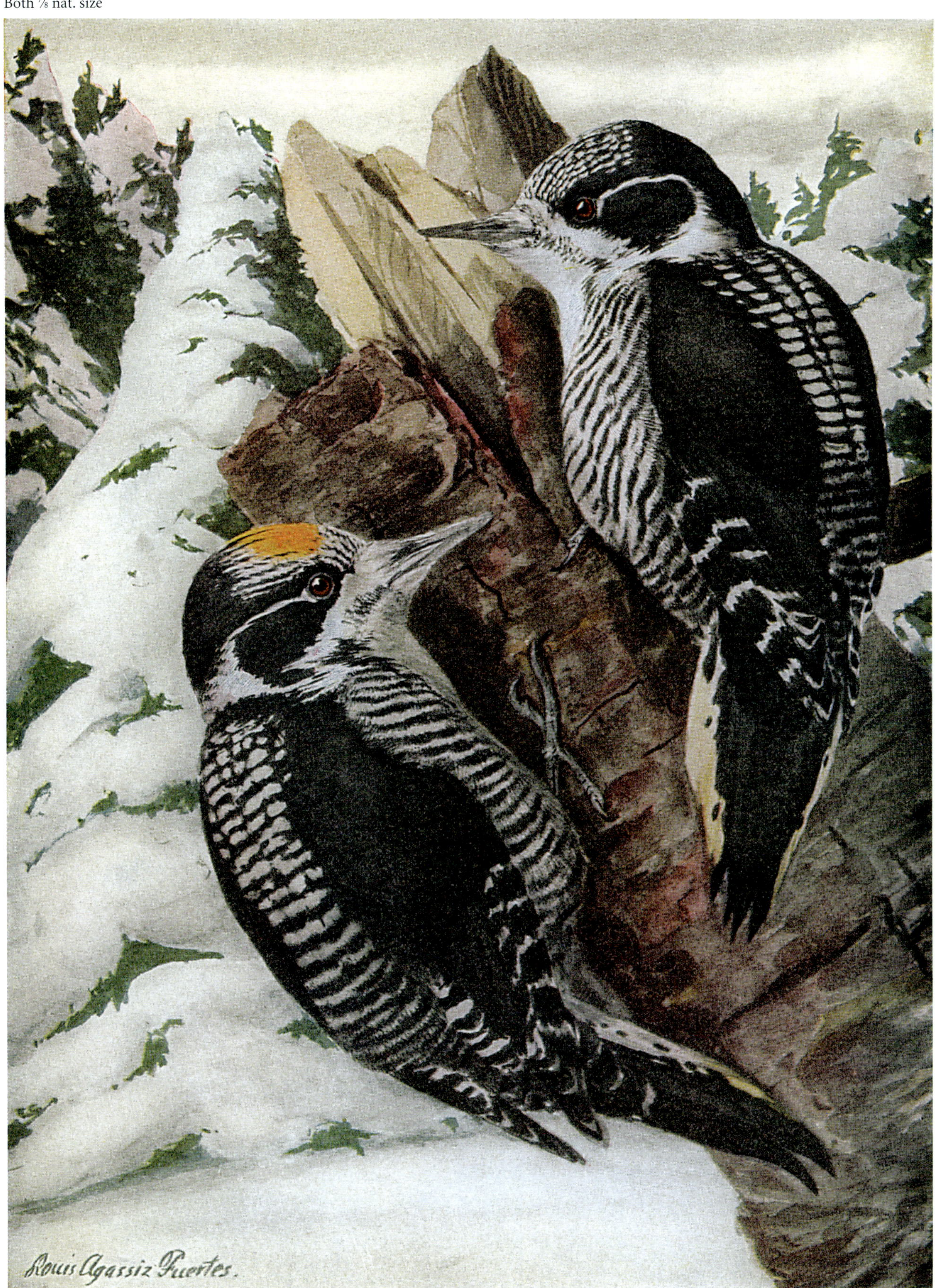

AMERICAN THREE-TOED WOODPECKER *Picoides americanus americanus* (Brehm)

MALE FEMALE

All ½ nat. size

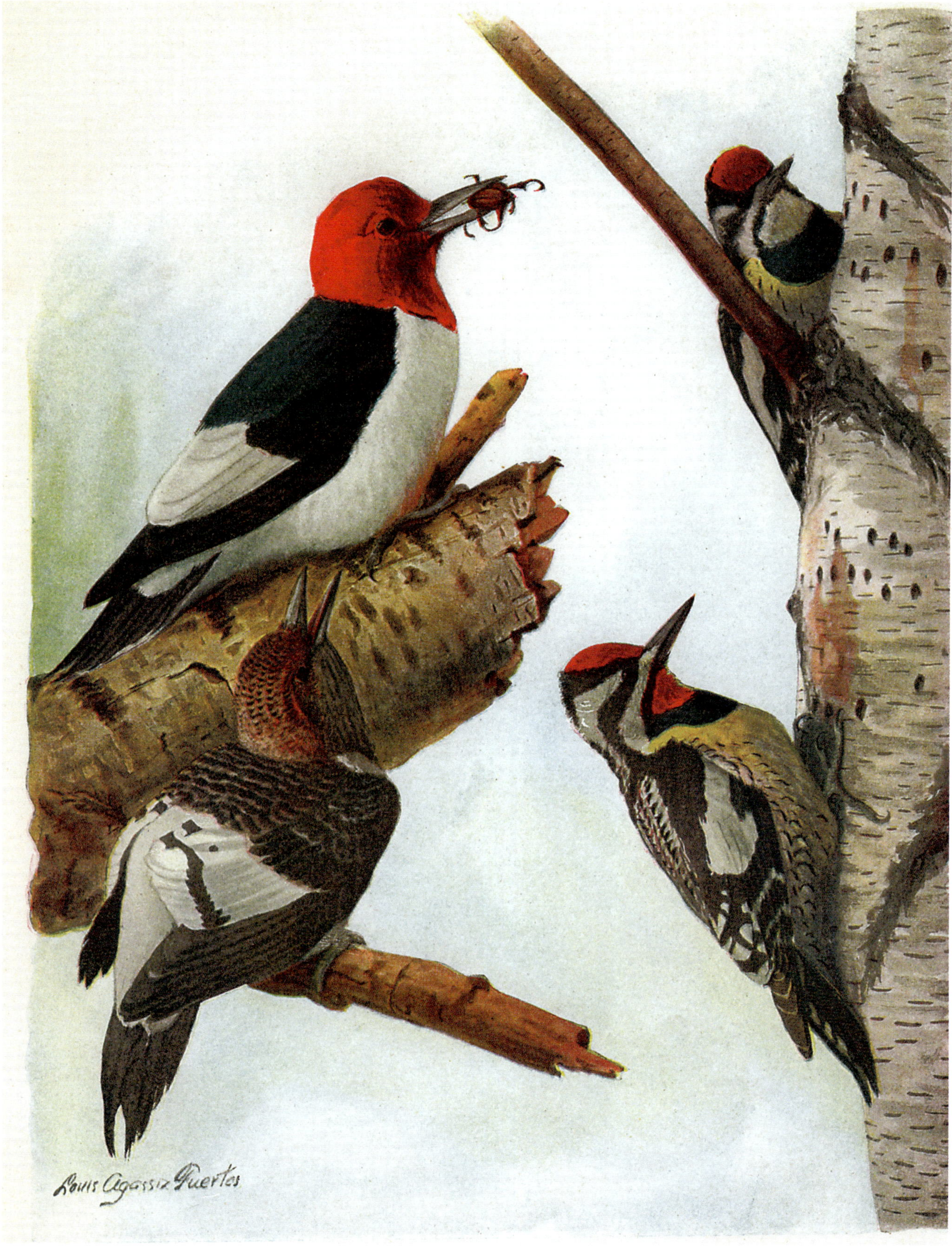

RED-HEADED WOODPECKER
Melanerpes erythrocephalus (Linnaeus)
ADULT
IMMATURE

YELLOW-BELLIED SAPSUCKER
Sphyrapicus varius varius (Linnaeus)
FEMALE
MALE

Both about ½ nat. size

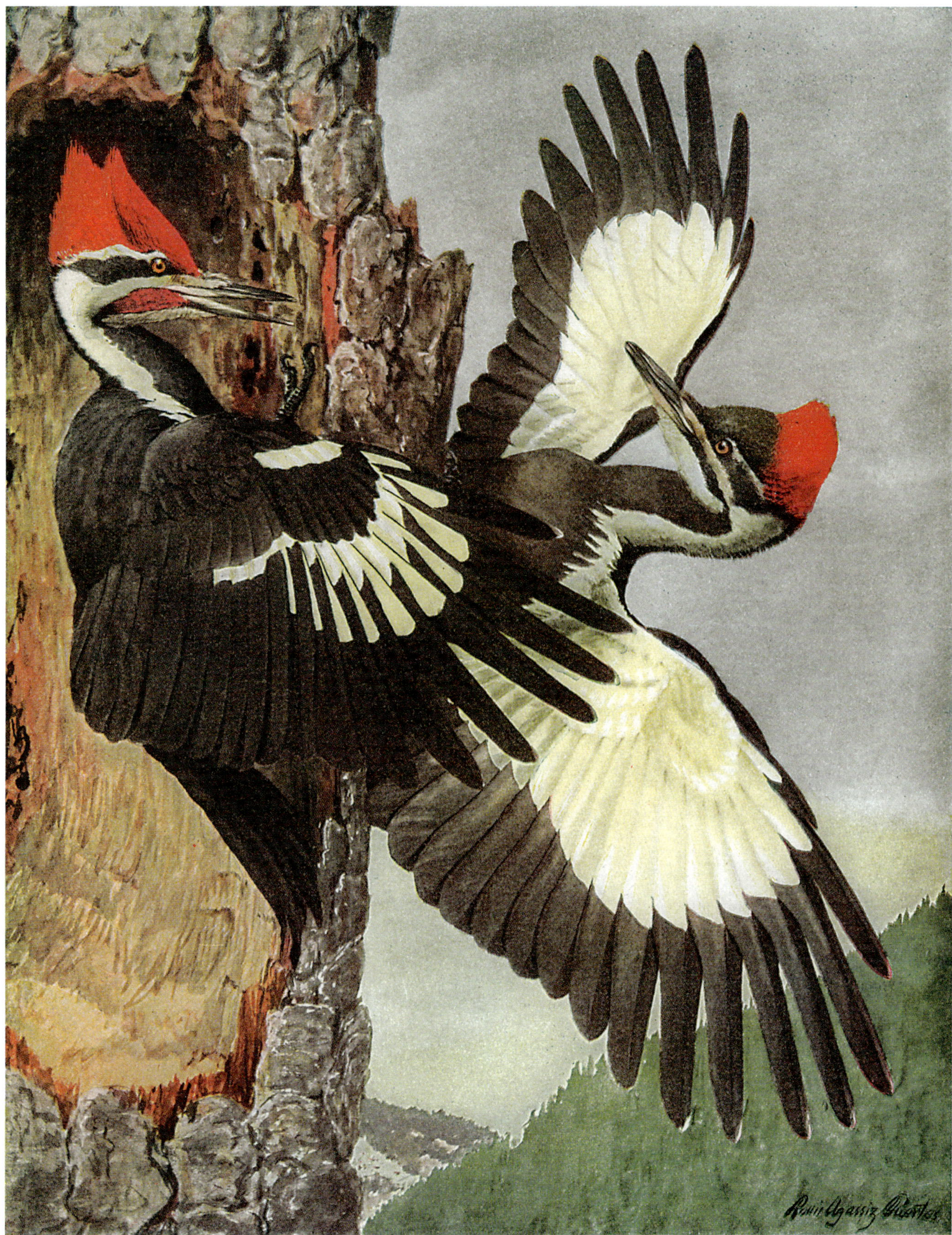

NORTHERN PILEATED WOODPECKER *Phloeotomus pileatus abieticola* (Bangs)

MALE FEMALE

All ⅓ nat. size

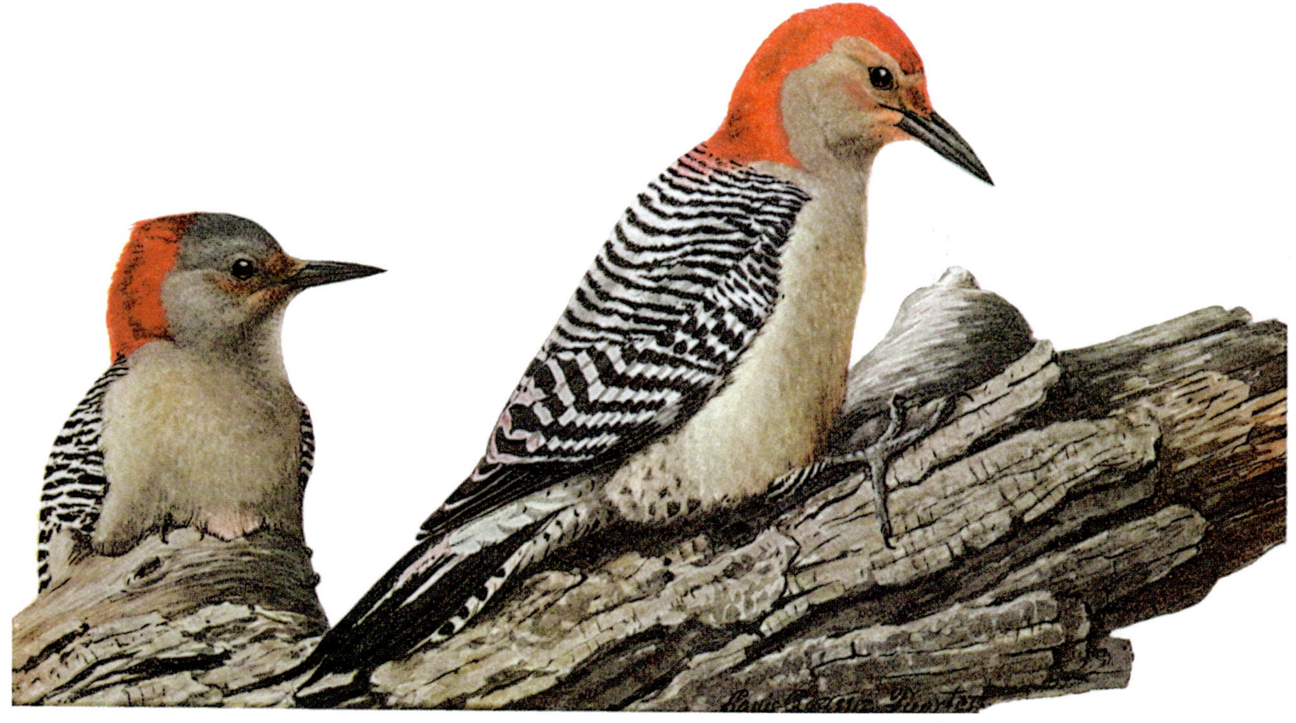

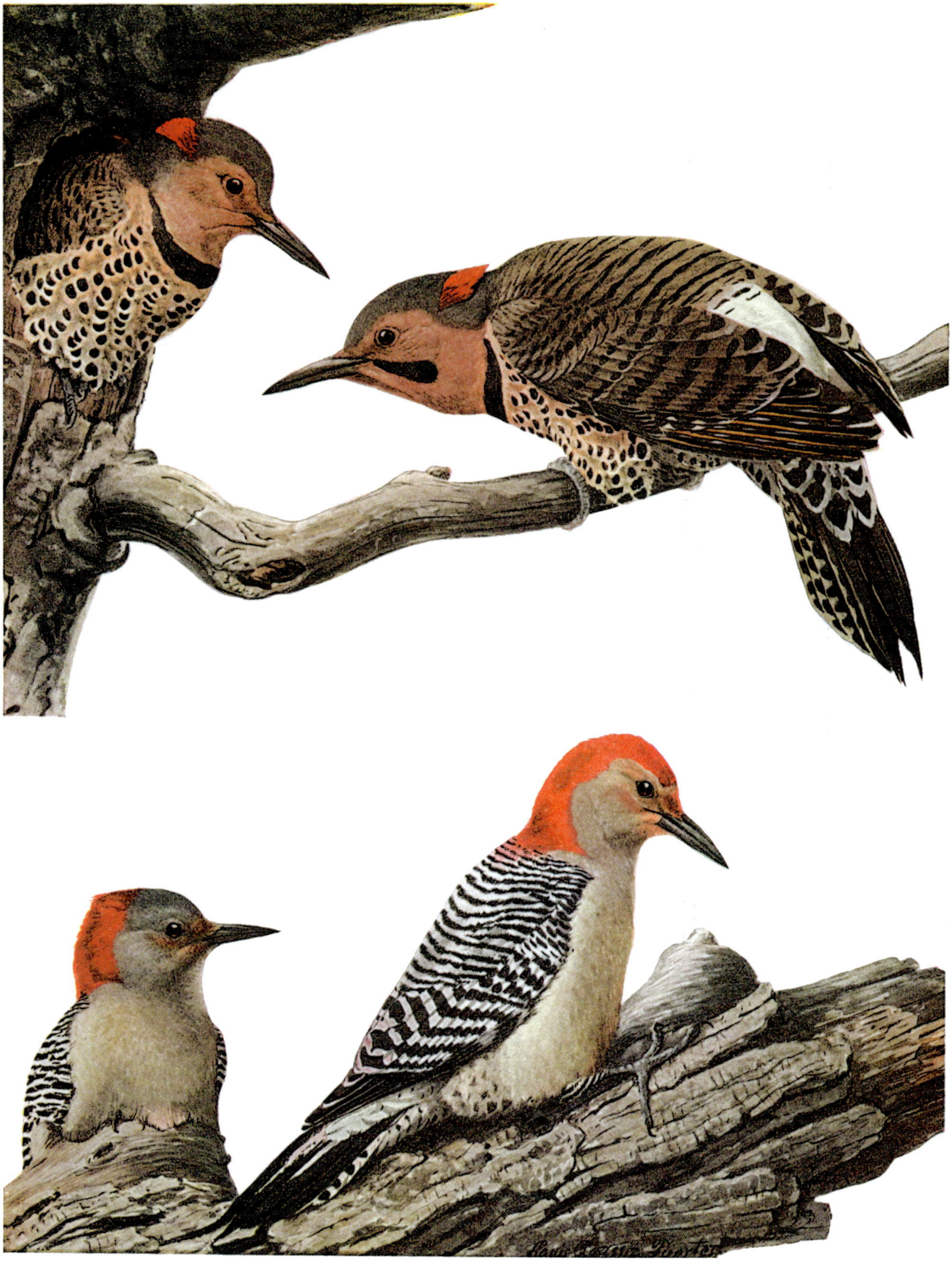

NORTHERN FLICKER *Colaptes auratus luteus* (Bangs)

FEMALE MALE

RED-BELLIED WOODPECKER *Centurus carolinus* (Linnaeus)

FEMALE MALE

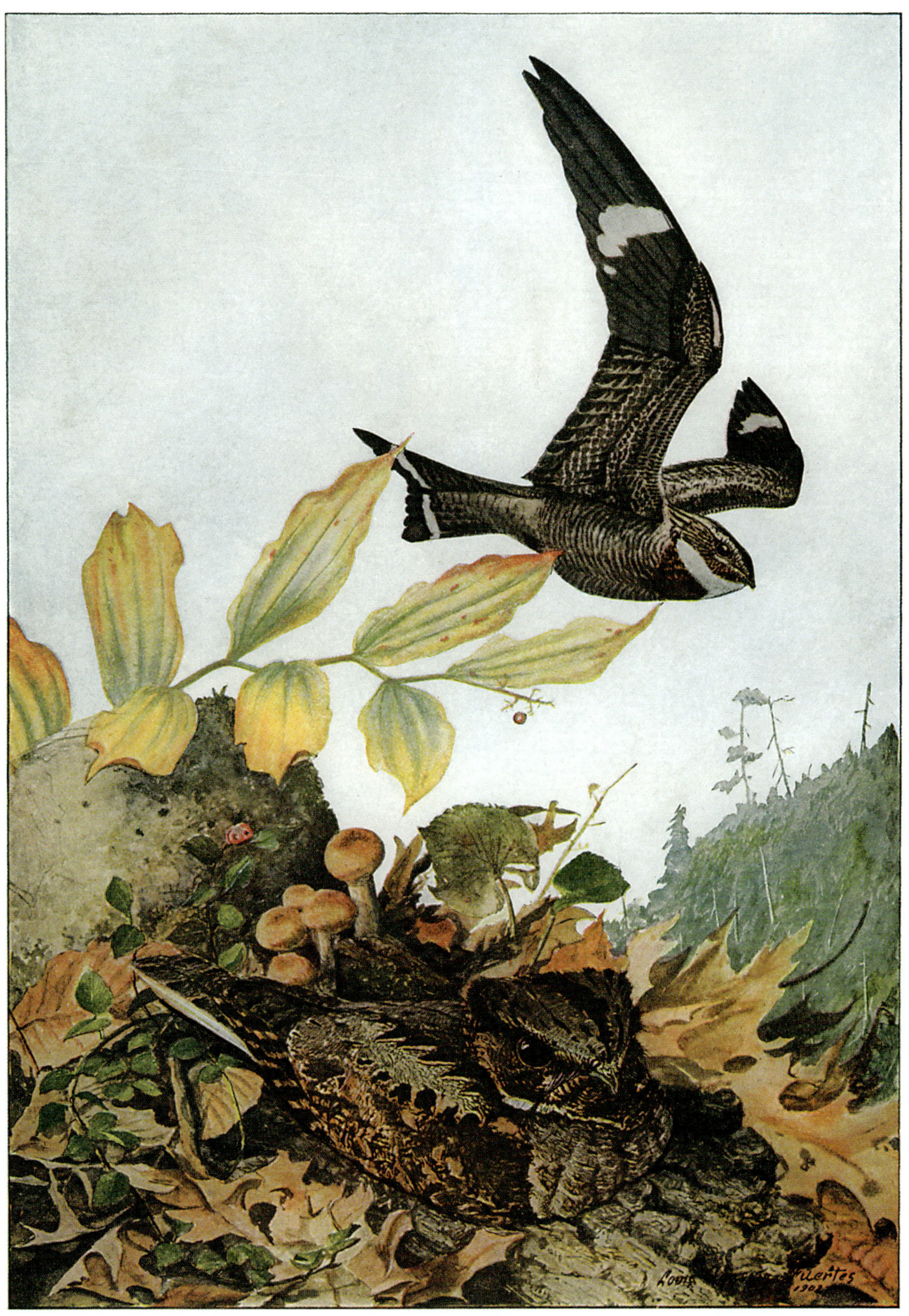

NIGHTHAWK *Chlordeiles virginianus virginianus* (Gmelin)
MALE ⅓ nat. size

WHIP-POOR-WILL *Antrostomus vociferus vociferus* (Wilson)
MALE ½ nat. size

All life size

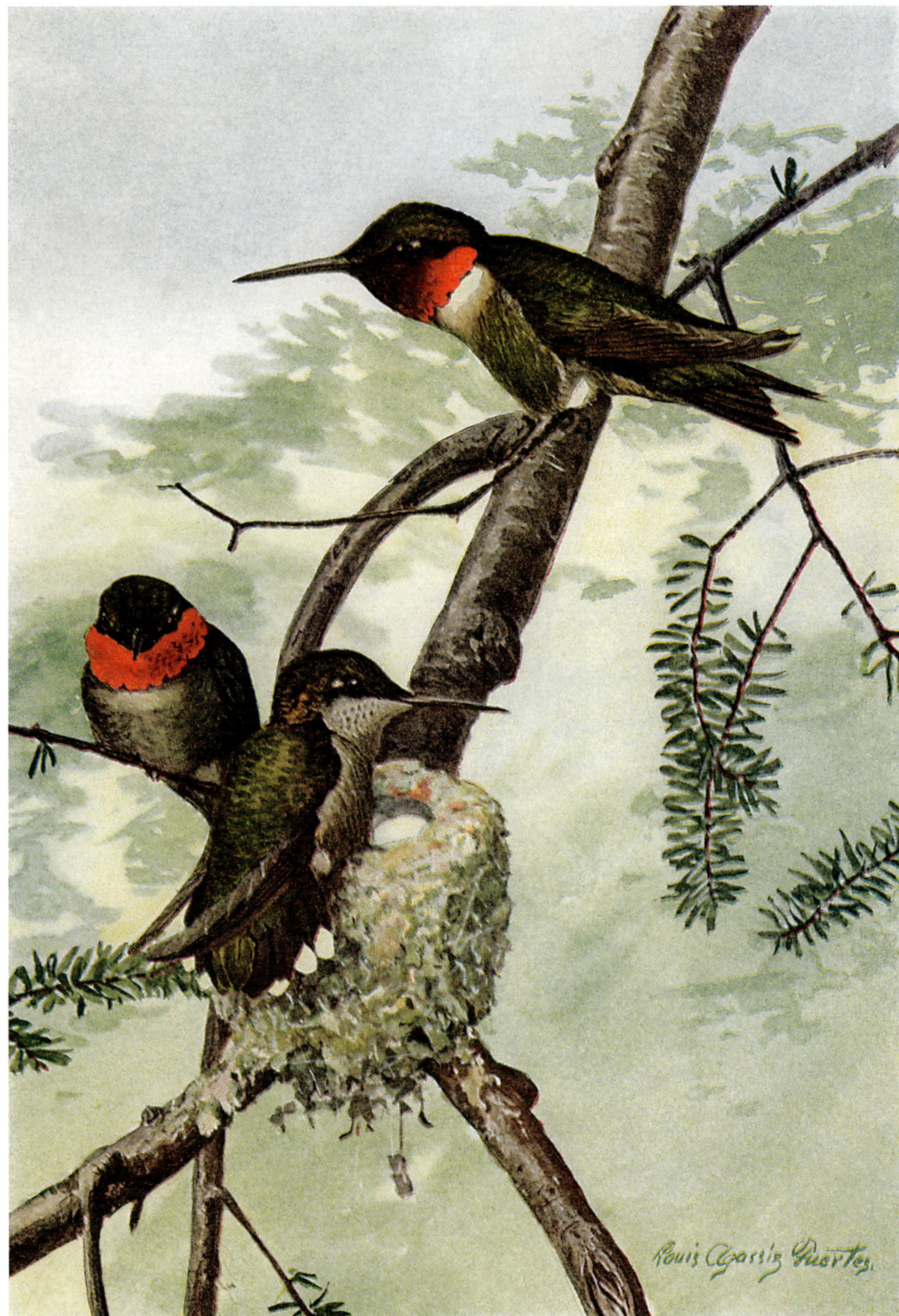

RUBY-THROATED HUMMINGBIRD *Archilochus colubris* (Linnaeus)

MALE FEMALE MALE

All ½ nat. size

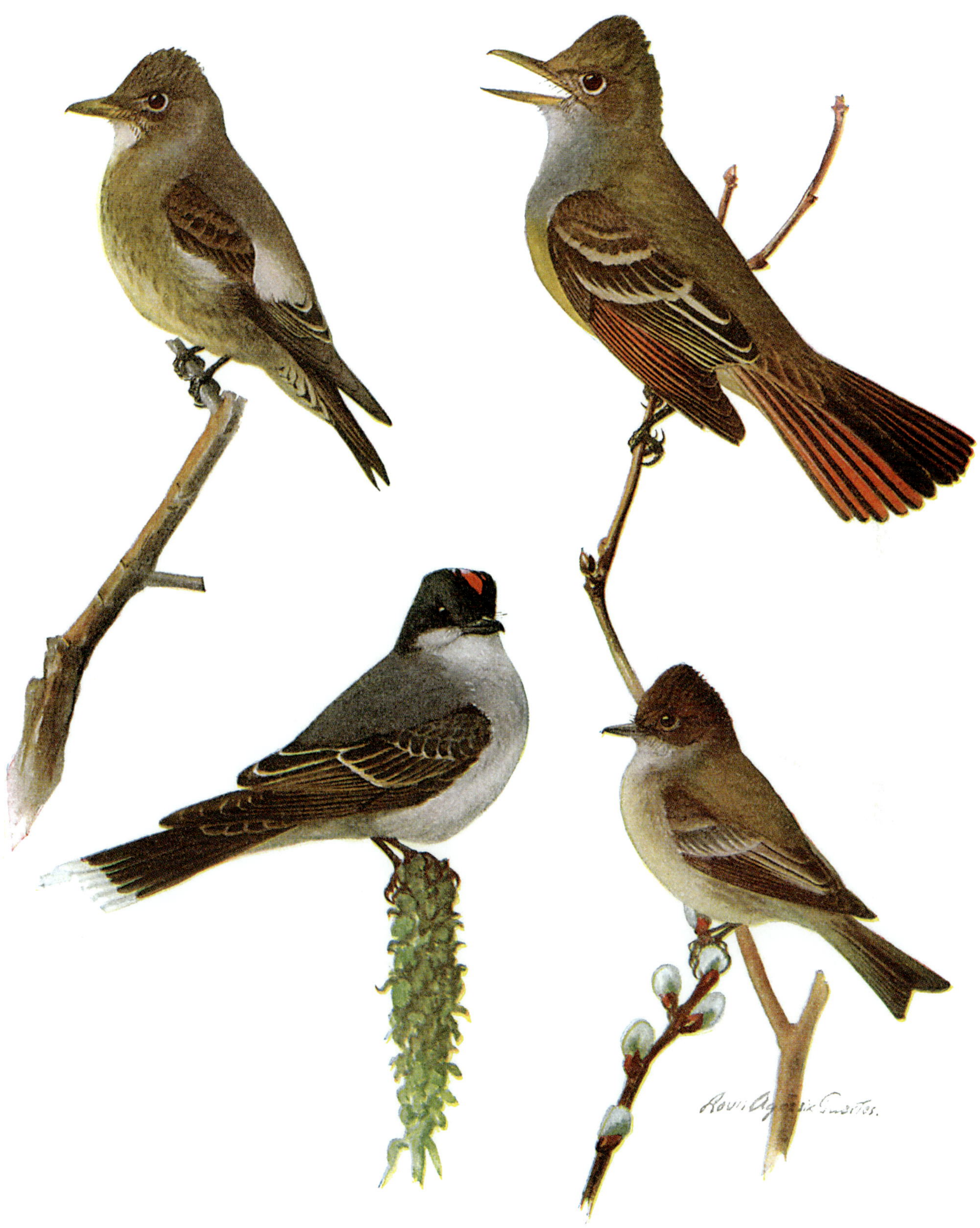

OLIVE-SIDED FLYCATCHER
Nuttallornis borealis (Swainson)

CRESTED FLYCATCHER
Myiarchus crinitus (Linnaeus)

KINGBIRD *Tyrannus tyrannus* (Linnaeus)

PHOEBE *Savornis phoebe* (Latham)

All ⅔ nat. size

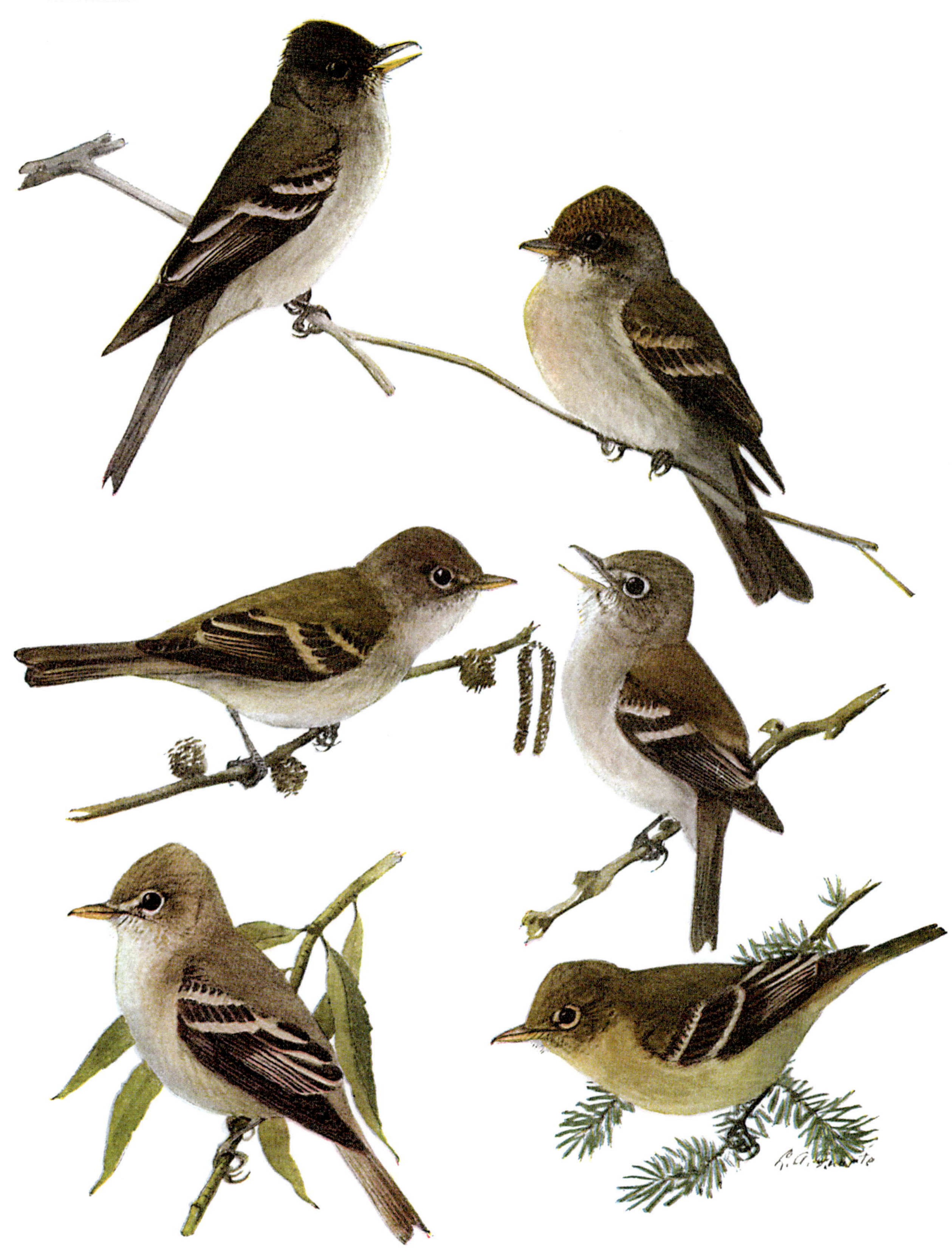

WOOD PEWEE *Myiochanes virens* (Linnaeus)

ADULT IMMATURE

ALDER FLYCATCHER
Empidonax trailli alnorum (Brewster)

LEAST FLYCATCHER
Empidonax minimus (W. M. & S. F. Baird)

ACADIAN FLYCATCHER
Empidonax virescens (Vieillot)

YELLOW-BELLIED FLYCATCHER
Empidonax flaviventris (W. M. & S. F. Baird)

All ½ nat. size

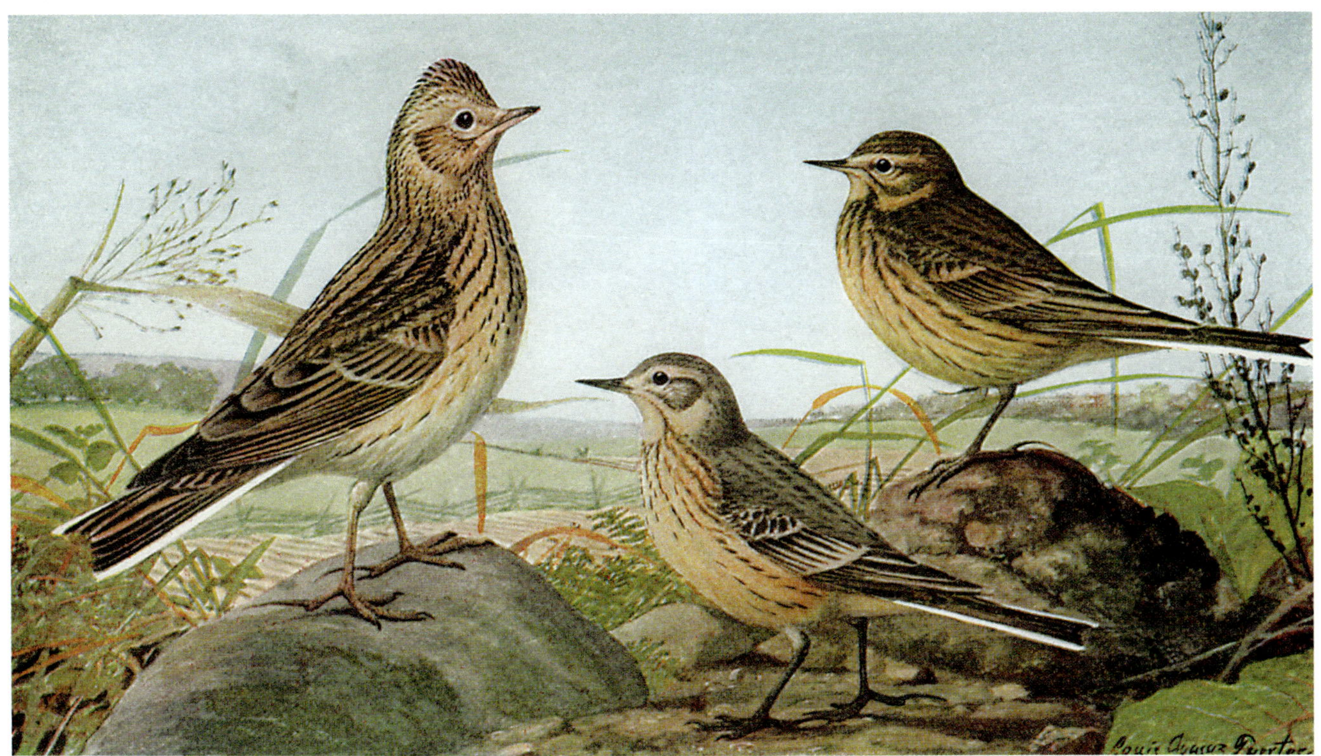

SKYLARK
Alauda arvensis (Linnaeus)

PIPIT *Anthus rubescens* (Tunstall)
SPRING AUTUMN

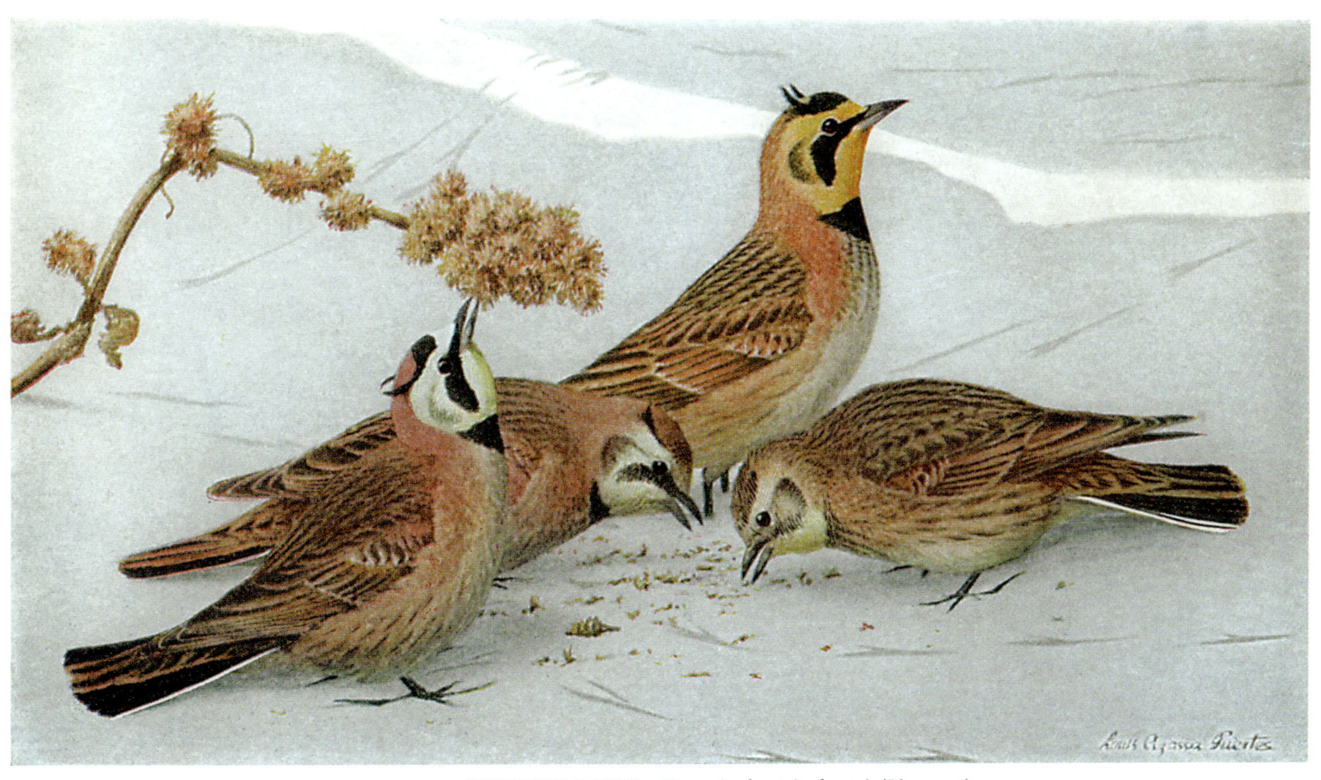

HORNED LARK *Otocoris alpestris alpestris* (Linnaeus)
MALE

PRAIRIE HORNED LARK *Otocoris alpestris praticola* (Henshaw)
MALE FEMALE IMMATURE

⅔ nat. size

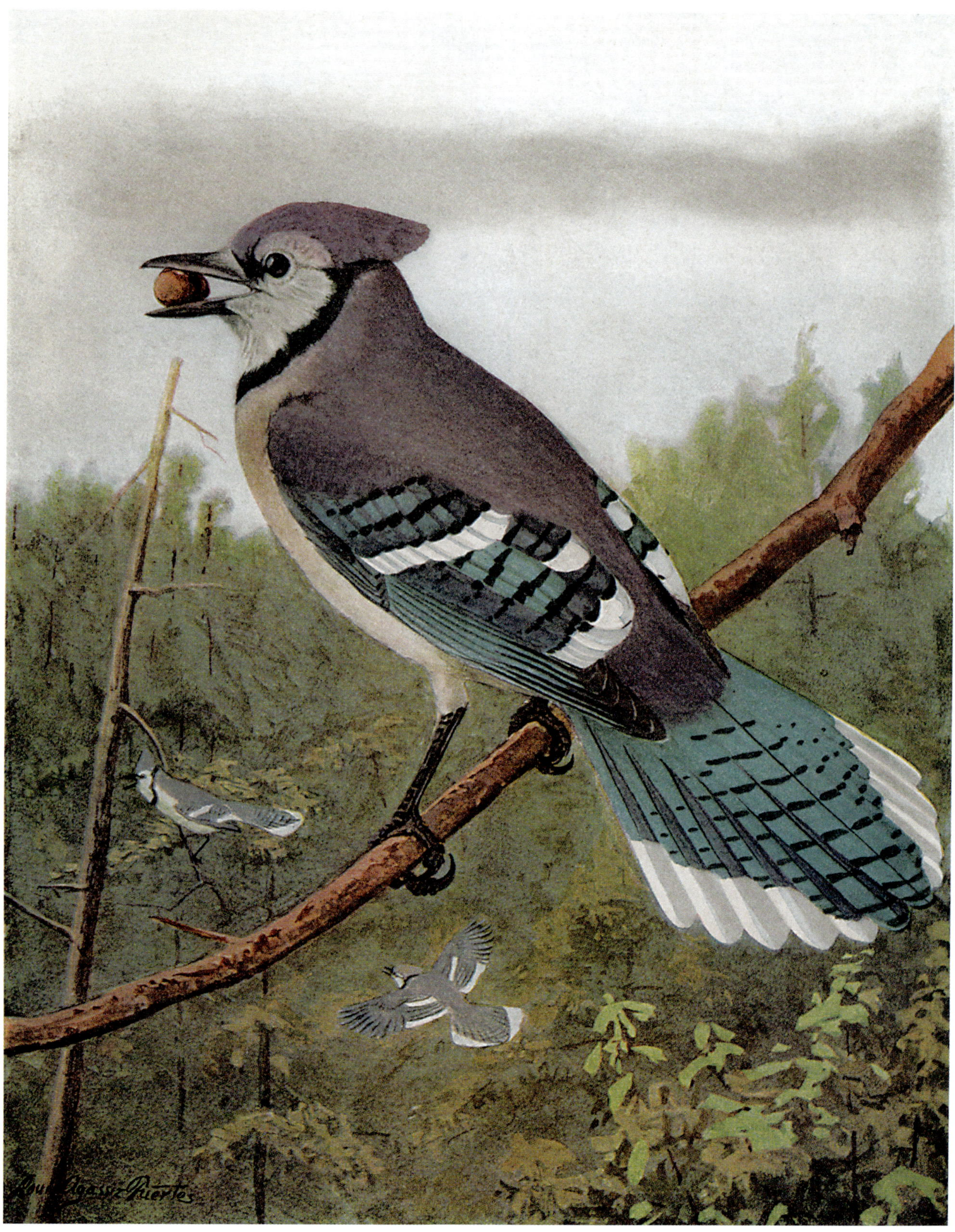

BLUE JAY
Cyanocitta cristata cristata (Linnaeus)

Both ¼ nat. size

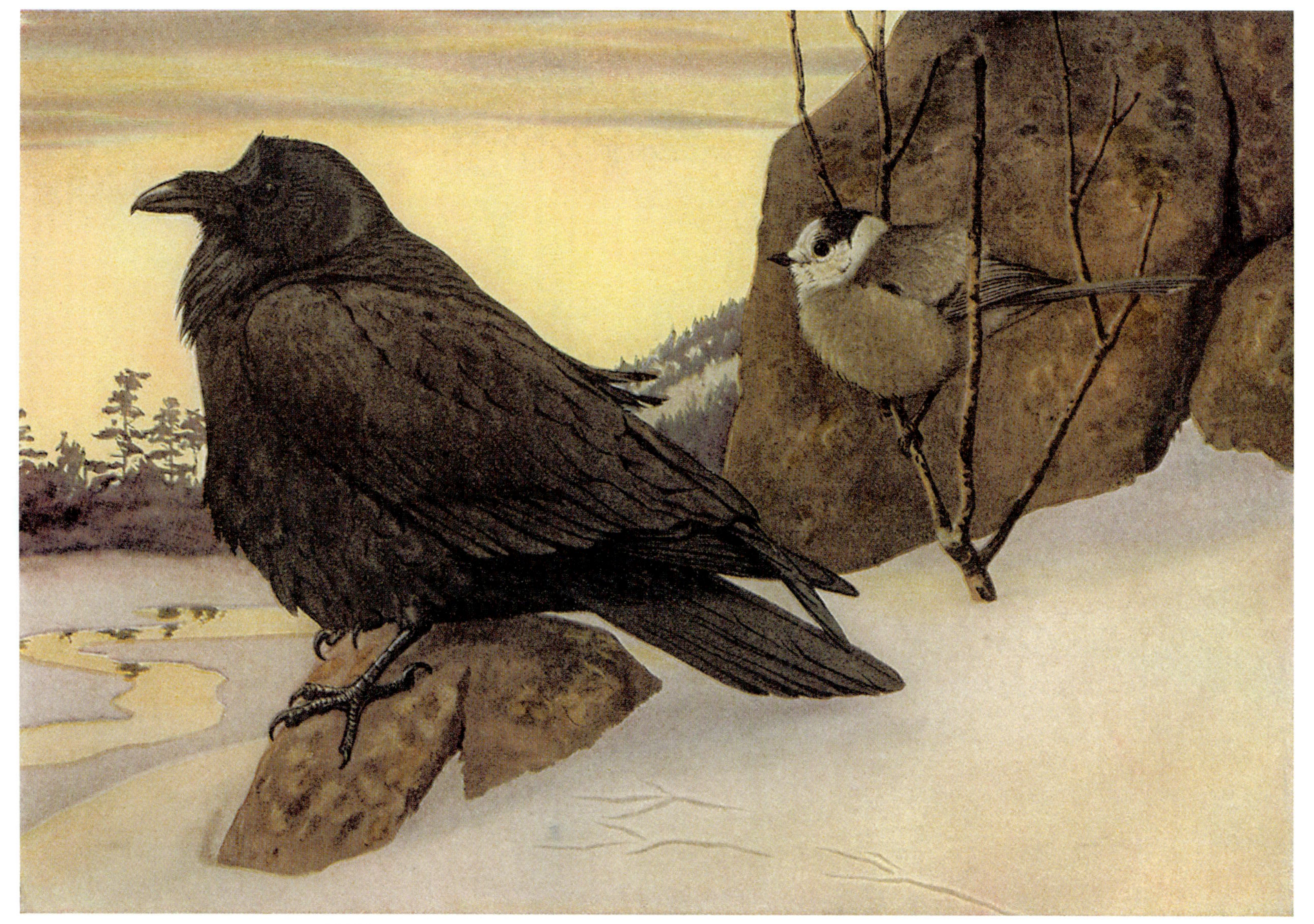

NORTHERN RAVEN
Corvus corax principalis (Ridgway)

CANADA JAY
Perisoreus canadensis canadensis (Linnaeus)

All ¼ nat. size

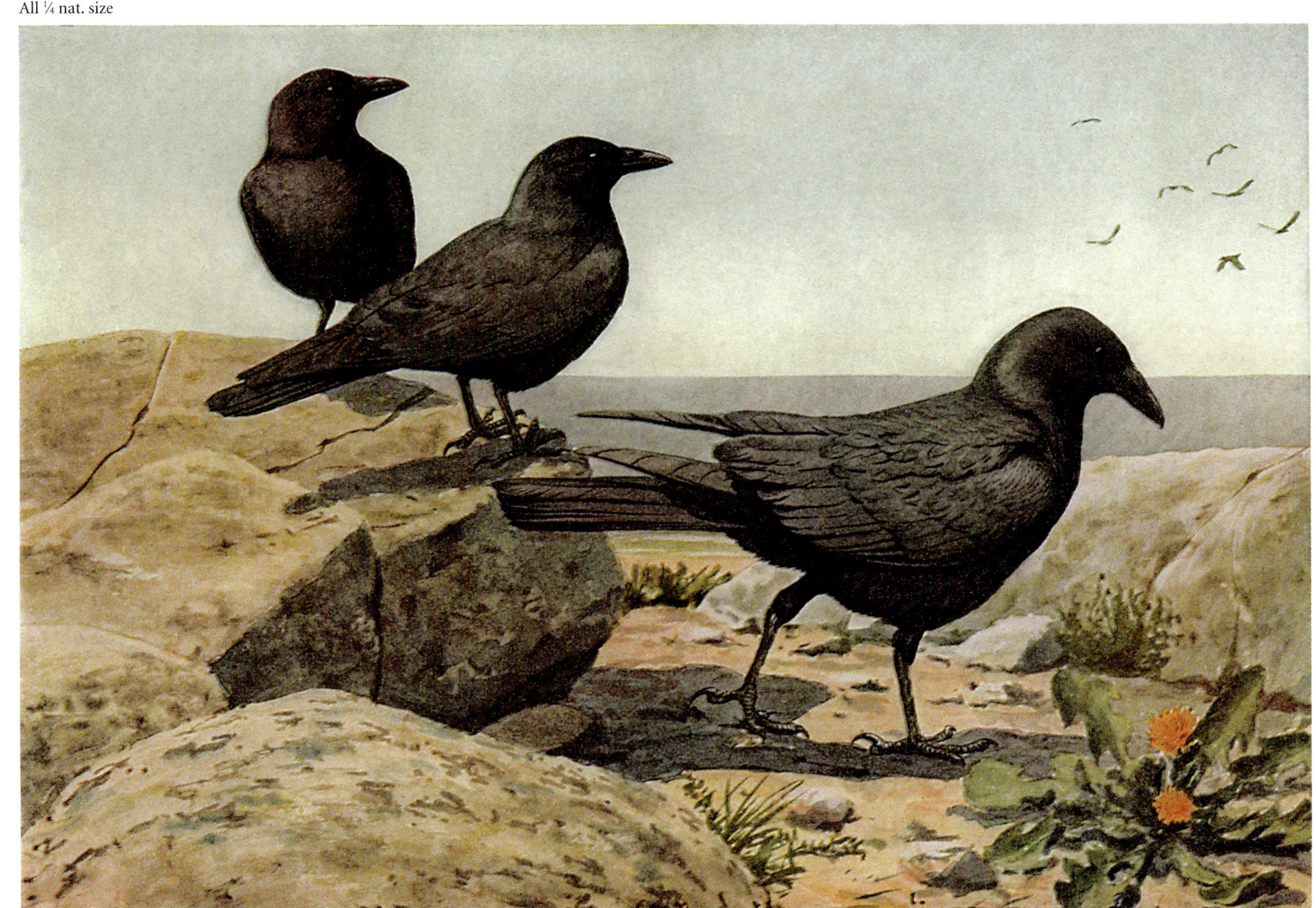

FISH CROW
Corvus ossifragus (Wilson)

CROW
Corvus brachyrhynchos brachyrhynchos (Brehm)

All ½ nat. size

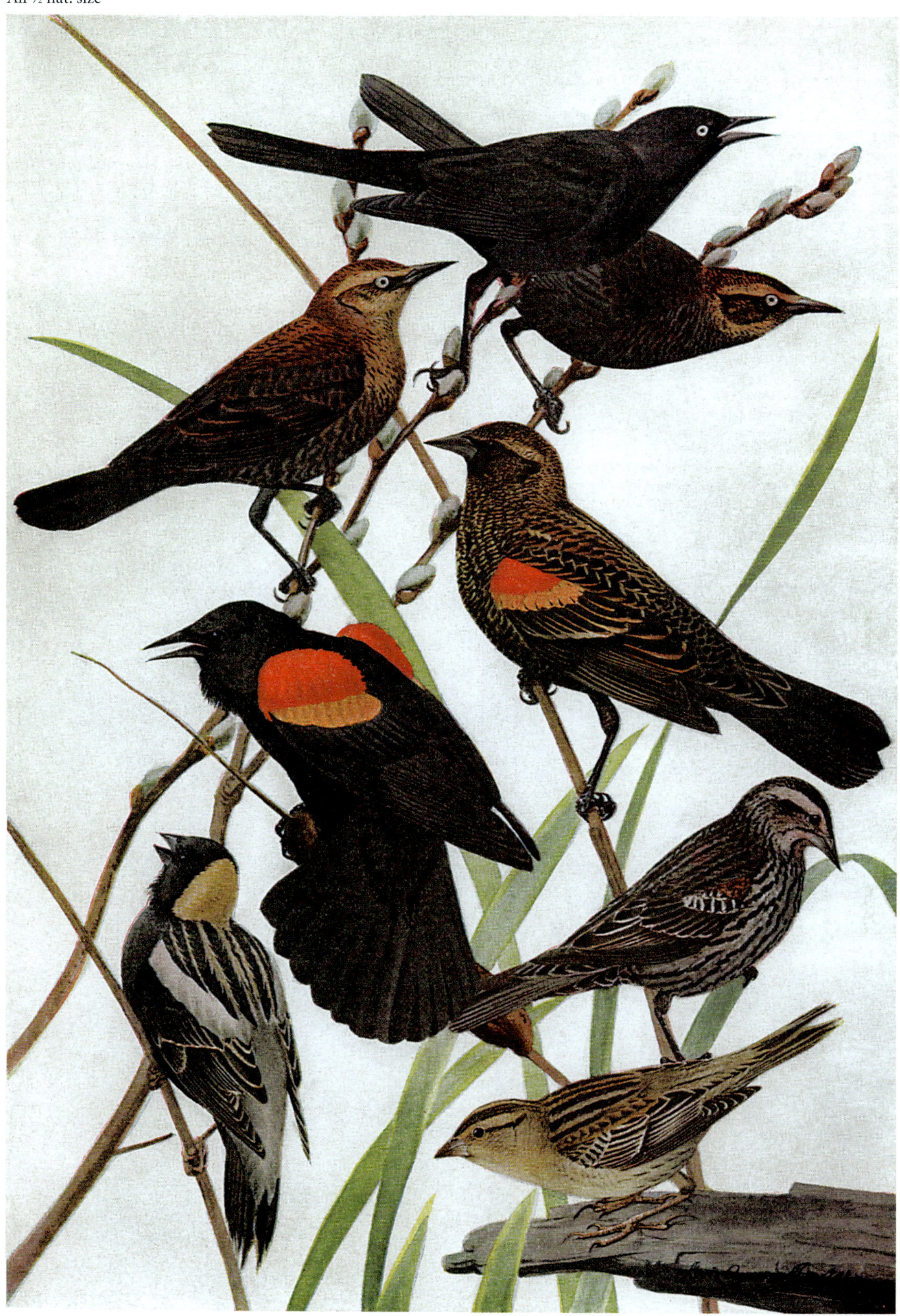

RUSTY BLACKBIRD *Euphagus carolinus* (Müller)
ADULT MALE IN SPRING
IMMATURE IN AUTUMN ADULT MALE IN AUTUMN
RED-WINGED BLACKBIRD *Agelaius phoenicieus phoeniceus* (Linnaeus)
MALE IN AUTUMN
MALE IN SPRING FEMALE
BOBOLINK *Dolichonyx oryzivorus* (Linnaeus)
MALE FEMALE

All ½ nat. size

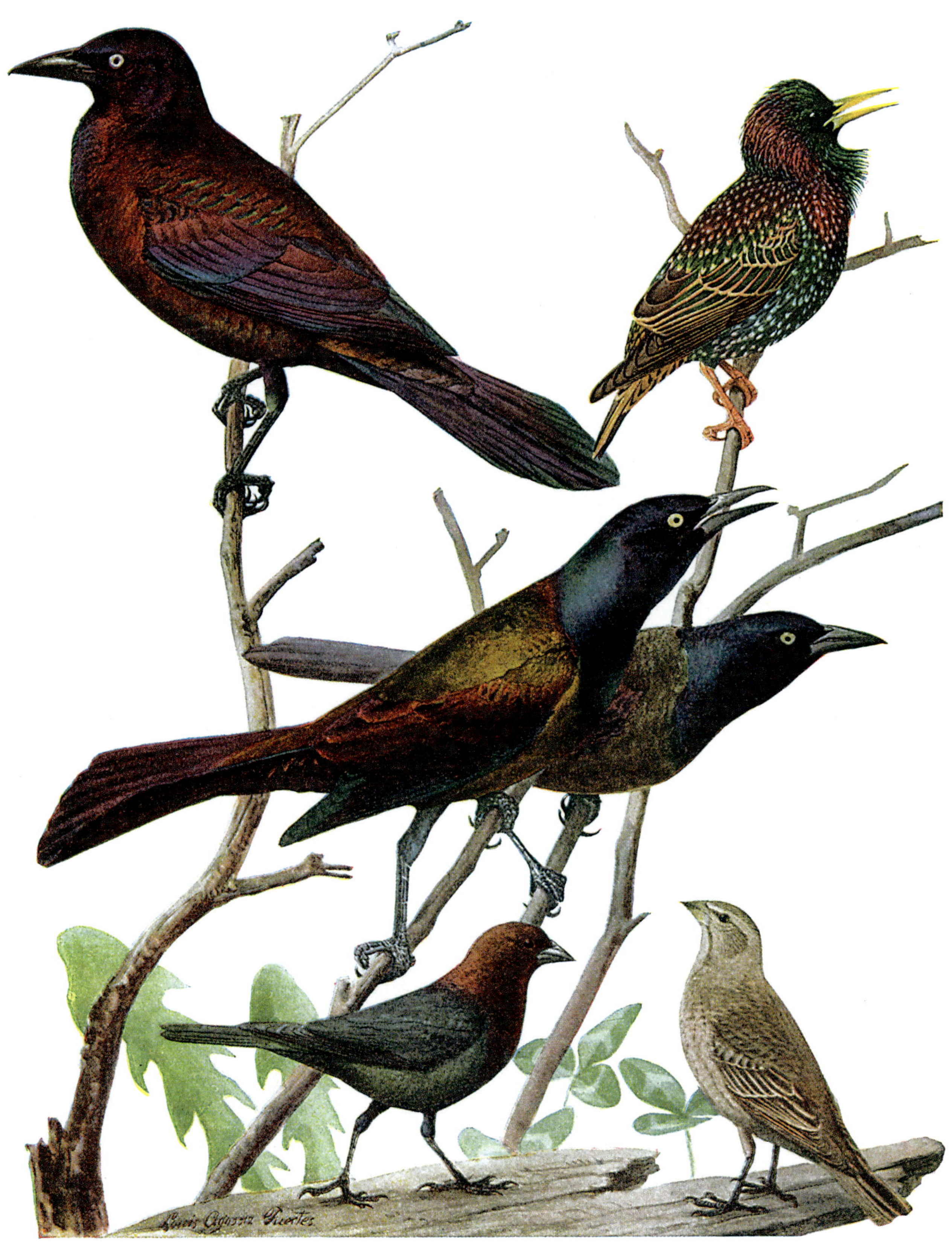

PURPLE GRACKLE
Quiscalus quiscula quiscula (Linnaeus)
MALE

STARLING
Sturnus vulgaris (Linnaeus)

BRONZED GRACKLE *Quiscalus quiscula aeneus* (Ridgway)
MALE FEMALE

COWBIRD *Molothrus ater ater* (Boddaert)
MALE FEMALE

All ½ nat. size

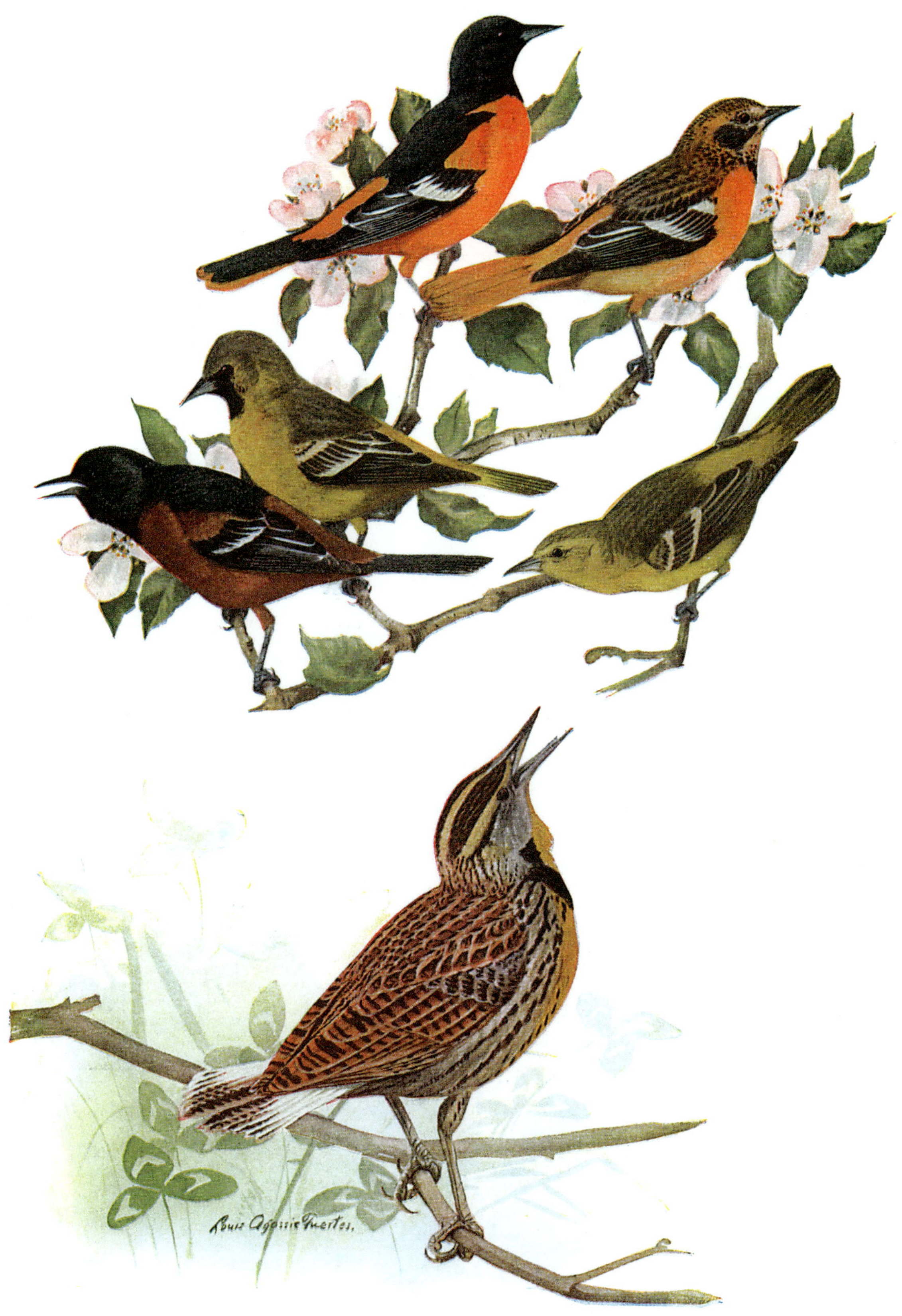

BALTIMORE ORIOLE *Icterus galbula* (Linnaeus)
MALE FEMALE
ORCHARD ORIOLE *Icterus spurius* (Linnaeus)
FIRST YEAR MALE FEMALE
ADULT MALE
MEADOWLARK *Sturnella magna magna* (Linnaeus)

All ⅔ nat. size

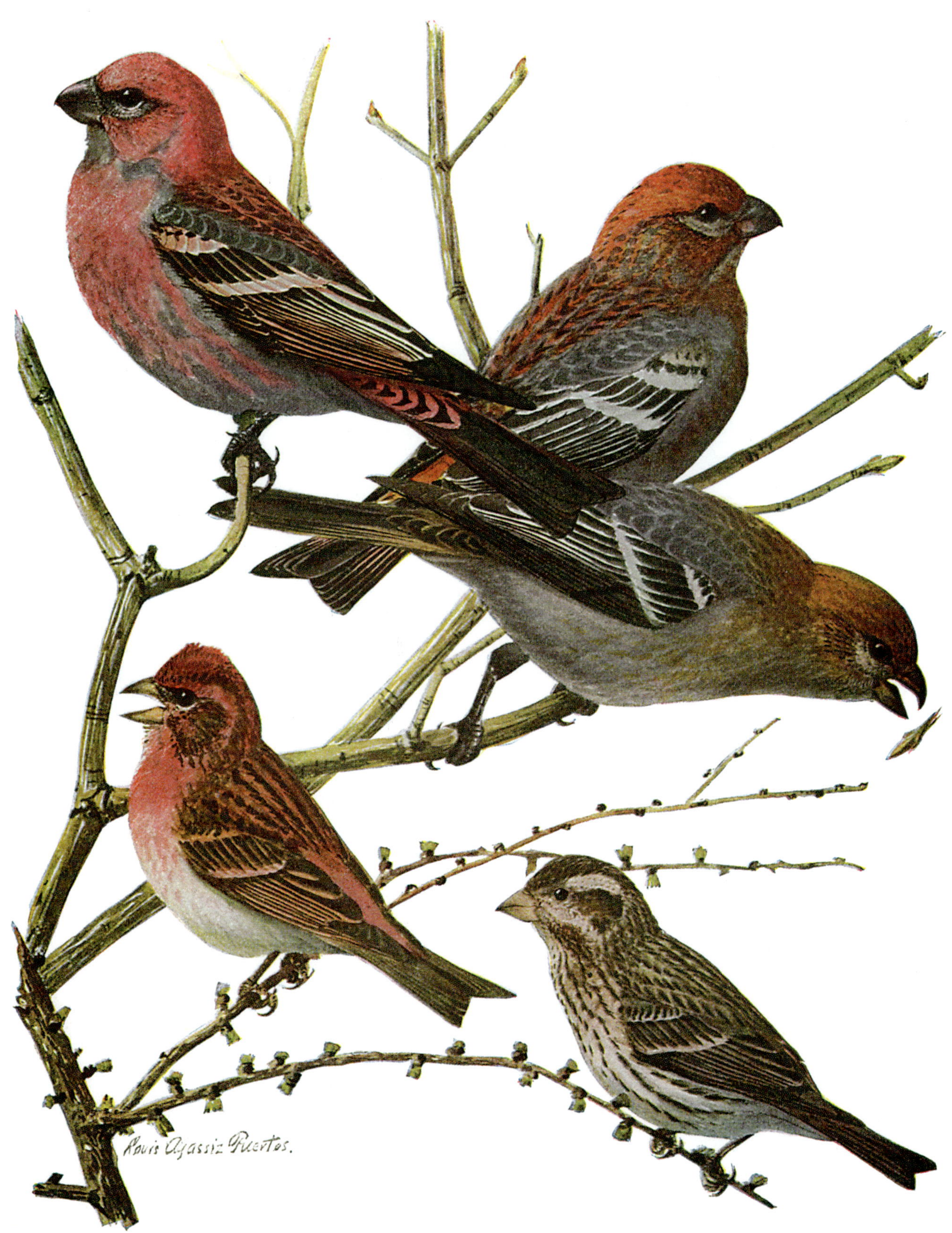

PINE GROSBEAK *Pinicola enucleator leucura* (Müller)
ADULT MALE IMMATURE MALE
FEMALE

PURPLE FINCH *Carpodacus purpureus purpureus* (Gmelin)
MALE FEMALE OR IMMATURE MALE

All ⅔ nat. size

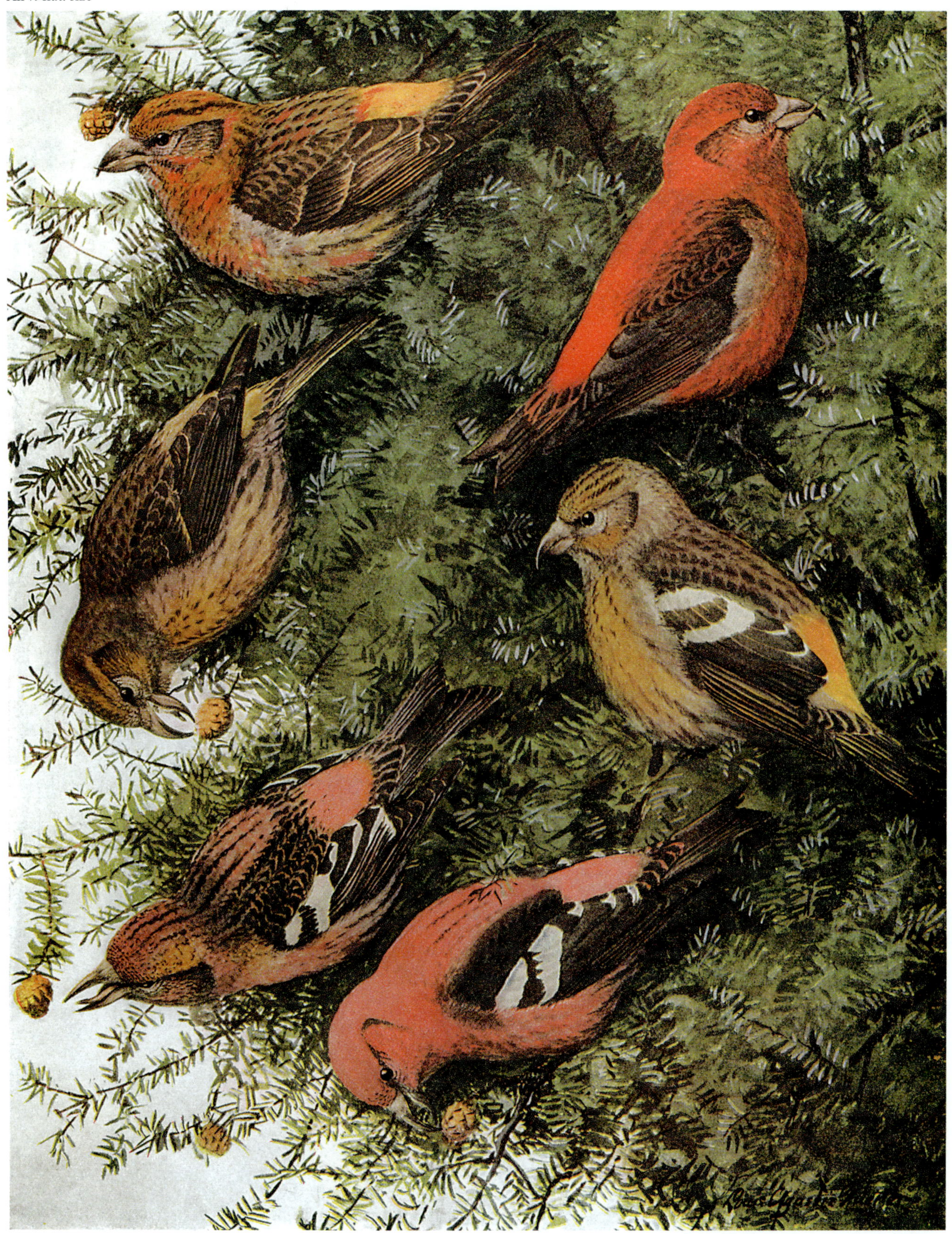

CROSSBILL *Loxia curvirostra minor* (Brehm)

IMMATURE MALE ADULT MALE

FEMALE

WHITE-WINGED CROSSBILL *Loxia leucoptera* (Gmelin)

IMMATURE MALE FEMALE

MALE

All ⅔ nat. size

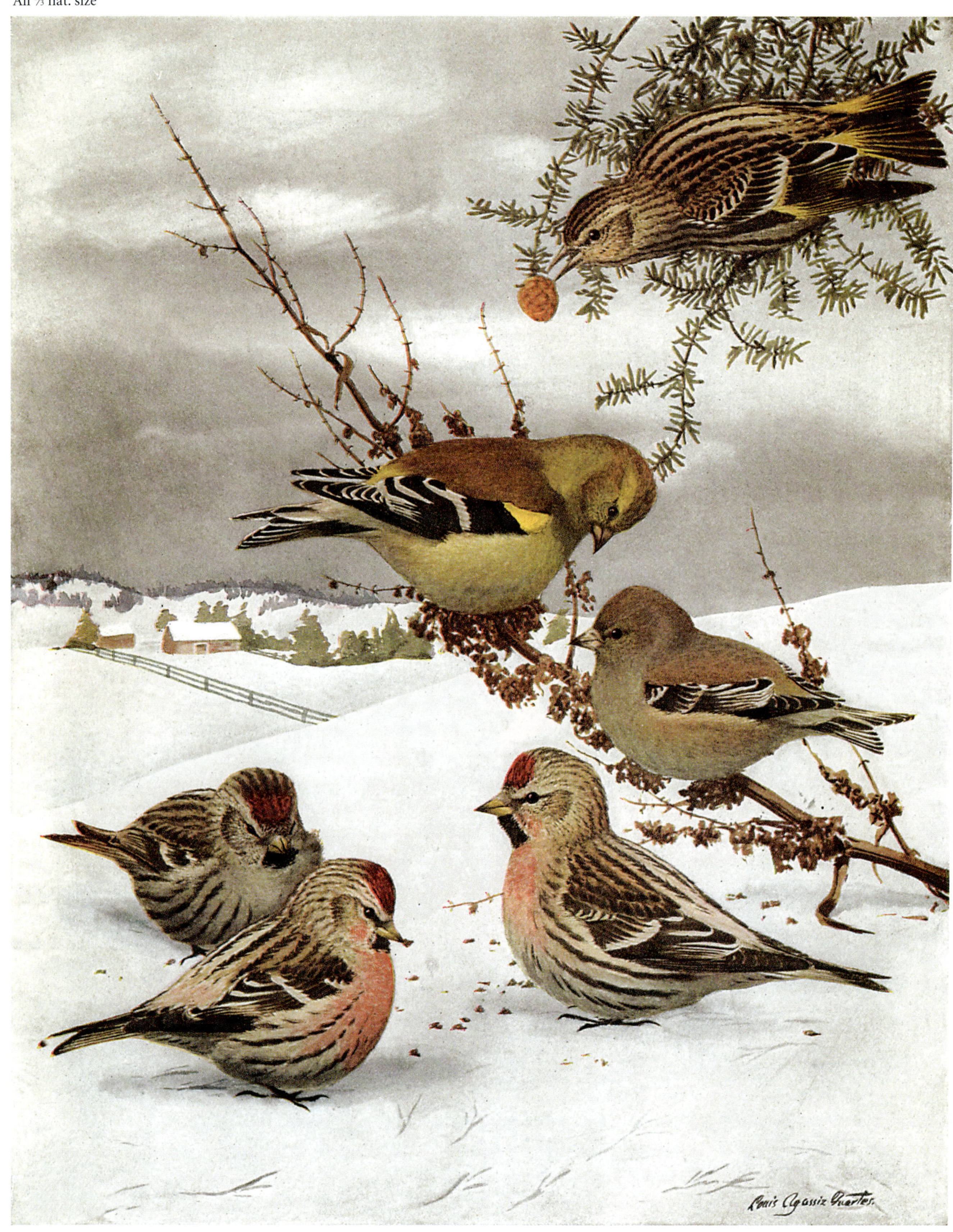

REDPOLL
Acanthis linaria linaria (Linnaeus)
FEMALE
MALE

PINE SISKIN *Spinus pinus* (Wilson)

GOLDFINCH *Astragalinus tristis tristis* (Linnaeus)
MALE AND FEMALE IN WINTER

GREATER REDPOLL *Acanthis linaria rostrata* (Coues)
MALE

All $\frac{2}{3}$ nat. size

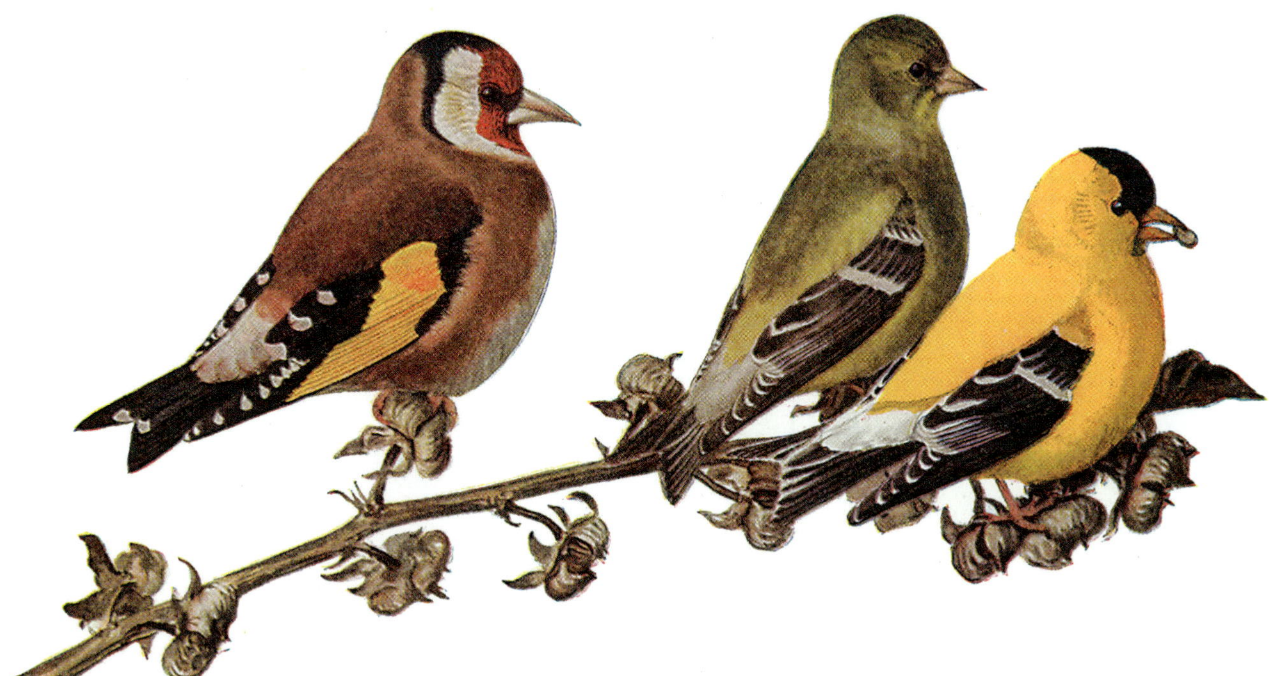

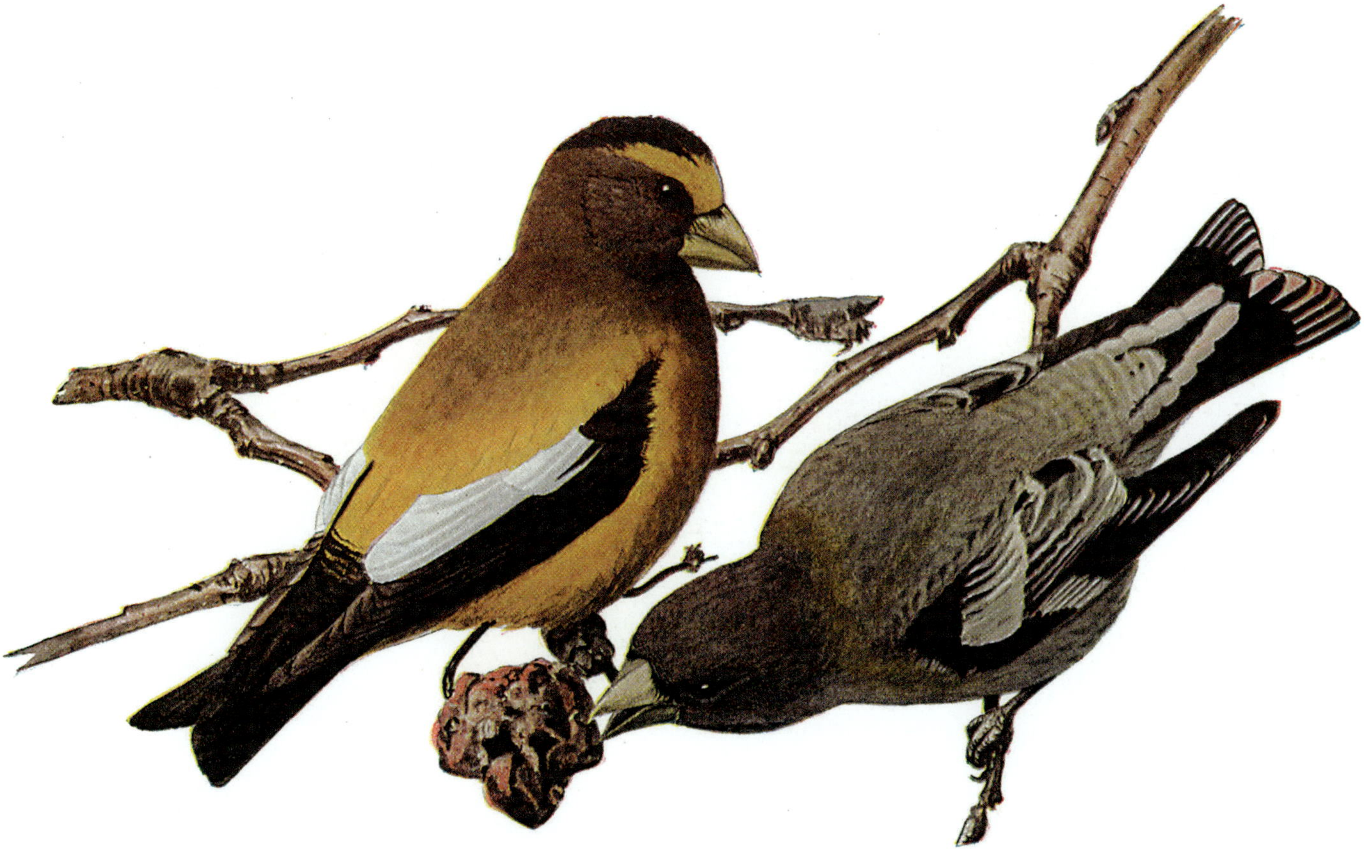

EUROPEAN GOLDFINCH
Carduelis carduelis (Linnaeus)

GOLDFINCH
Astragalinus tristis tristis (Linnaeus)
FEMALE AND MALE IN SUMMER

EVENING GROSBEAK *Hesperiphona vespertina vespertina* (W. Cooper)
MALE FEMALE

Both ⅔ nat. size

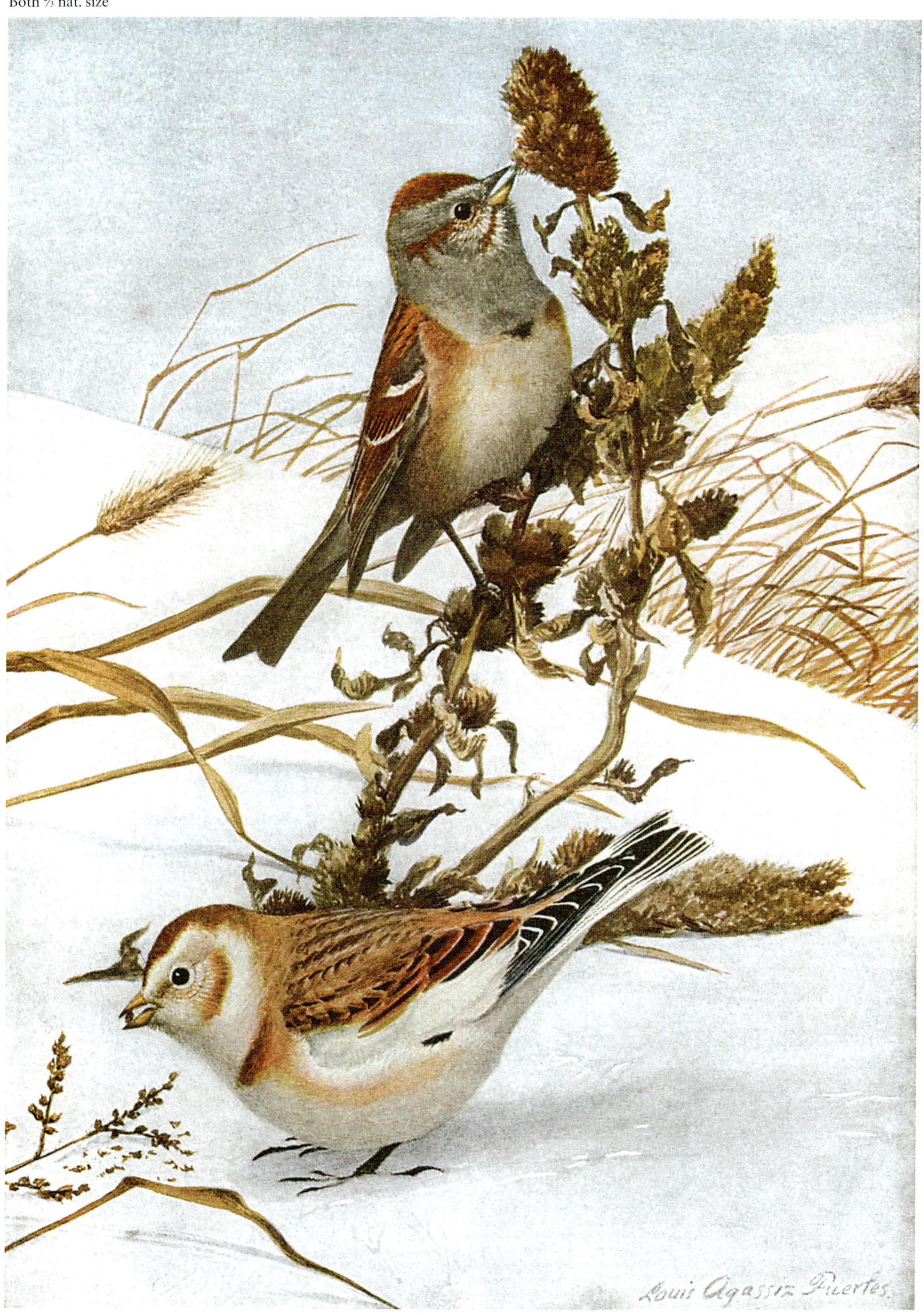

TREE SPARROW *Spizella monticola monticola* (Gmelin)
SNOW BUNTING *Piectrophenax nivalis nivalis* (Linnaeus)

All ½ nat. size

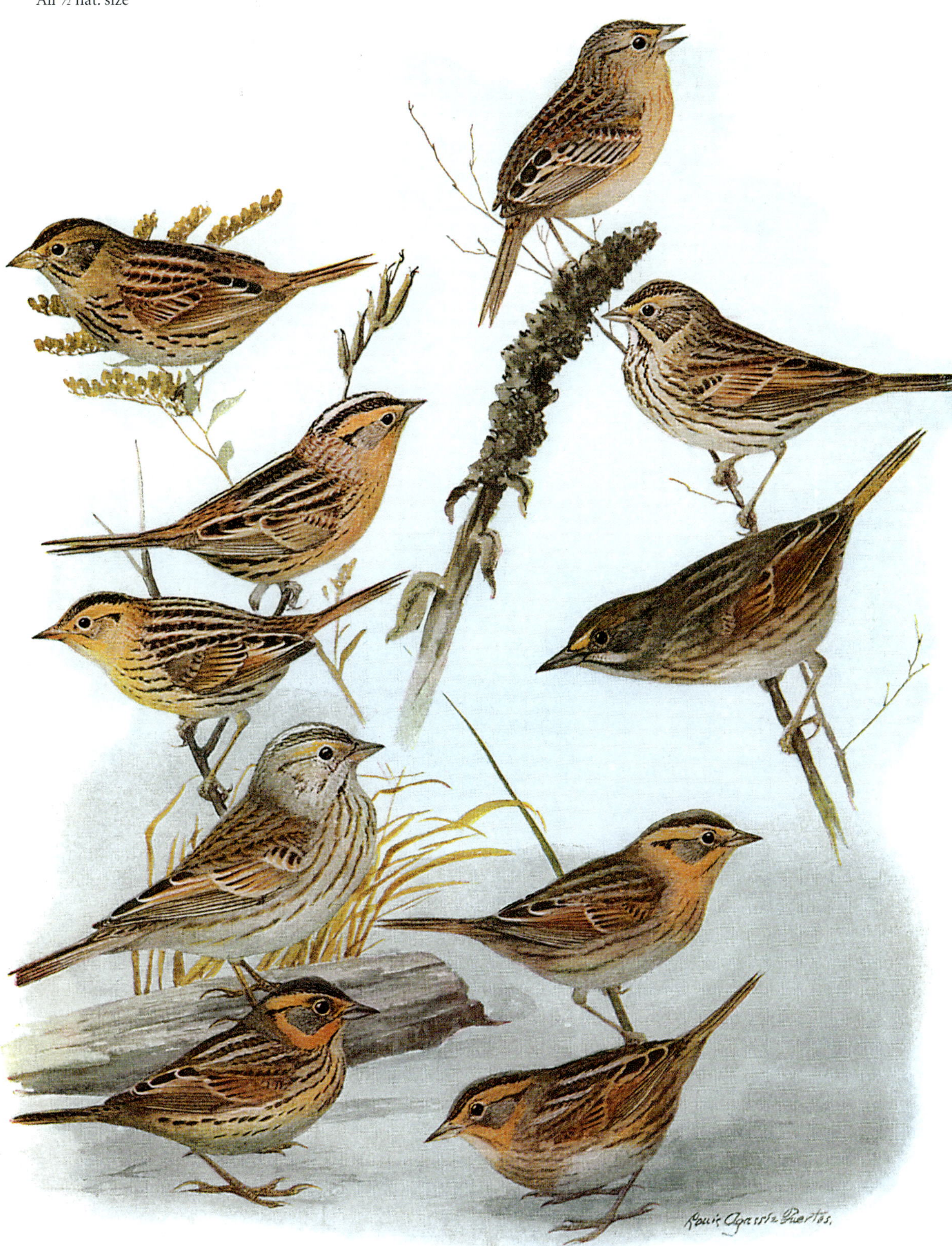

HENSLOW'S SPARROW
Passerherbulus henslowi henslowi (Audubon)
LECONTE'S SPARROW
Passerherbulus lecontei (Audubon)
ADULT
IMMATURE
IPSWICH SPARROW
Passerculus princeps (Maynard)
SHARP-TAILED SPARROW
Passerherbulus caudacutus (Gmelin)

GRASSHOPPER SPARROW
Ammodramus savannarum australis (Maynard)
SAVANNAH SPARROW
Passerculus sandwichensis savanna (Wilson)
SEASIDE SPARROW
Passerherbulus maritimus maritimus (Wilson)
ACADIAN SHARP-TAILED SPARROW
Passerherbulus nelsoni subvirgatus (Dwight)
NELSON'S SPARROW
Passerherbulus nelsoni nelsoni (Allen)

All ⅔ nat. size

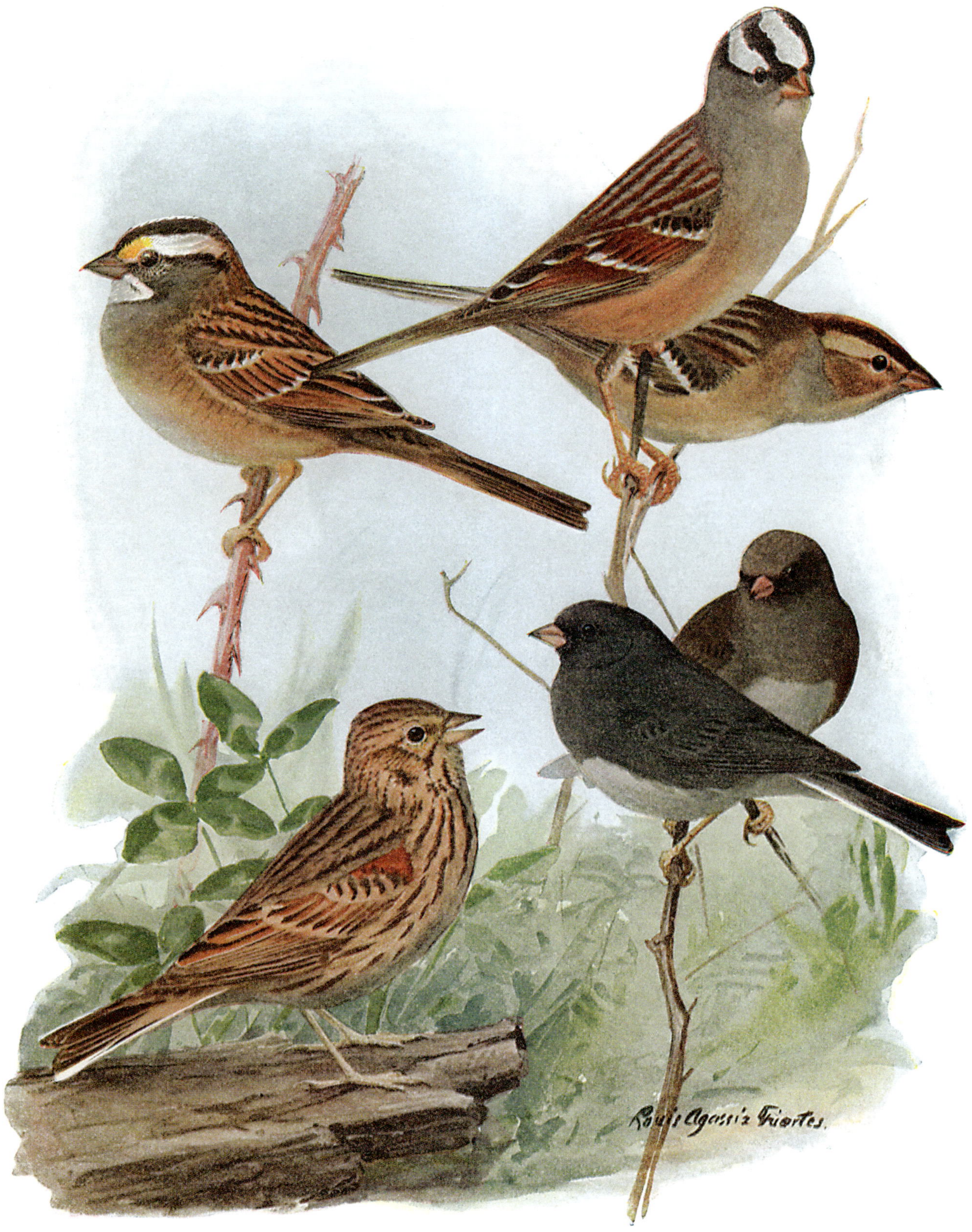

WHITE-THROATED SPARROW
Zonotrichia albicollis (Gmelin)

VESPER SPARROW
Pooecetes gramineus gramineus (Gmelin)

WHITE-CROWNED SPARROW
Zonotrichia leucophrys leucophrys (J. R. Forster)
ADULT
IMMATURE

SLATE-COLORED JUNCO
Junco hyemalis hyemalis (Linnaeus)
MALE FEMALE

All ⅔ nat. size

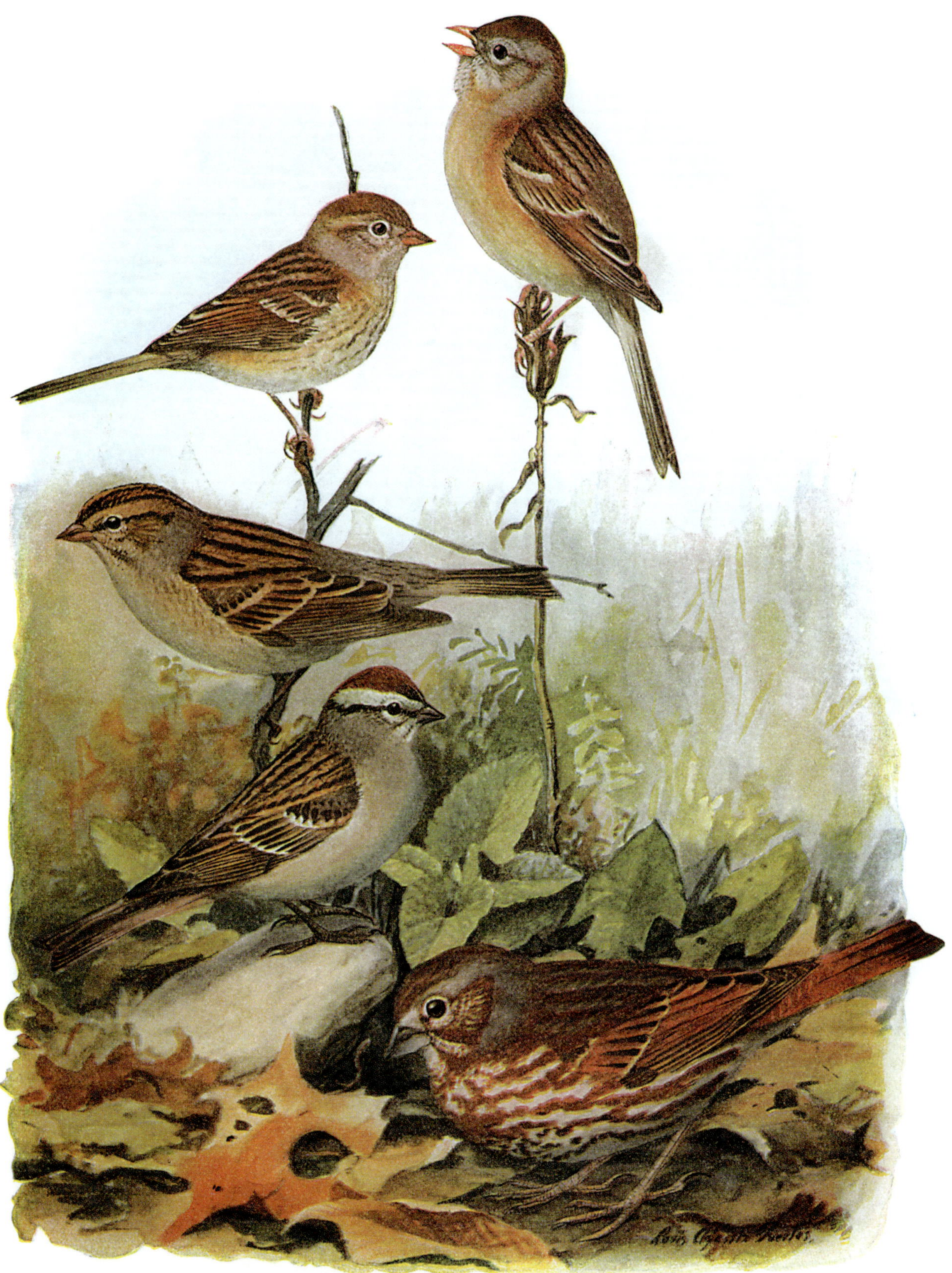

FIELD SPARROW *Spizella pusilla pusilla* (Wilson)
IMMATURE MALE

CHIPPING SPARROW *Spizella passerina passerina* (Bechstein)
IMMATURE
MALE

FOX SPARROW *Passerella iliaca iliaca* (Merrem)

All ⅔ nat. size

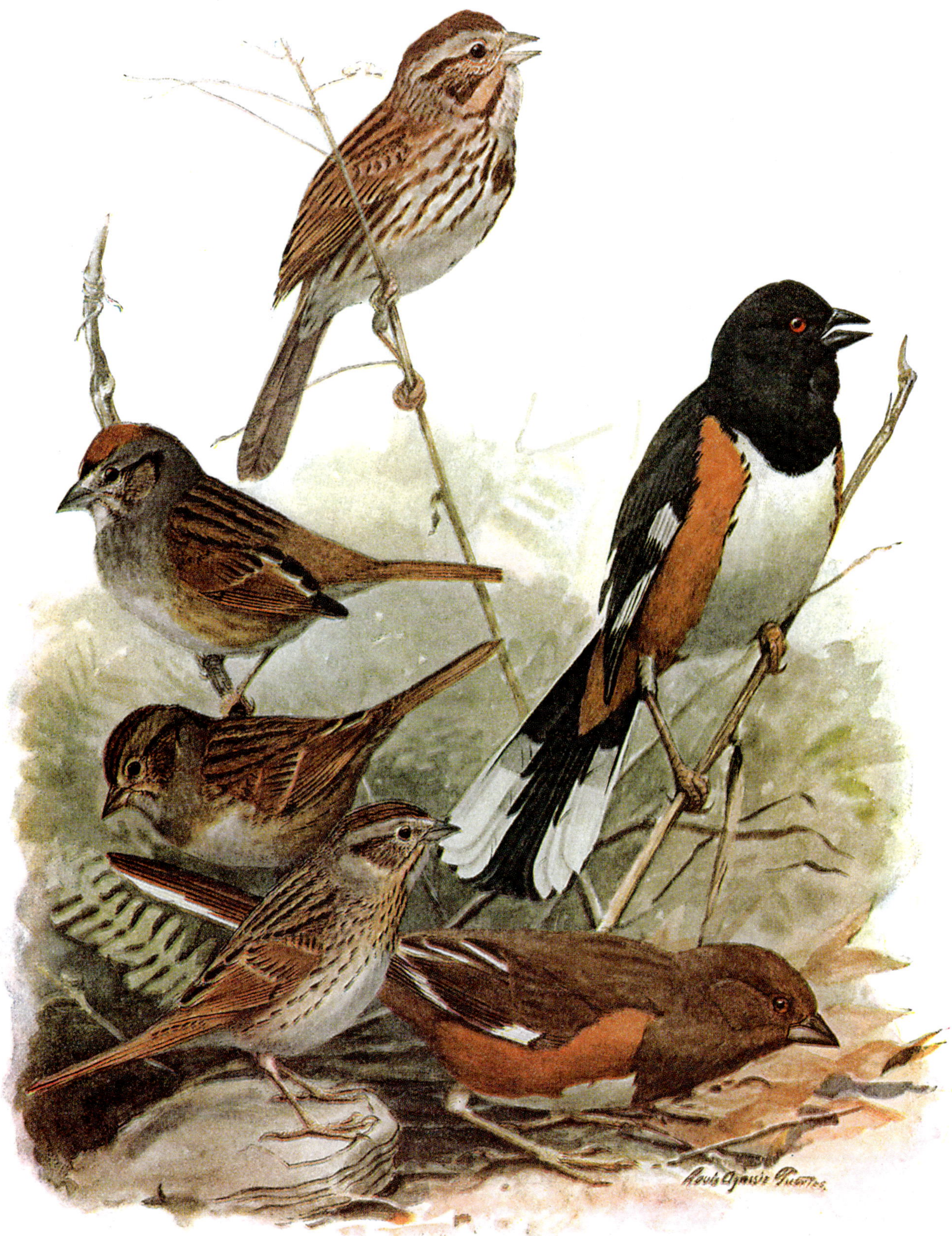

SONG SPARROW *Meliospiza melodia melodia* (Wilson)

SWAMP SPARROW
Melospiza georgiana (Latham)
SPRING
AUTUMN

LINCOLN'S SPARROW
Melospiza lincolni lincolni (Audubon)

TOWHEE
Pipilo erythrophthalmus erythrophthalmus
(Linnaeus)
MALE
FEMALE

All ⅔ nat. size

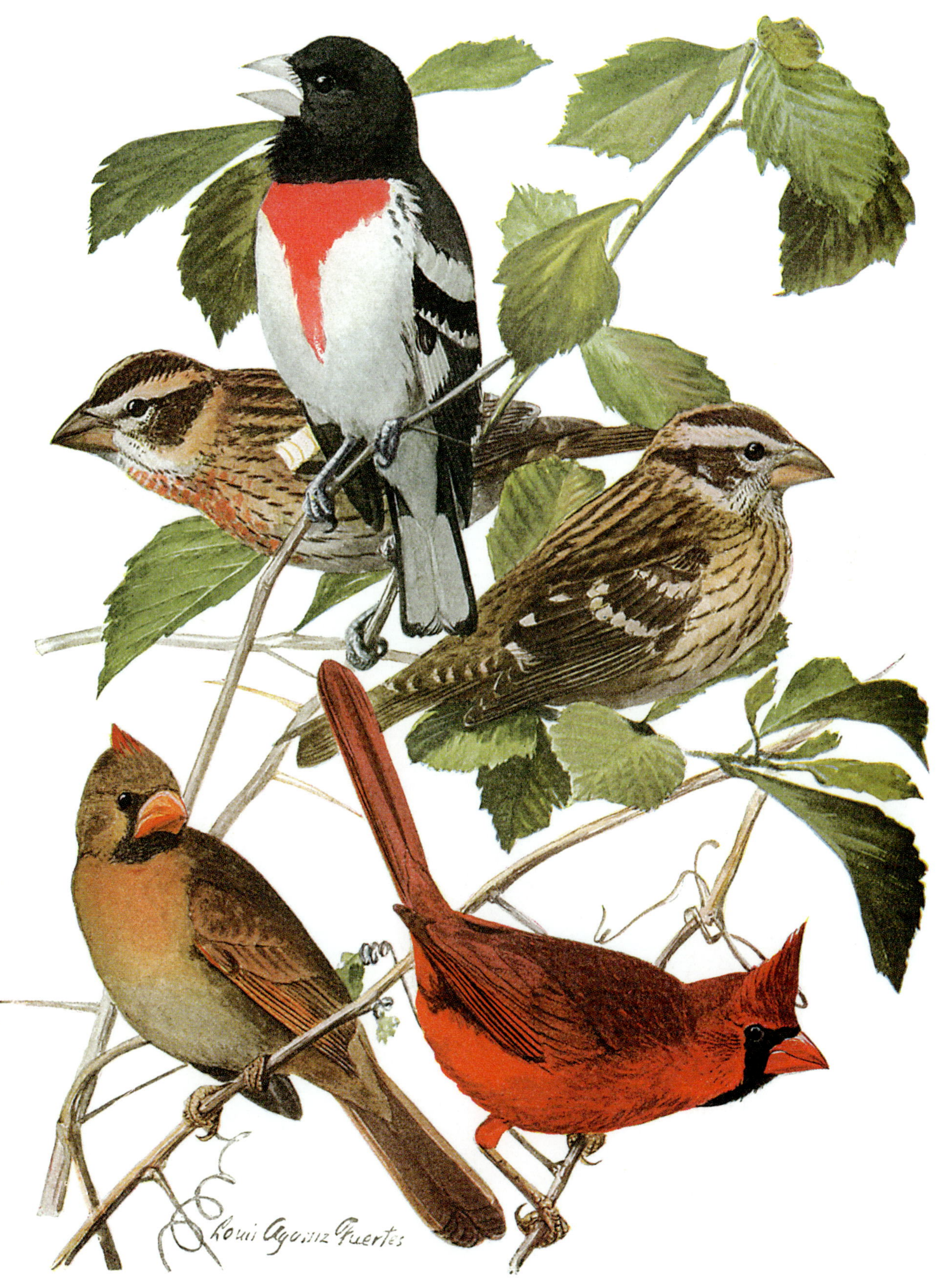

ROSE-BREASTED GROSBEAK *Zamelodia ludoviciana* (Linnaeus)
ADULT MALE
IMMATURE MALE IN AUTUMN
FEMALE
CARDINAL *Cardinalis cardinalis cardinalis* (Linnaeus)
FEMALE
MALE

All ⅔ nat. size

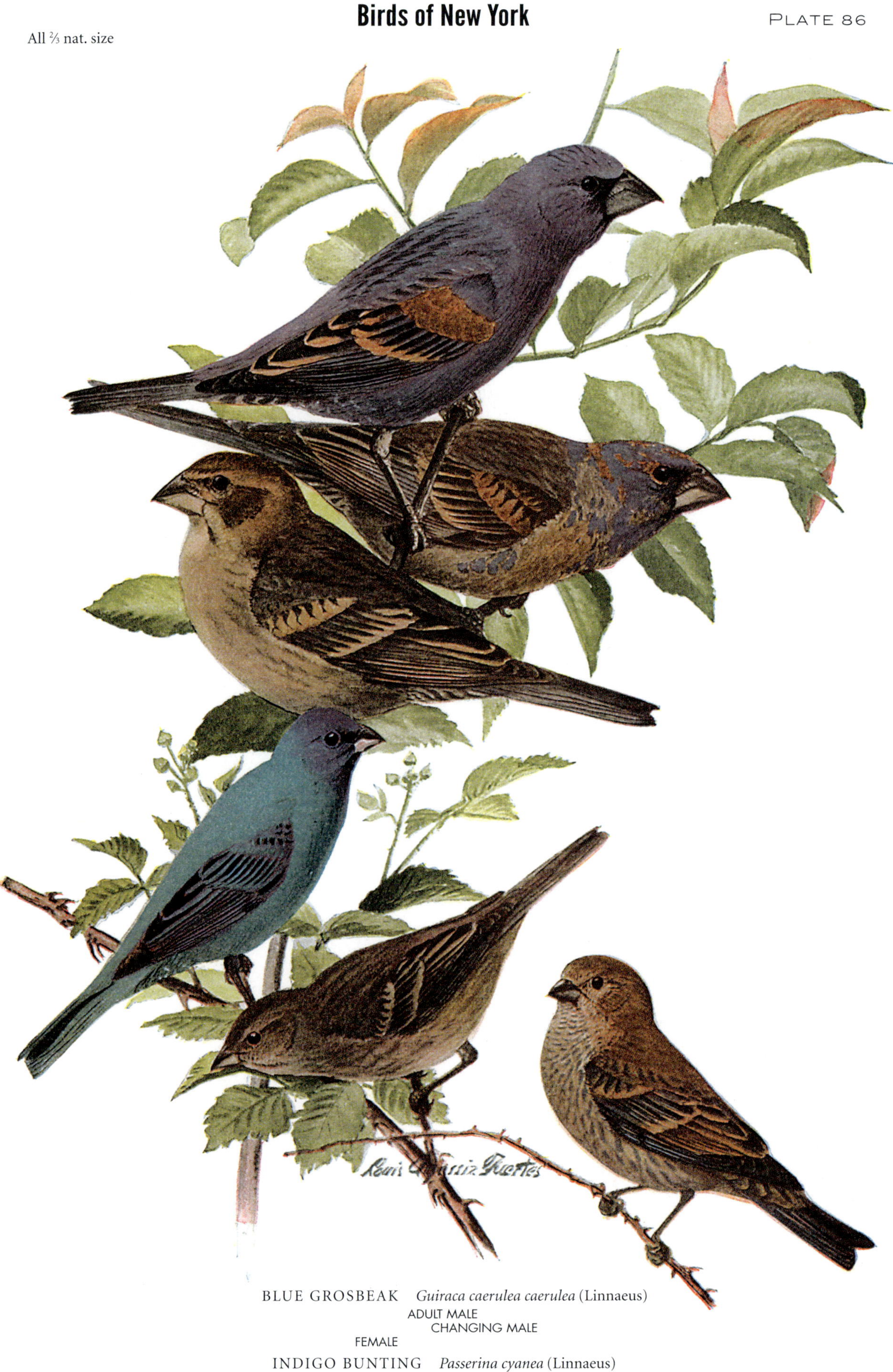

BLUE GROSBEAK *Guiraca caerulea caerulea* (Linnaeus)

ADULT MALE

CHANGING MALE

FEMALE

INDIGO BUNTING *Passerina cyanea* (Linnaeus)

MALE IN SUMMER

FEMALE

MALE IN AUTUMN

All ½ nat. size

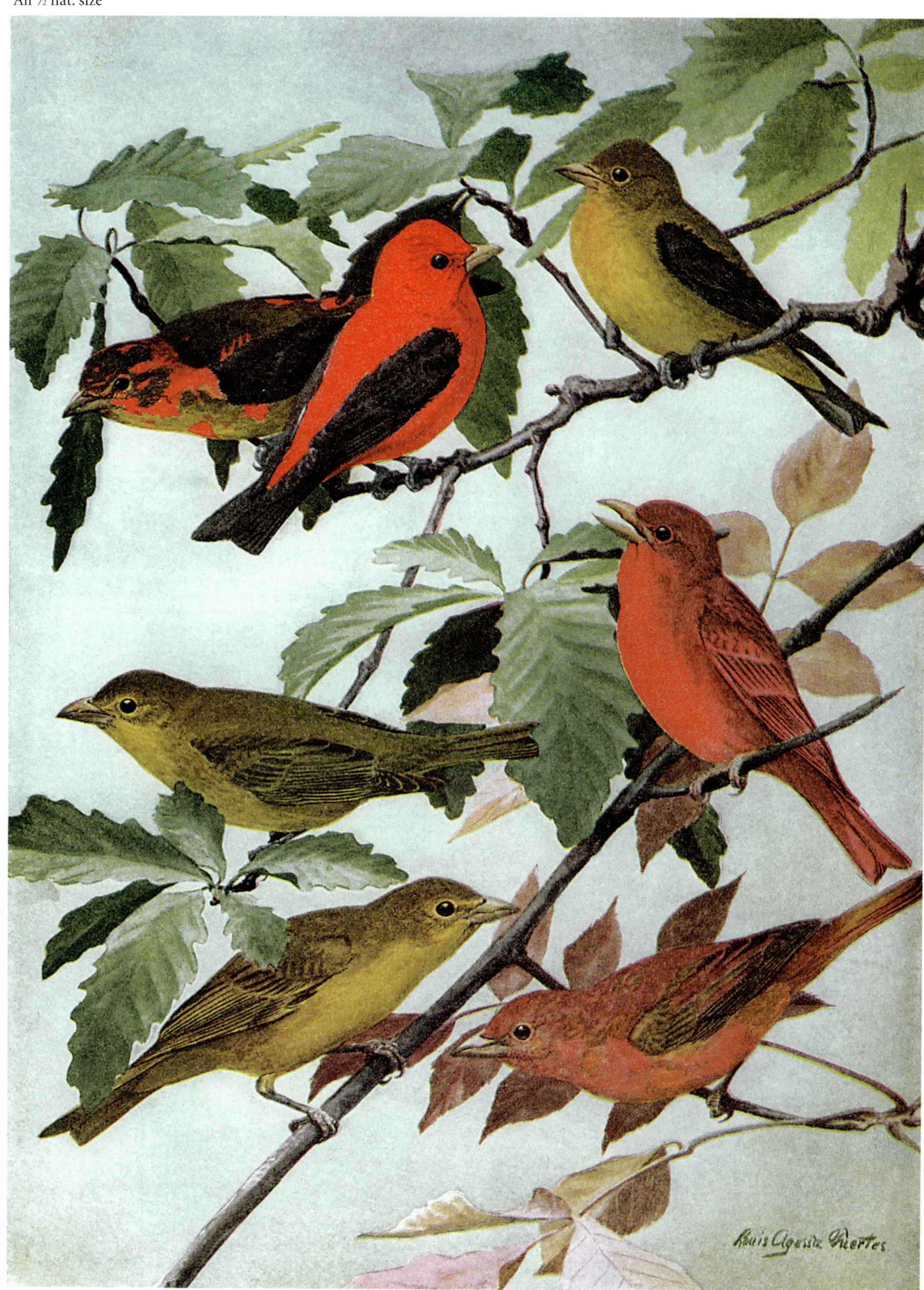

SCARLET TANAGER *Piranga erythromelas* (Vieillot)
CHANGING MALE MALE IN SUMMER MALE IN WINTER
FEMALE

SUMMER TANAGER *Piranga rubra rubra* (Linnaeus)
MALE
FEMALE CHANGING MALE

All ½ nat. size

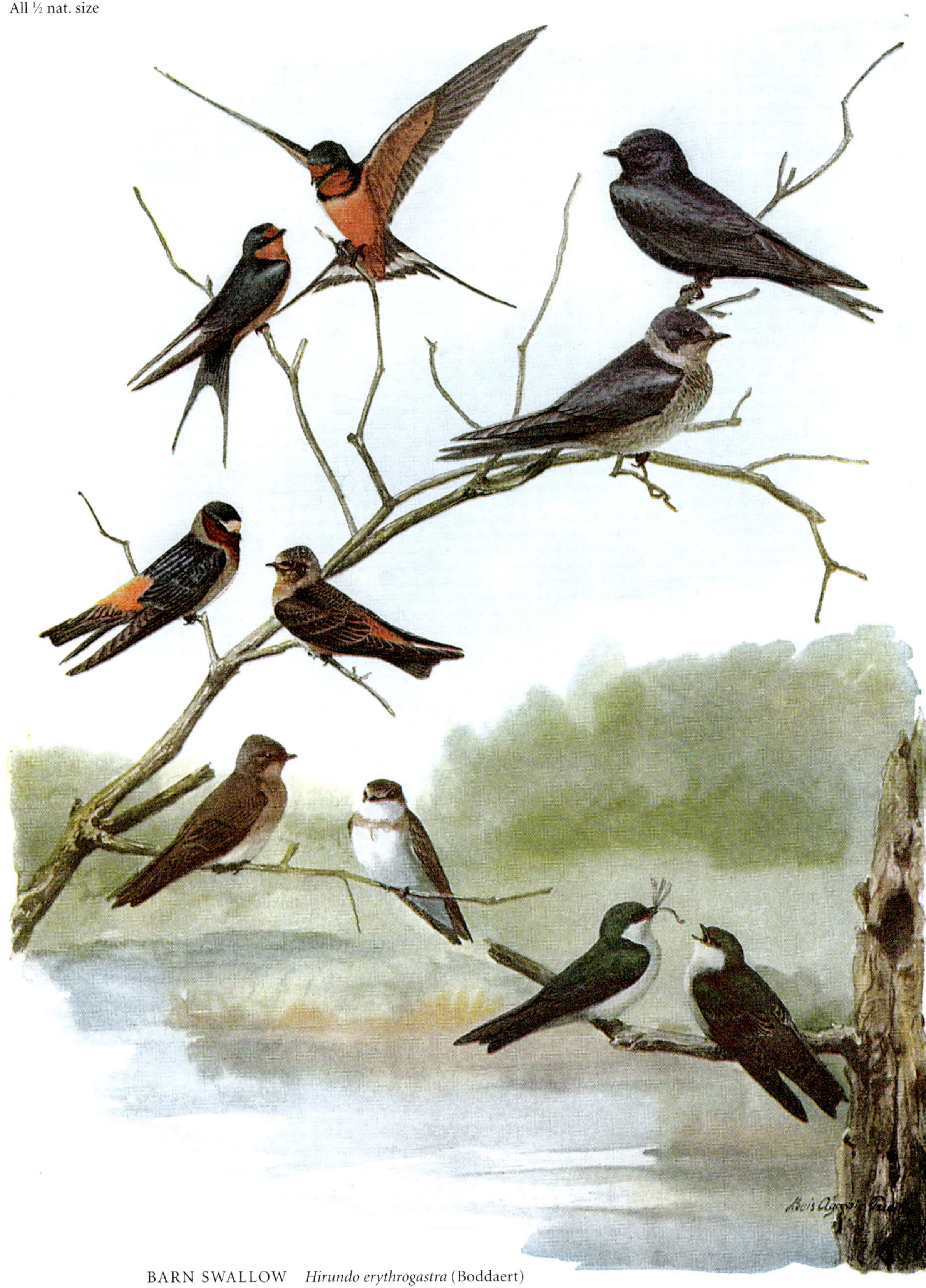

BARN SWALLOW *Hirundo erythrogastra* (Boddaert)
FEMALE MALE

CLIFF SWALLOW *Petrochelidon lunifrons lunifrons* (Say)
ADULT IMMATURE

ROUGH-WINGED SWALLOW
Stelgidopteryx serripennis (Audubon)

BANK SWALLOW
Riparia riparia (Linnaeus)

PURPLE MARTIN *Progne subis subis* (Linnaeus)
MALE
FEMALE

TREE SWALLOW
Iridoprocne bicolor (Vieillot)
ADULT IMMATURE

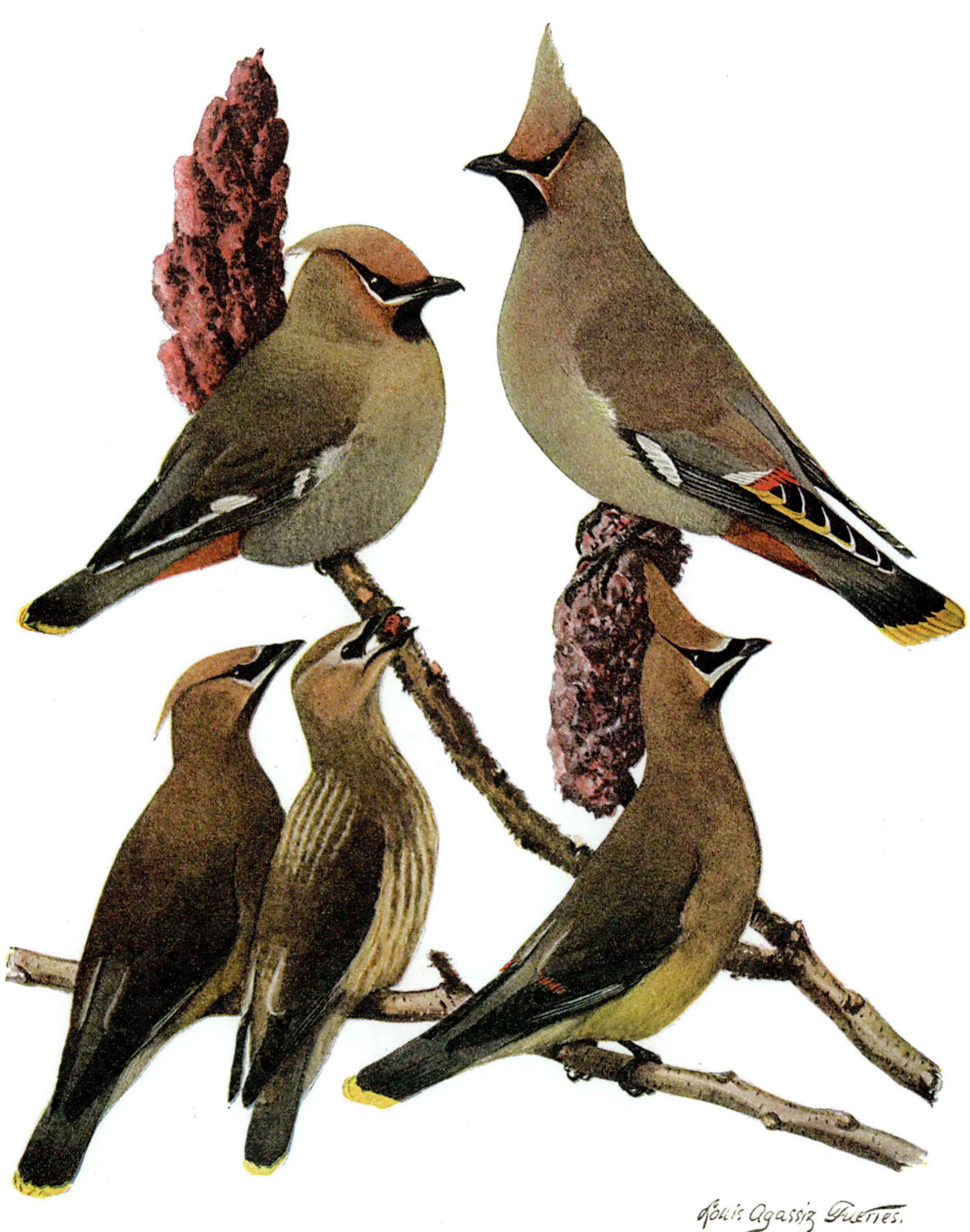

BOHEMIAN WAXWING *Bombycilla garrula* (Linnaeus)
FEMALE MALE
CEDAR WAXWING *Bombycilla cedrorum* (Vieillot)
FEMALE IMMATURE MALE

All ½ nat. size

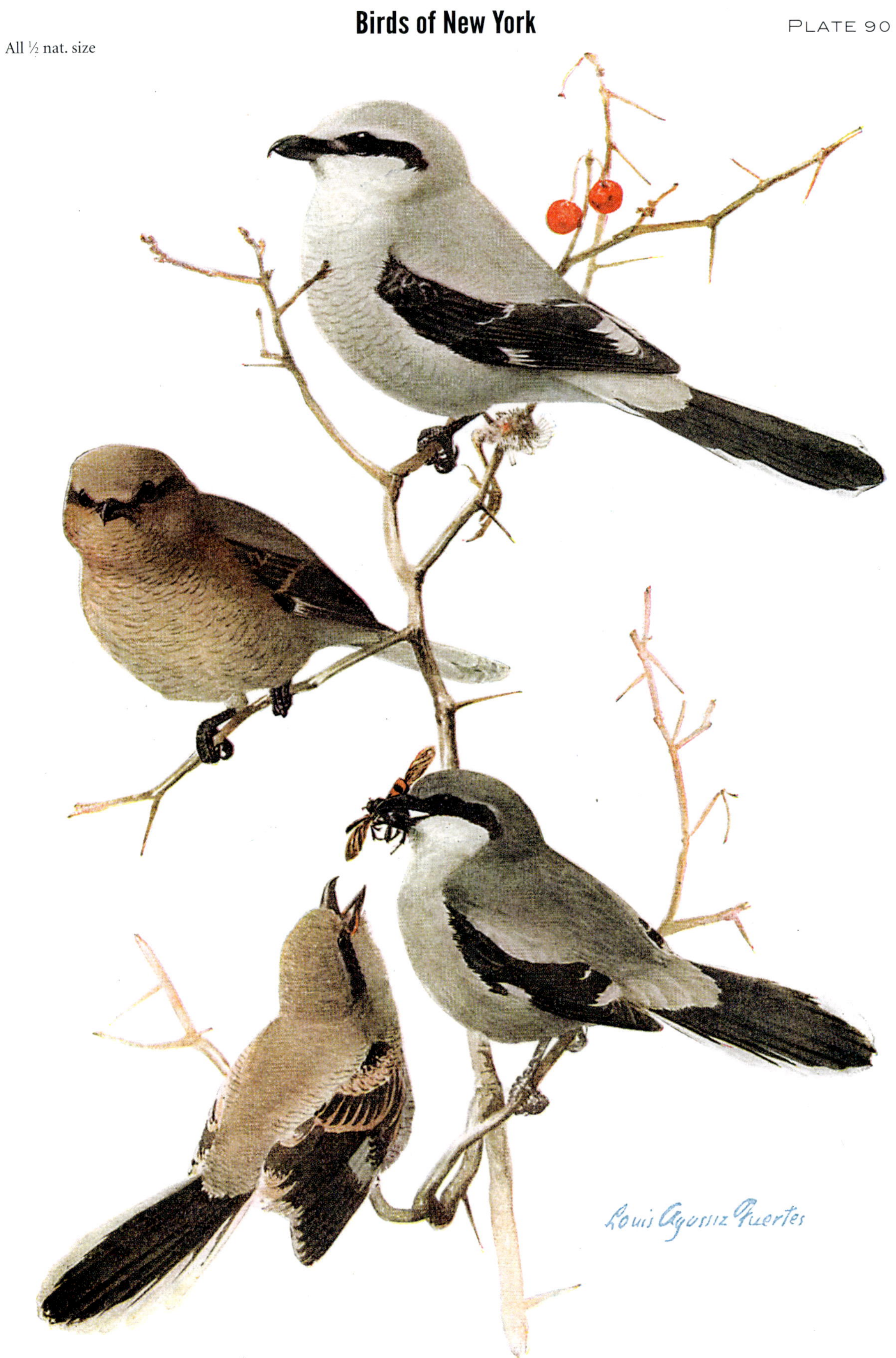

NORTHERN SHRIKE *Lanius borealis* (Vieillot)
ADULT MALE
IMMATURE
MIGRANT SHRIKE *Lanius ludovicianus migrans* (W. Palmer)
IMMATURE ADULT

All ½ nat. size

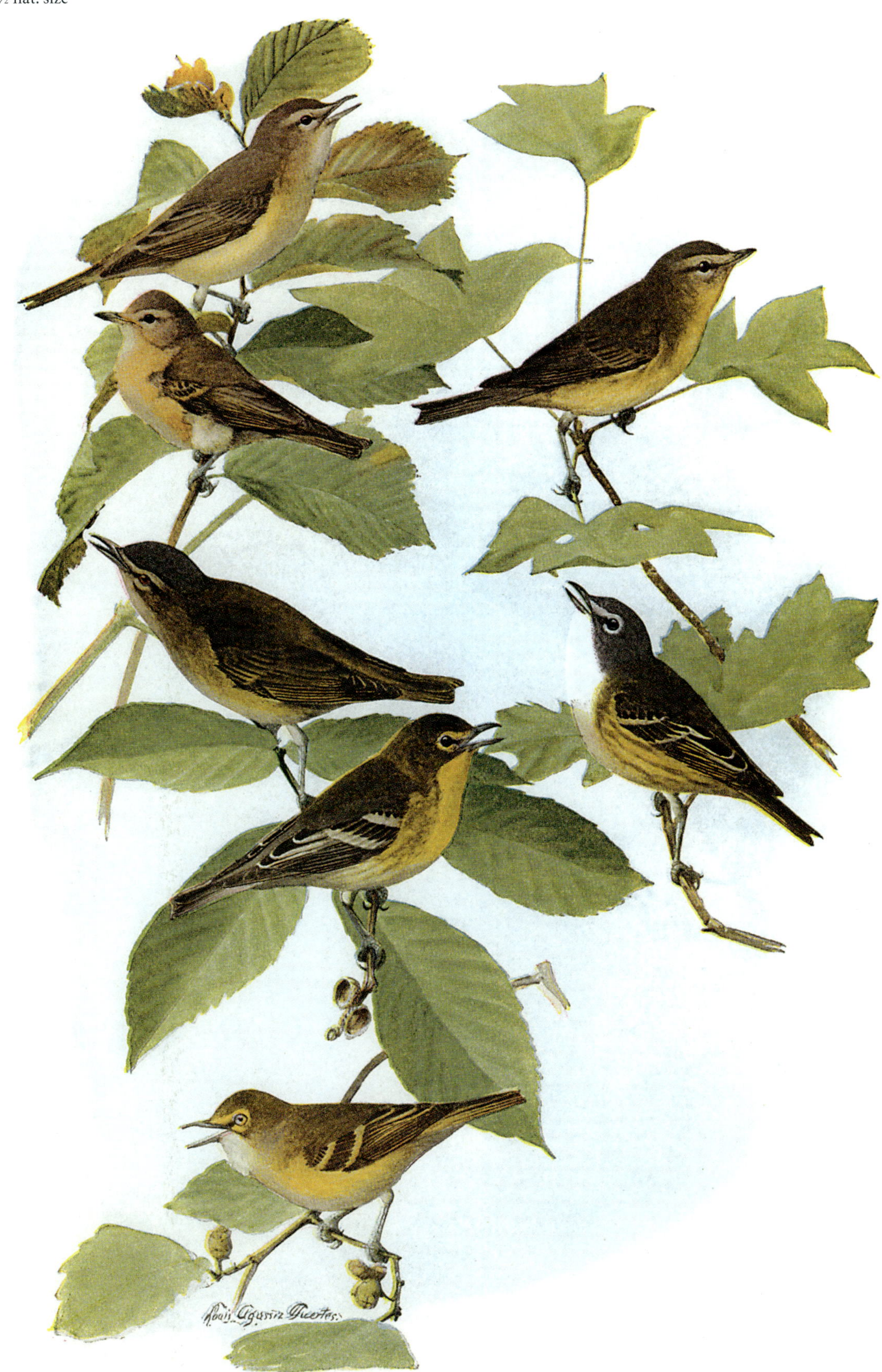

WARBLING VIREO *Vireosylva gilva gilva* (Vieillot)
ADULT
YOUNG
RED-EYED VIREO *Vireosylva olivacea* (Linnaeus)
YELLOW-THROATED VIREO *Lanivireo flavifrons* (Vieillot)
WHITE-EYED VIREO *Vireo griseus griseus* (Boddaert)

PHILADELPHIA VIREO
Vireosylva philadelphica (Cassin)
BLUE-HEADED VIREO
Lanivireo solitaries (Wilson)

All ½ nat. size

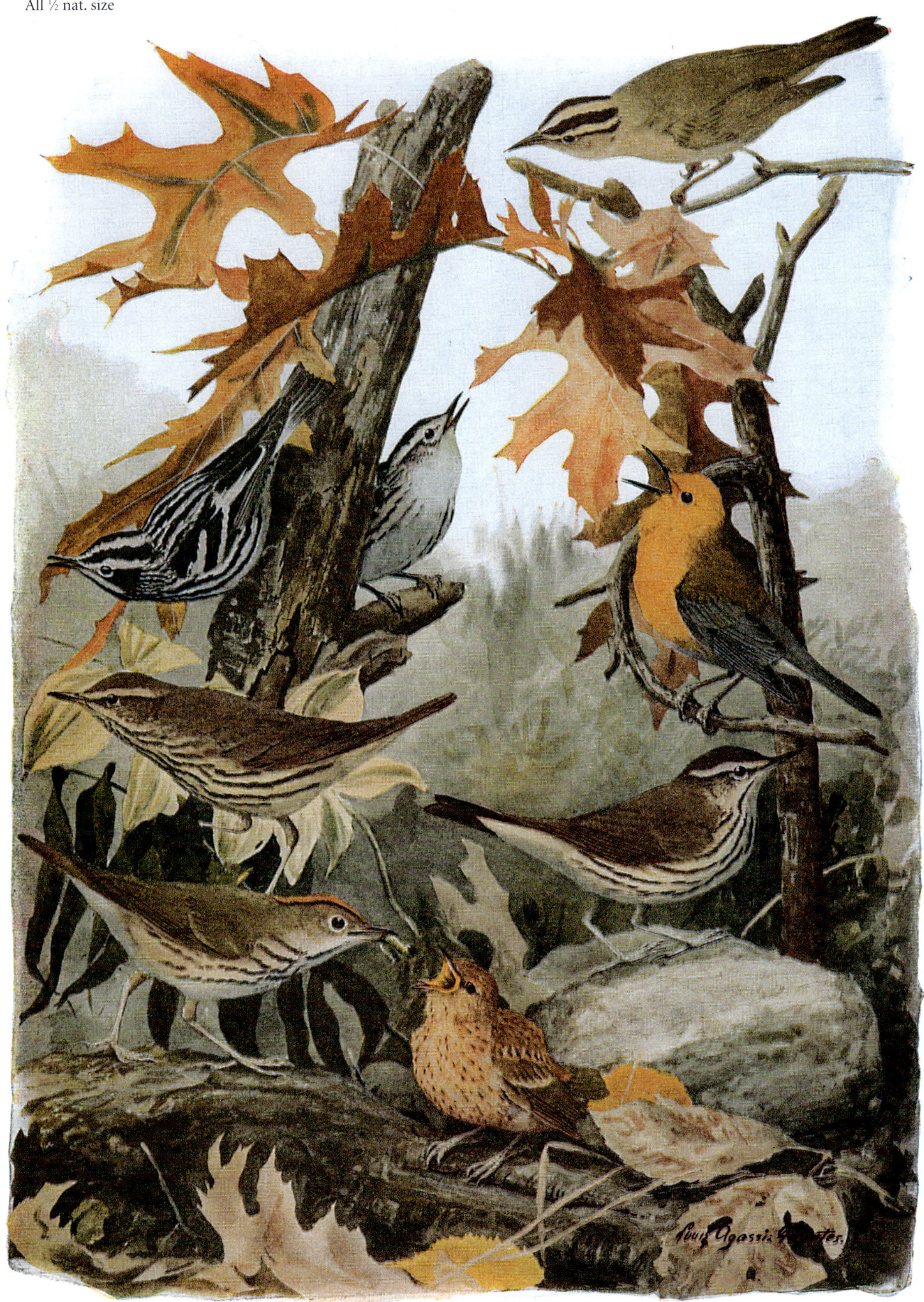

BLACK AND WHITE WARBLER *Mniotilta varia* (Linnaeus)
MALE FEMALE

WATER-THRUSH
Seiurus noveboracensis noveboracensis (Gmelin)

OVEN-BIRD *Seiurus aurocapillus* (Linnaeus)
ADULT JUVENAL

WORM-EATING WARBLER
Helmitheros verminivorus (Gmelin)

PROTHONOTARY WARBLER
Protonotaria citrea (Boddaert)

LOUISIANA WATER-THRUSH
Seiurus motacilla (Vieillot)

All ½ nat. size

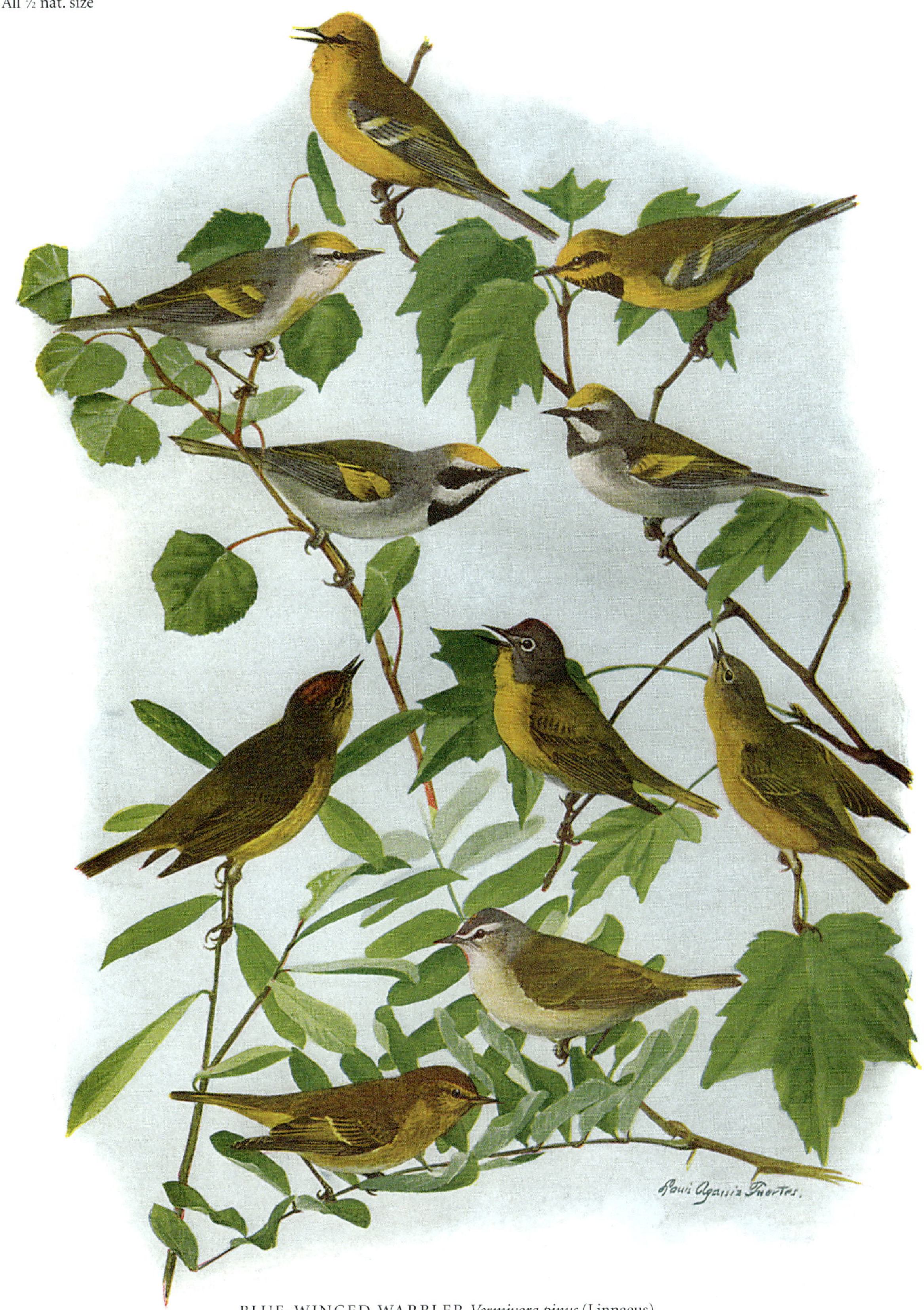

BLUE-WINGED WARBLER *Vermivora pinus* (Linnaeus)

BREWSTER'S WARBLER *Vermivora leucobronchialis* (Brewster)

LAWRENCE'S WARBLER *Vermivora lawrencei* (Herrick)

GOLDEN-WINGED WARBLER *Vermivora chrysoptera* (Linnaeus)
MALE FEMALE

ORANGE-CROWNED WARBLER *Vermivora celata celata* (Say)

NASHVILLE WARBLER *Vermivora rubricapilla rubricapilla* (Wilson)
MALE IMMATURE

TENNESSEE WARBLER *Vermivora peregrina* (Wilson)
IMMATURE MALE

All ¼ nat. size

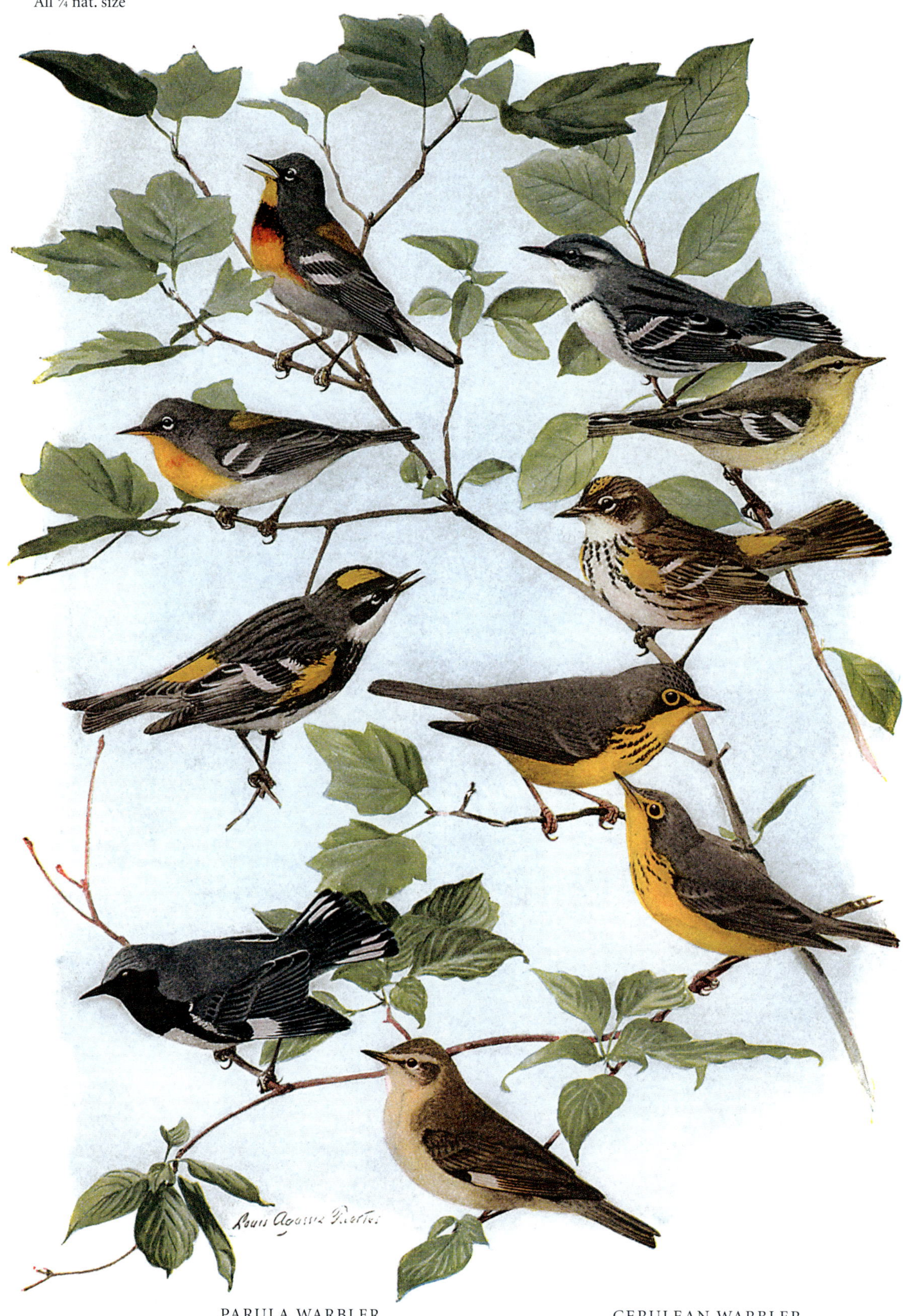

PARULA WARBLER
Compsothlypis americana americana (Linnaeus)
MALE
FEMALE

CERULEAN WARBLER
Dendroica cerulean (Wilson)
MALE
FEMALE

MYRTLE WARBLER *Dendroica coronata* (Linnaeus)
MALE
FEMALE

BLACK-THROATED BLUE WARBLER
Dendroica caerulescens caerulescens (Gmelin)
MALE
FEMALE

CANADA WARBLER
Wilsonia canadensis (Linnaeus)
MALE
FEMALE

All ½ nat. size

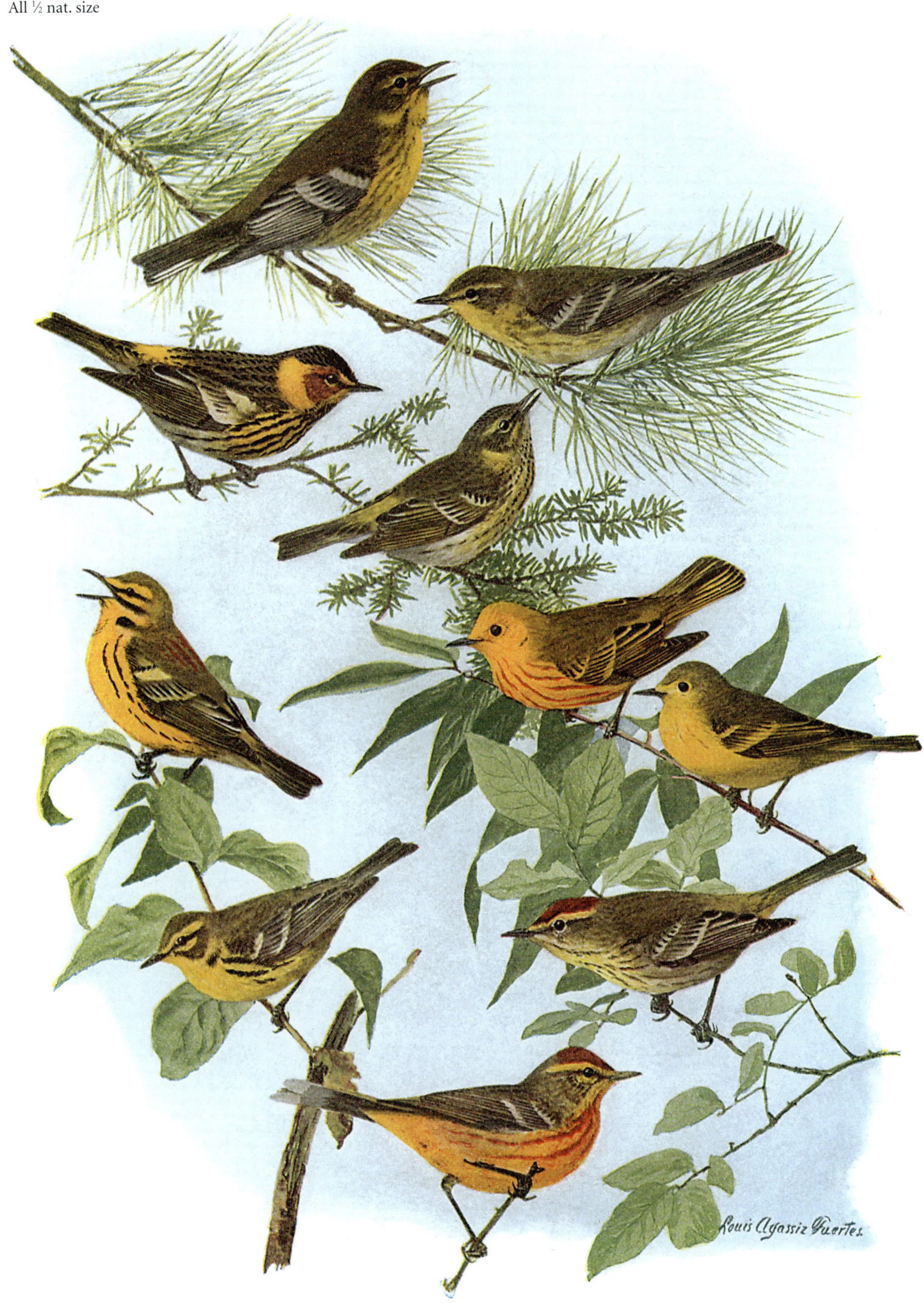

PINE WARBLER *Dendroica vigorsi* (Audubon)
MALE FEMALE
CAPE MAY WARBLER
MALE FEMALE
YELLOW WARBLER
Dendroica aestiva aestiva (Gmelin)
MALE FEMALE
PRAIRIE WARBLER
Dendroica discolor (Vieillot)
MALE
FEMALE
PALM WARBLER *Dendroica palmarum palmarum* (Gmelin)
YELLOW PALM WARBLER *Dendroica palmarum hypochrysea* (Ridgway)

All ½ nat. size

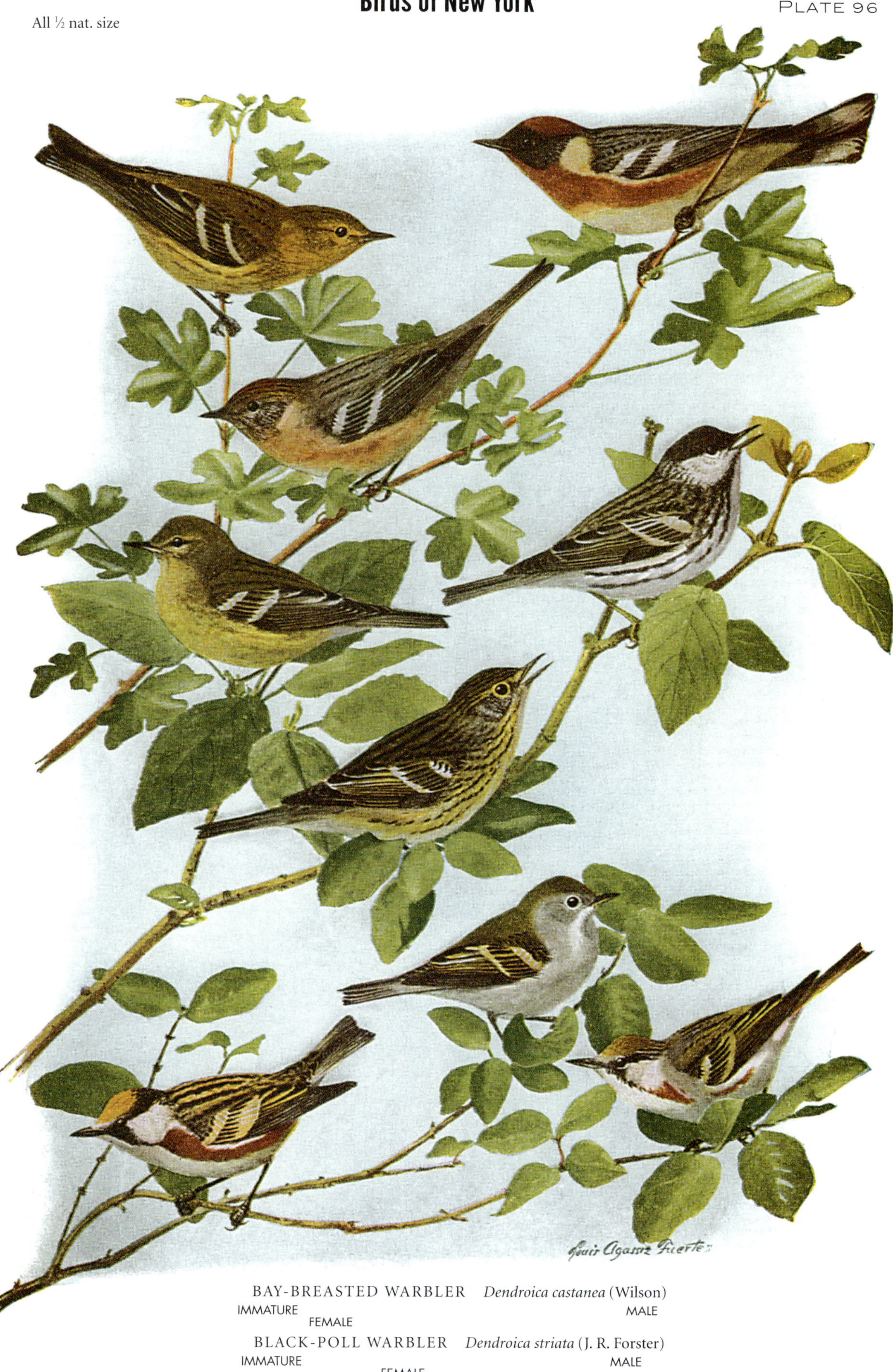

BAY-BREASTED WARBLER *Dendroica castanea* (Wilson)

IMMATURE FEMALE MALE

BLACK-POLL WARBLER *Dendroica striata* (J. R. Forster)

IMMATURE FEMALE MALE

CHESTNUT-SIDED WARBLER *Dendroica pensylvanica* (Linnaeus)

MALE IMMATURE FEMALE

All ½ nat. size

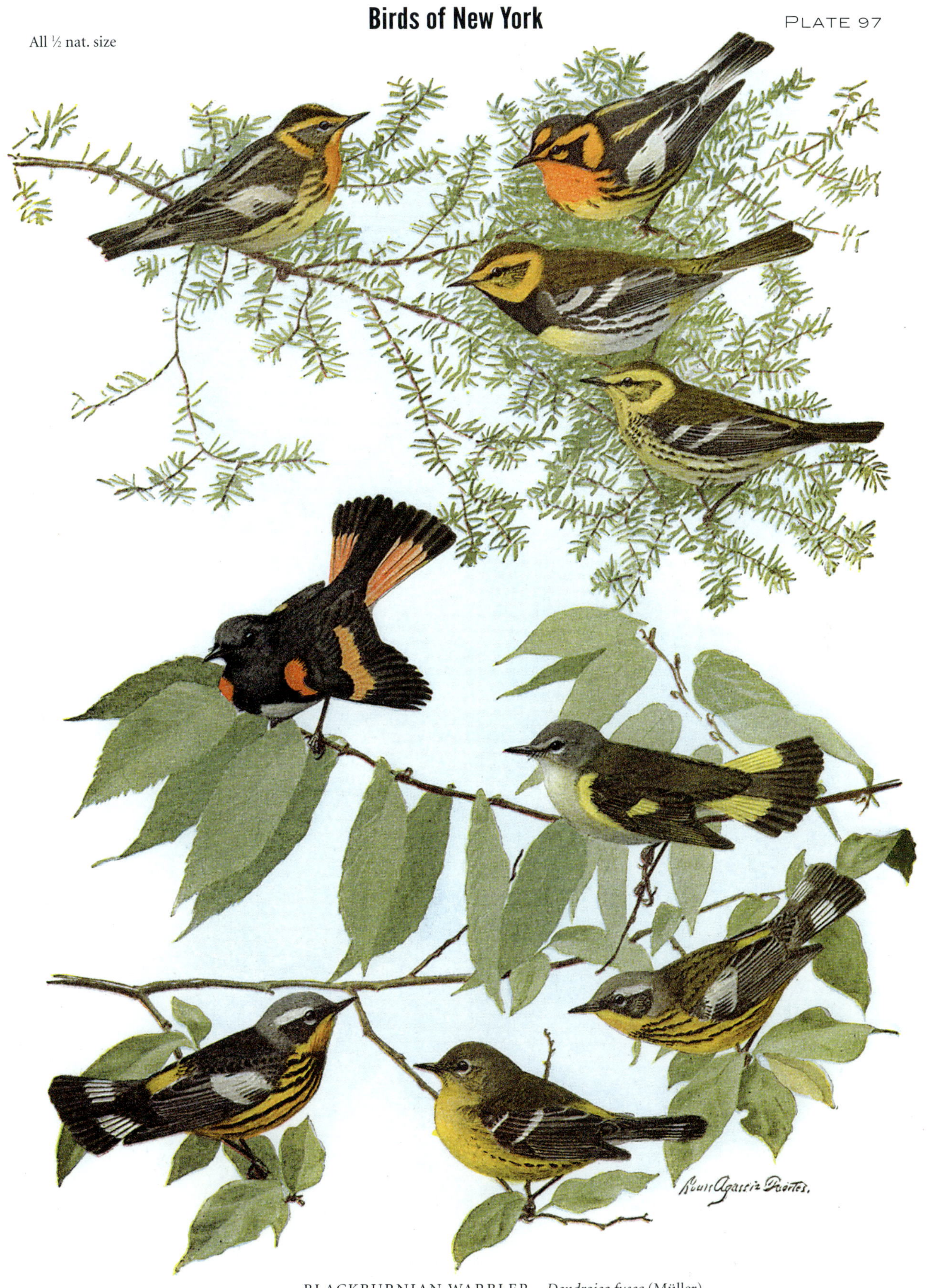

BLACKBURNIAN WARBLER *Dendroica fusca* (Müller)
FEMALE MALE
BLACK-THROATED GREEN WARBLER *Dendroica virens* (Gmelin)
MALE FEMALE
REDSTART *Setophaga ruticilla* (Linnaeus)
MALE FEMALE
MAGNOLIA WARBLER *Dendroica magnolia* (Wilson)
MALE IMMATURE FEMALE

All ½ nat. size

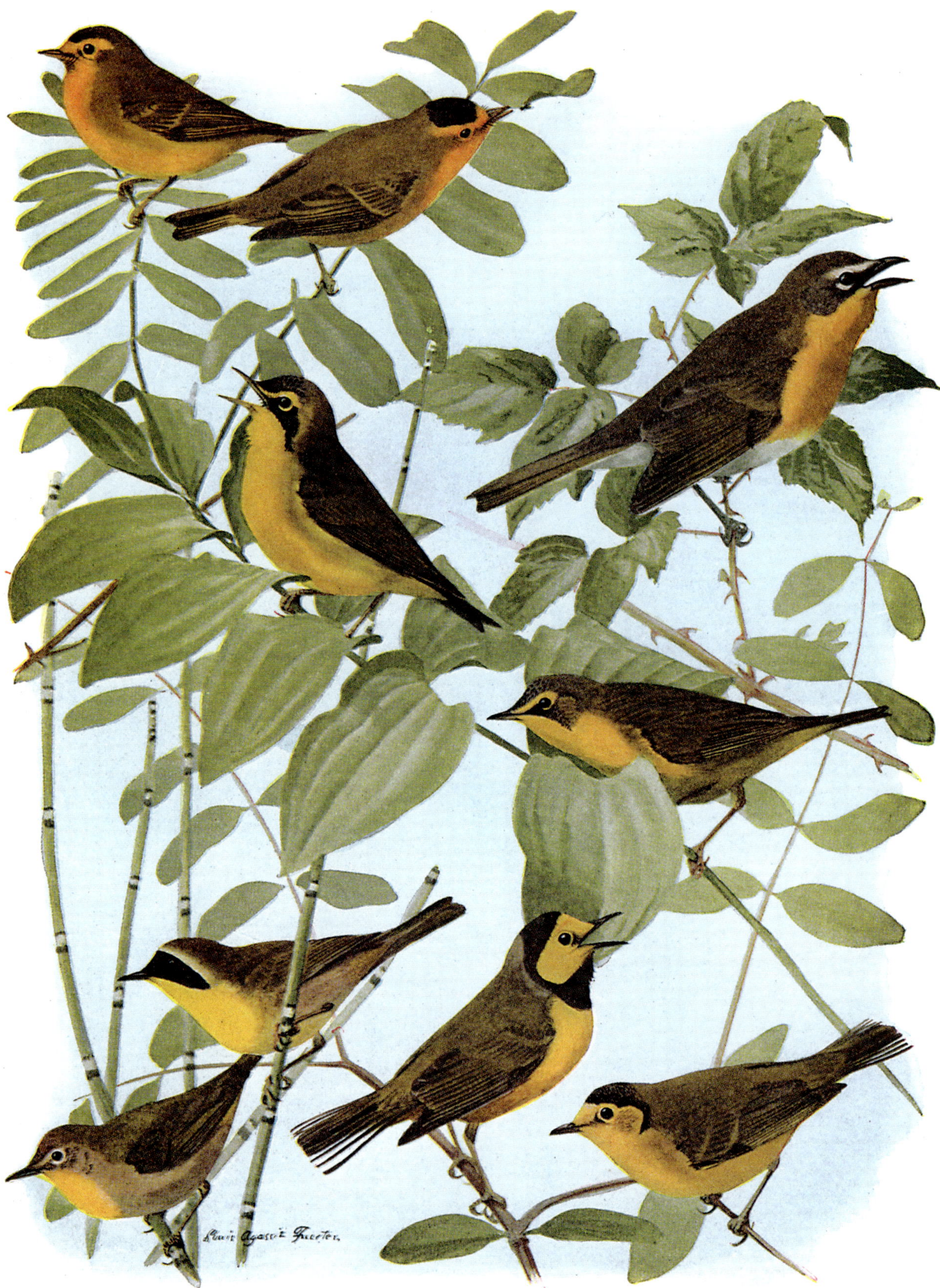

WILSON'S WARBLER *Wilsonia pusilla pusilla* (Wilson)
FEMALE MALE

YELLOW-BREASTED CHAT
Icteria virens virens (Linnaeus)

KENTUCKY WARBLER *Oporornis formosus* (Wilson)
MALE FEMALE

MARYLAND YELLOW-THROAT
Geothlypis trichas trichas (Linnaeus)
FEMALE MALE

HOODED WARBLER *Wilsonia citrina* (Boddaert)
MALE FEMALE

Both life size

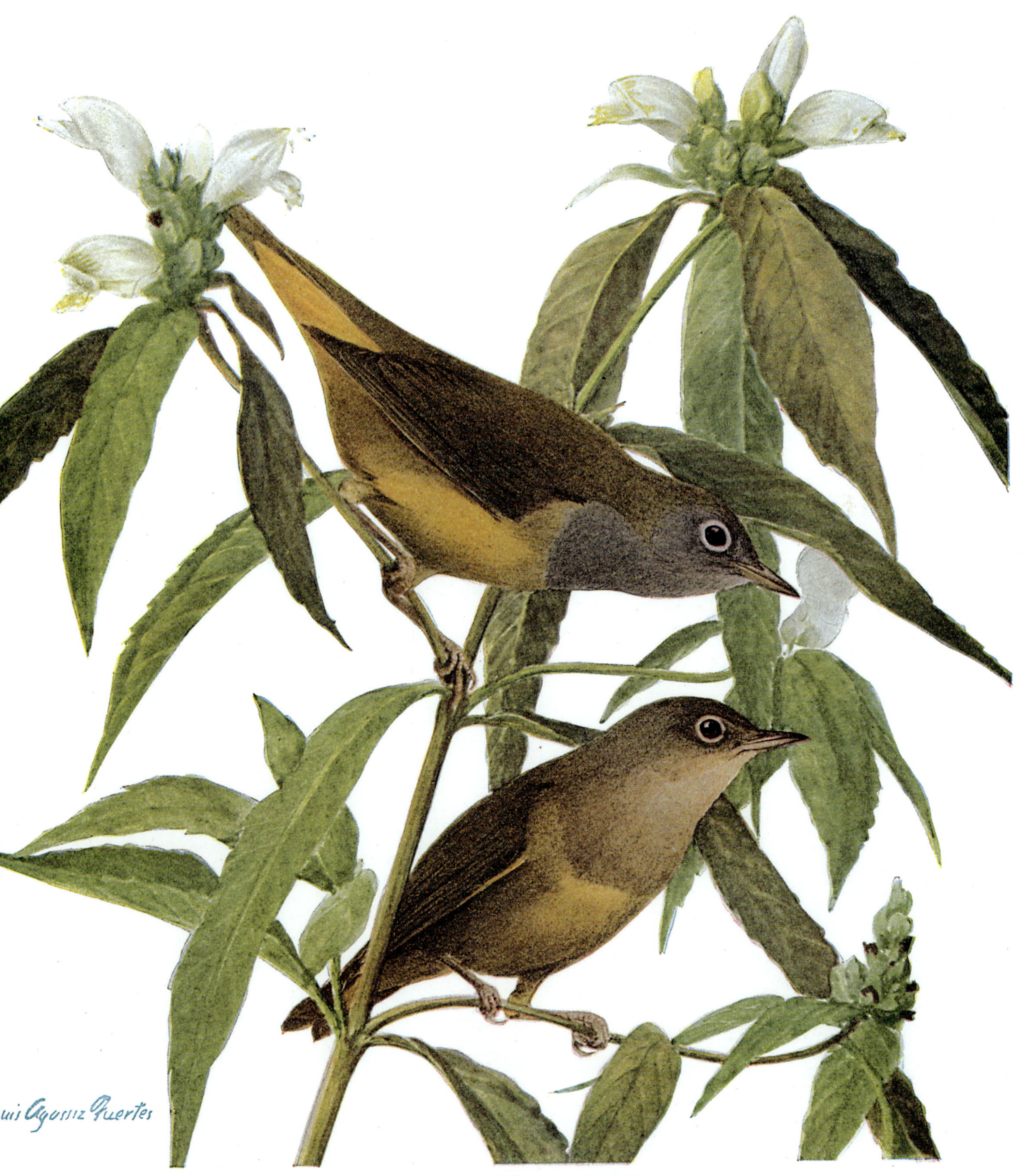

CONNECTICUT WARBLER *Oporonis agilis* (Wilson)
ADULT
IMMATURE

Both ⅔ nat. size

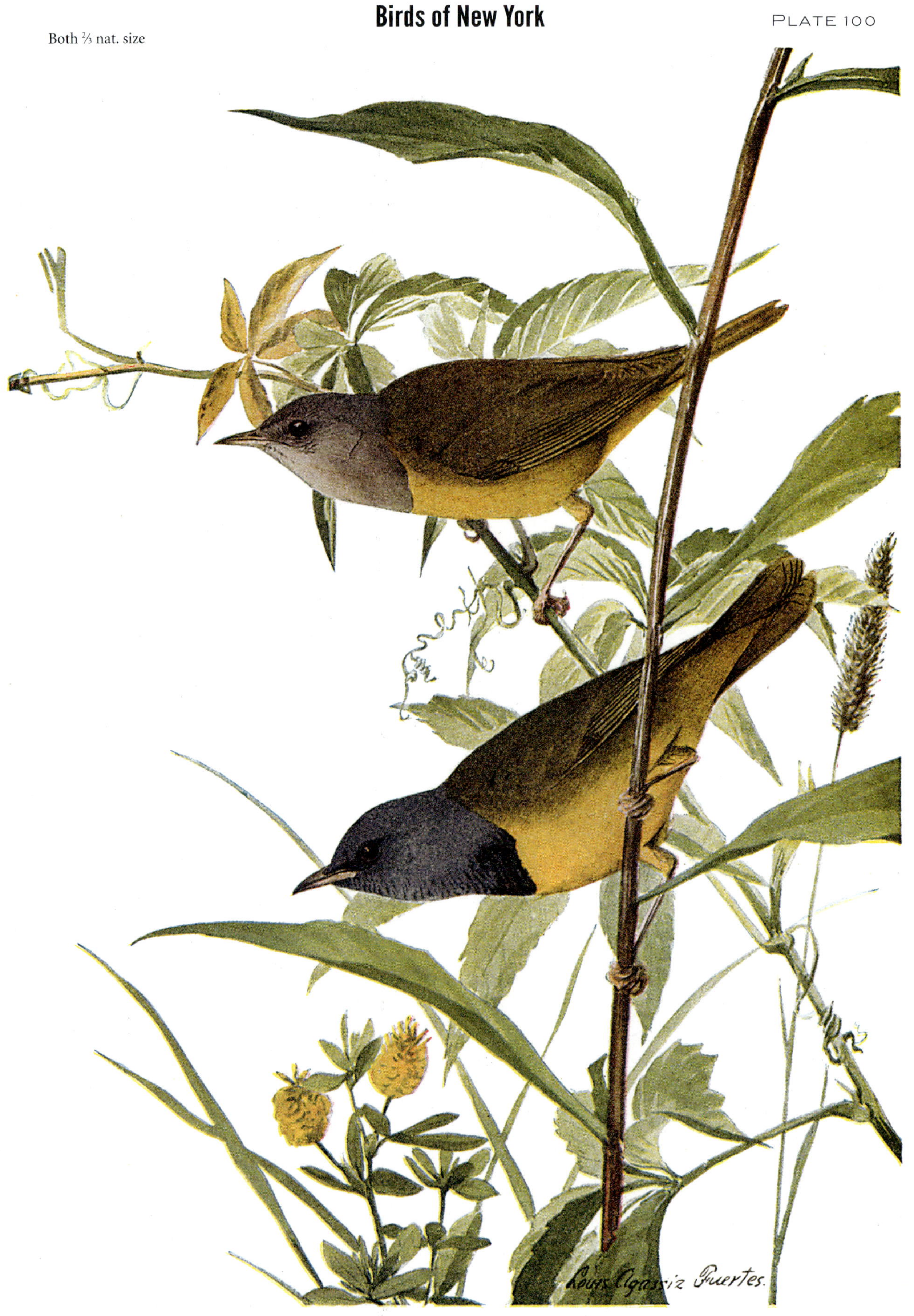

MOURNING WARBLER *Oporornis philadelphia* (Wilson)
FEMALE
MALE

All ½ nat. size

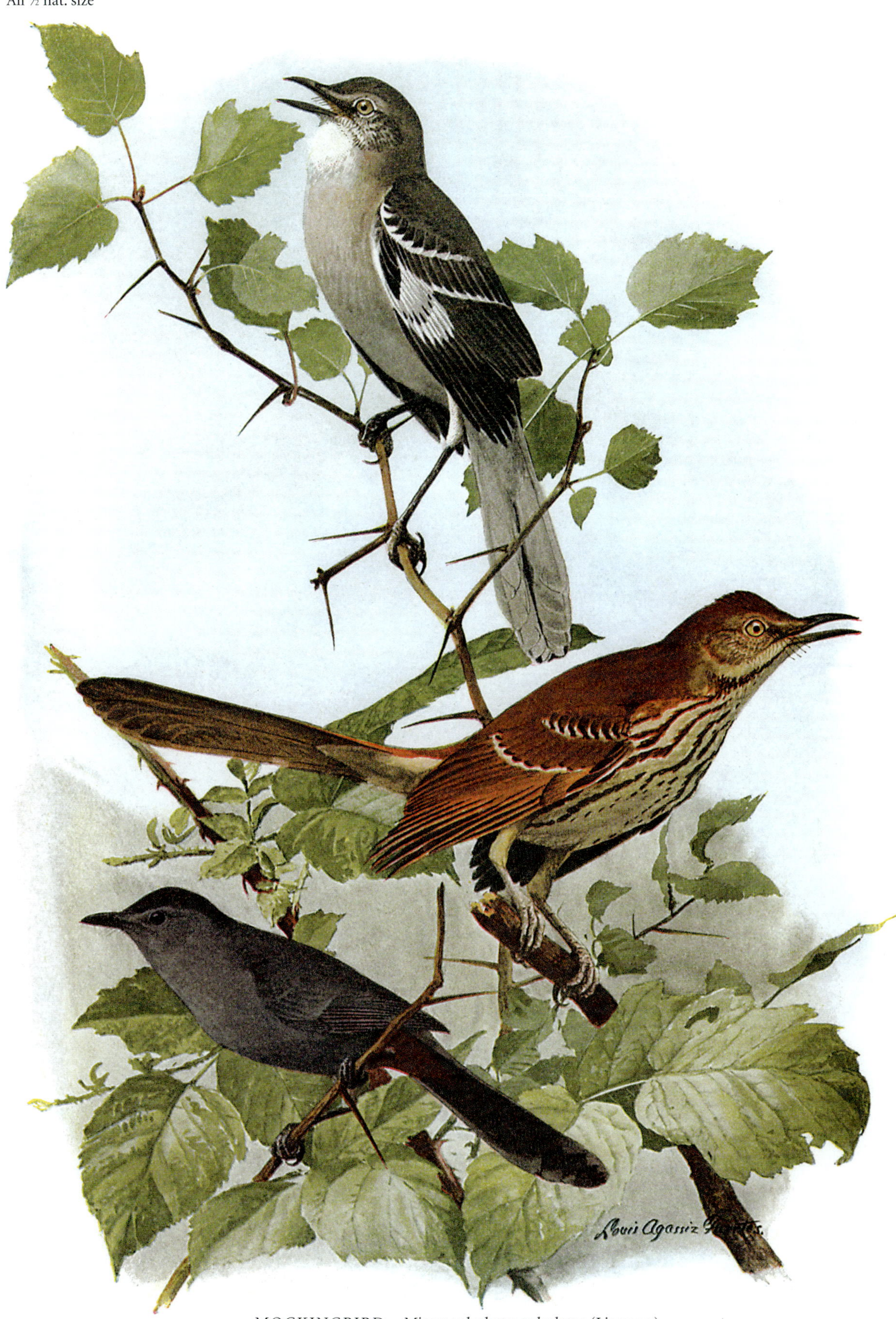

MOCKINGBIRD *Mimus polyglottos polyglottos* (Linnaeus)
BROWN THRASHER *Toxostoma rufum* (Linnaeus)
CATBIRD *Dumetella colinensis* (Linnaeus)

All ⅔ nat. size

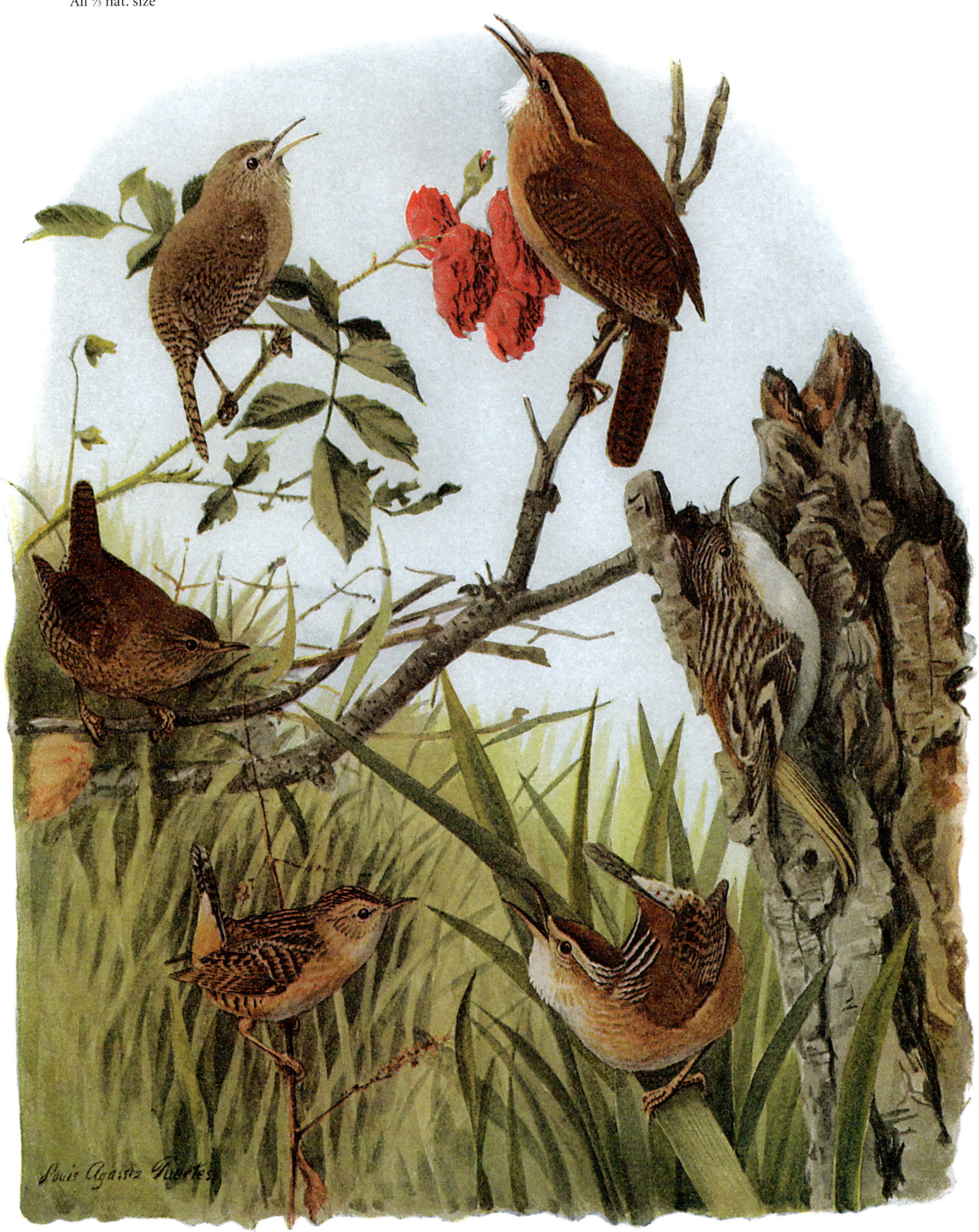

HOUSE WREN
Troglodytes aëdon aëdon (Vieillot)

CAROLINA WREN
Thryotharus ludovicianus ludovicianus (Latham)

WINTER WREN
Nannus hiemalis hiemalis (Vieillot)

BROWN CREEPER
Certhia familiaris americana (Bonaparte)

SHORT-BILLED MARSH WREN
Cistothorus stellaris (Naumann)

LONG-BILLED MARSH WREN
Telmatodytes palustris palustris (Wilson)

All ⅔ nat. size

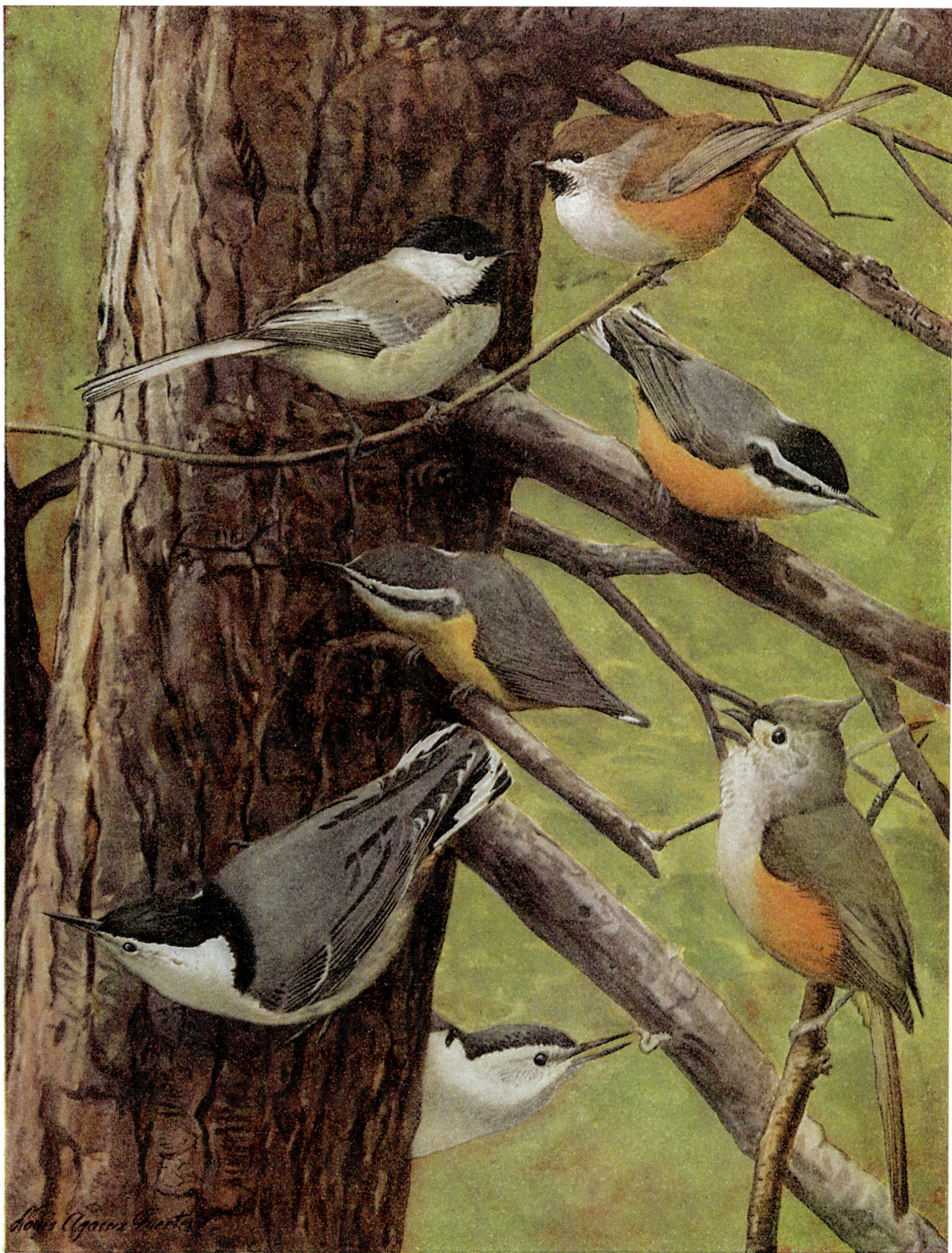

ACADIAN CHICKADEE
Pethestes hudsonicus littoralis (H. Bryant)

CHICKADEE
Penthestes atricapillus atricapillus (Linnaeus)

RED-BREASTED NUTHATCH
Sitta canadensis (Linnaeus)

FEMALE   MALE

WHITE-BREASTED NUTHATCH
Sitta carolinensis carolinensis (Latham)
MALE   FEMALE

TUFTED TITMOUSE
Baeolophus bicolor (Linnaeus)

All ⅔ nat. size

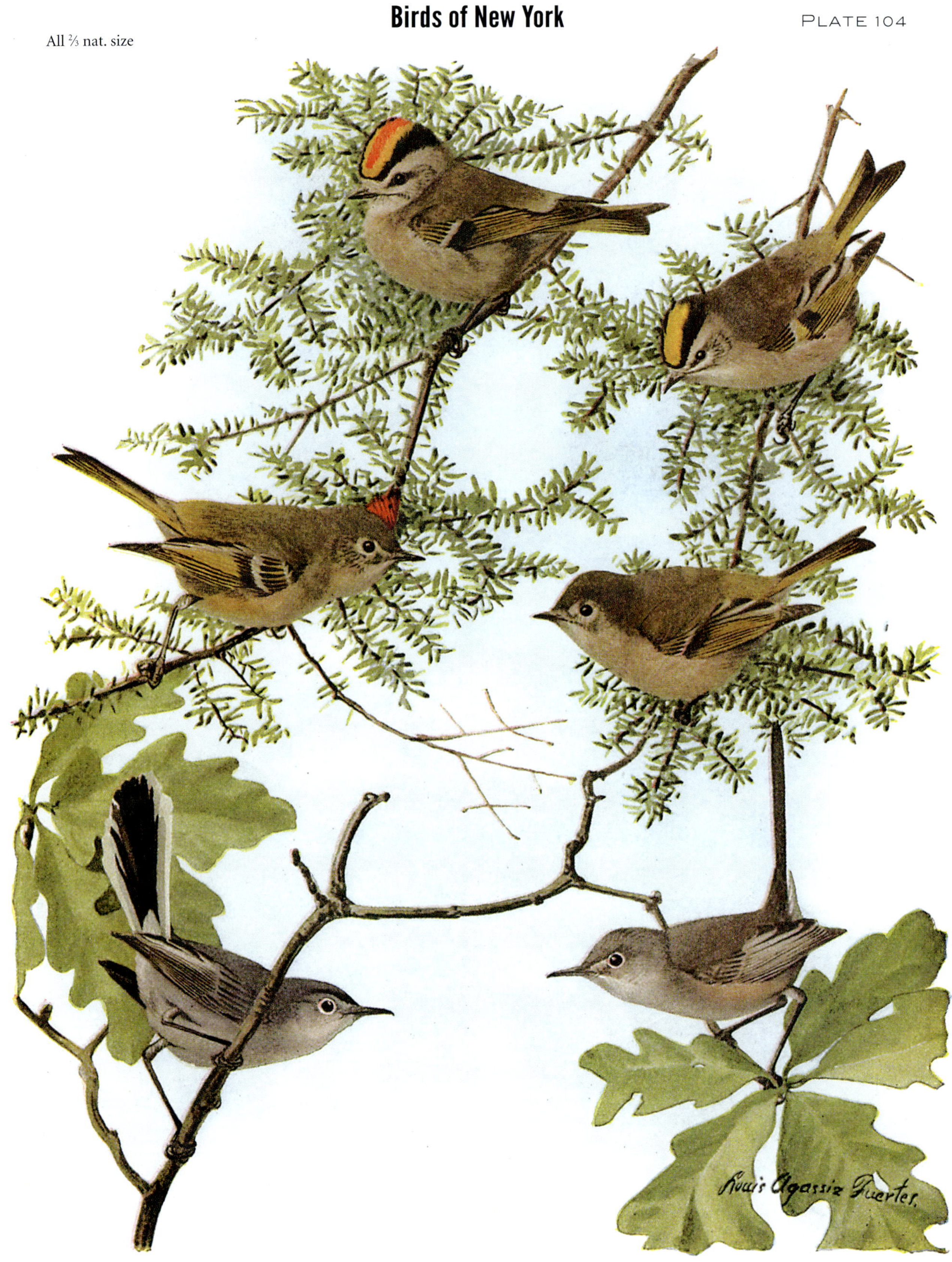

GOLDEN-CROWNED KINGLET
Regulus satrapa satrapa (Lichtenstein)
MALE FEMALE

RUBY-CROWNED KINGLET
Regulus calendula calendula (Linnaeus)
MALE FEMALE

BLUE-GRAY GNATCATCHER
Polioptila caerulea caerulea (Linnaeus)
MALE FEMALE

All ½ nat. size

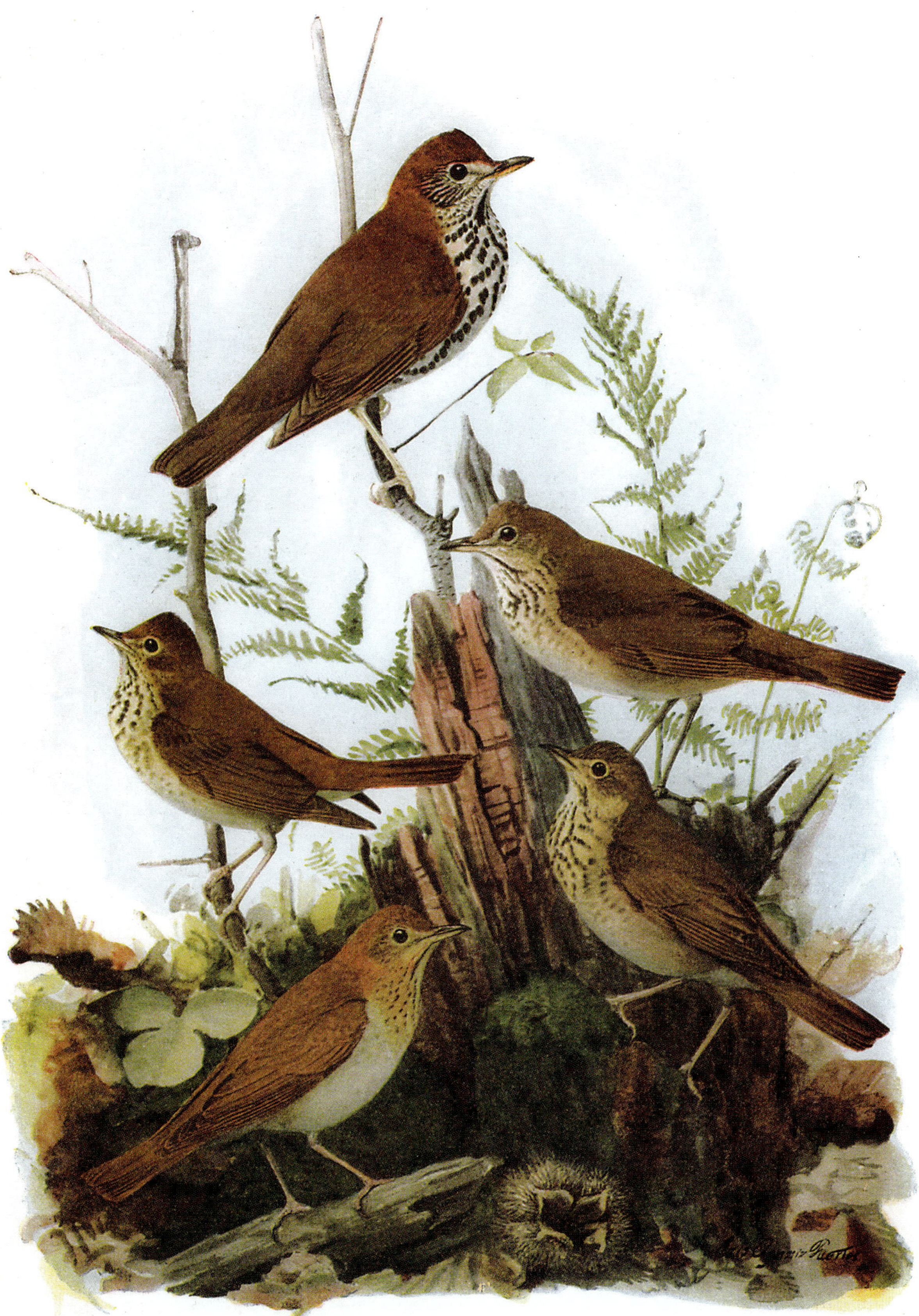

WOOD THRUSH
Hylocichla mustelina (Gmelin)
HERMIT THRUSH
Hylocichla guttata pallasi (Cabanis)
VEERY
Hylocichla fuscescens fuscescens (Stephens)
GRAY-CHEEKED THRUSH
Hylocichla aliciae aliciae (Baird)
OLIVE-BACKED THRUSH
Hylocichla ustulata swainsoni (Tschudi)

All ½ nat. size

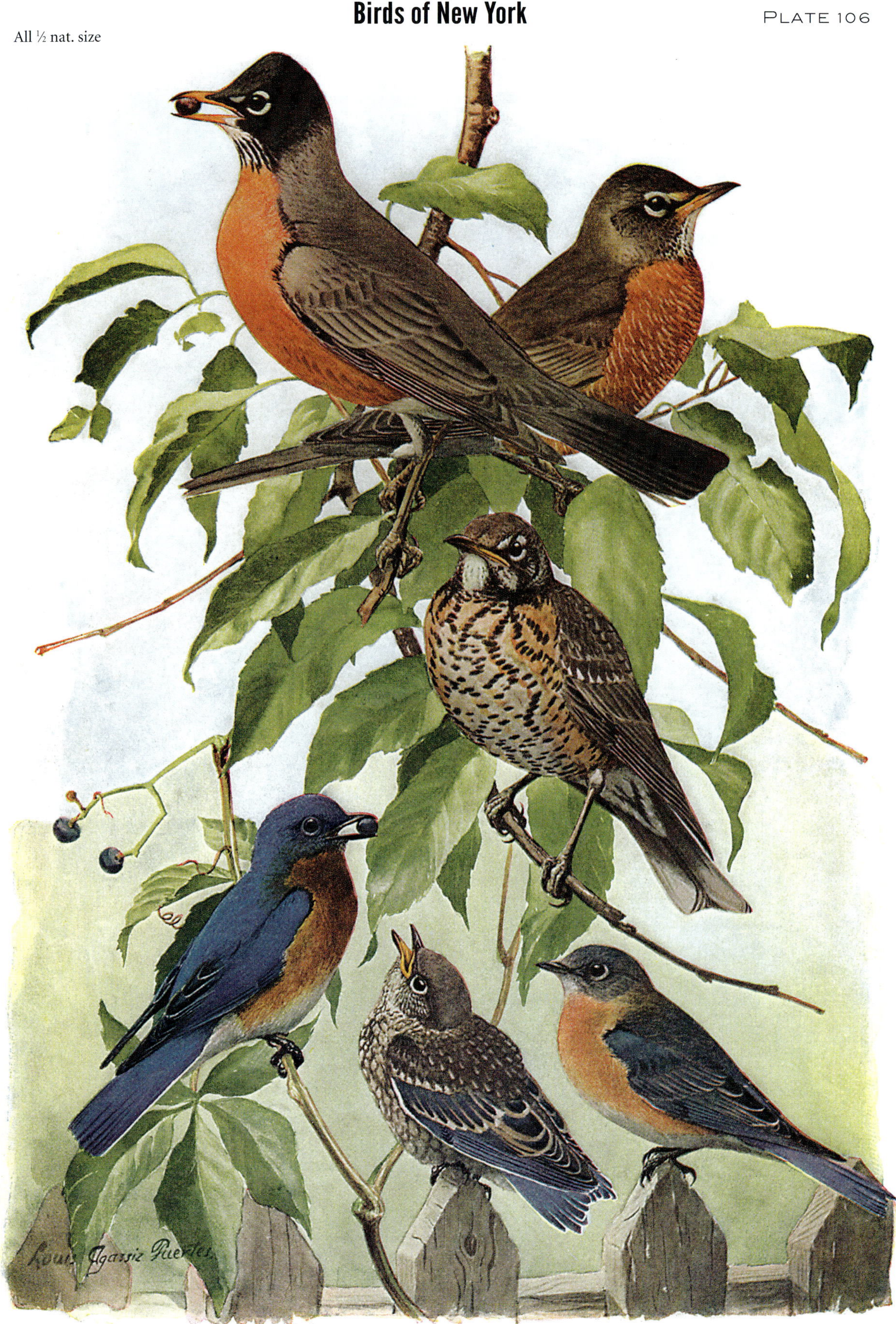

ROBIN *Planesticus migratorius migratorius* (Linnaeus)

ADULT IN SPRING IMMATURE FALL

BLUEBIRD *Sialia sialis sialis* (Linnaeus)

MALE IMMATURE FEMALE